First World War

and Army of Occupation

War Diary

France, Belgium and Germany

18 DIVISION
Divisional Troops
Machine Gun Corps
18 Battalion
19 February 1918 - 31 March 1919

WO95/2028/2

The Naval & Military Press Ltd
www.nmarchive.com
Published in association with The National Archives

Published by

The Naval & Military Press Ltd

Unit 10 Ridgewood Industrial Park,

Uckfield, East Sussex,

TN22 5QE England

Tel: +44 (0) 1825 749494

www.naval-military-press.com

www.nmarchive.com

This diary has been reprinted in facsimile from the original. Any imperfections are inevitably reproduced and the quality may fall short of modern type and cartographic standards.

Contents

Document type	Place/Title	Date From	Date To
Heading	WO95/2028/2		
Heading	18th Division 18th Bn Machine Gun Corps Feb 1918-Mar 1919.		
Heading	War Diary 18th Bn Machine Gun Corps. From 19th Feby 1918 To 28th Feby 1918. Vol 1		
War Diary	Mondescourt	19/02/1918	26/02/1918
War Diary	Villequier Aumont	27/02/1918	28/02/1918
Miscellaneous	Appendix 1 18th Div. M.G. Battalion Order 1.		
Heading	18th Div. War Diary 18th Battalion, Machine Gun Corps. March 1918		
Heading	War Diary of 18th Battn. Machine Gun Corps From March 1918 To 31st March 1918 Volume II		
War Diary	Rouez	01/03/1918	26/03/1918
War Diary	Caignes	26/03/1918	26/03/1918
War Diary	Audignicourt	27/03/1918	31/03/1918
Miscellaneous	10th Division Machine Gun Battalion. Defence Scheme. Appendix 2	01/03/1918	01/03/1918
Operation(al) Order(s)	18th. Battn. Machine Gun Corps Order No 2 Appendix 3	02/03/1918	02/03/1918
Operation(al) Order(s)	18th Battn. Machine Gun Corps. Order No 3. Appendix 4		
Operation(al) Order(s)	18th Battalion Machine Gun Corps Order No.4. Appendix 5	04/03/1918	04/03/1918
Miscellaneous	18th Bn. M.G.C. No. S.11. Appendix 6	13/03/1918	13/03/1918
Miscellaneous	18'th Div. G. 918. 18th Battn. M.G.C. No. S. 14.	15/03/1918	15/03/1918
Miscellaneous	III Corps Defence Scheme. Appendix VIII.		
Miscellaneous	18th Battn. M.G.C. No.S. 22 Appendix. 8.	20/03/1918	20/03/1918
Operation(al) Order(s)	18th Battn. Machine Gun Corps Order No. 6. Appendix 9	21/03/1918	21/03/1918
Miscellaneous	Appendix 10		
Miscellaneous	Losses of Machine Guns During Operations From 21st To 26th March 1918 Appendix. 11.	28/03/1918	28/03/1918
Miscellaneous	Appendix 12.		
Miscellaneous	Appendix 12	22/04/1918	22/04/1918
Miscellaneous	Narrative Relating To The Part Played During The Operations From The 21st To 26th March 1918 by the-18th Battalion Machine Gun Corps.	26/03/1918	26/03/1918
Map	Appendix 'A'		
Miscellaneous	Casualties Incurred During The Operations from 21st To 26th March 1918, by the 18th Battalion Machine Gun Corps. Appendix 'B'		
Miscellaneous	18th Battalion Machine Gun Corps. Lessons Learnt From The Recent Operations From March 21st To 28th. 1918	20/04/1918	20/04/1918
Operation(al) Order(s)	18th Battn. M.G. Corps. Order No. 9. Appendix 13	29/03/1918	29/03/1918
Miscellaneous	A Form. Messages And Signals. Appendix 14		
Miscellaneous	A Form. Messages And Signals.		
Miscellaneous	Changes In Establishment And Strength of Battalion During The Month of March 1918. Appendix 14.a		
Heading	18th Battalion, Machine Gun Corps. April 1918		

Heading	War Diary of 18th Bn Machine Gun Corps From 1st April 1918 To 30th April 1918		
War Diary	Boves	01/04/1918	13/04/1918
War Diary	Amiens	14/04/1918	17/04/1918
War Diary	Camp	18/04/1918	24/04/1918
War Diary	Camp. N of Hebecourt	25/04/1918	26/04/1918
War Diary	Camp M.35 d 90	27/04/1918	27/04/1918
War Diary	Saleux	28/04/1918	28/04/1918
War Diary	Cavillon	29/04/1918	29/04/1918
War Diary	Allery	30/04/1918	30/04/1918
Miscellaneous	Narrative of Operations Describing The Part Played-by the-18th Battalion Machine Gun Corps. During The Operations Near Villers Bretonneux From 31st March 1918. To 13th April 1918. Appendix 19		
Miscellaneous	Narrative of Operations Showing The Part Played by-The-18th Battn. Machine Gun Corps During The Period, 31st March 1918-13th April 1918.	18/05/1918	18/05/1918
Miscellaneous	Casualties Incurred by The 18th Battn. Machine Gun Corps During The Operation Covering The Period 31.3.18 to 13.4.18. Appendix "A"	13/04/1918	13/04/1918
Miscellaneous	Appendices		
Operation(al) Order(s)	18th Battn. M.G.C. Order No. 11. Appendix 15	02/04/1918	02/04/1918
Operation(al) Order(s)	18th Bn. Machine Gun Corps. Operation Order No. 12 Appendix 16	04/04/1918	04/04/1918
Miscellaneous	Appendix. "A"		
Operation(al) Order(s)	18th Battalion Machine Gun Corps Order No. 13. Appendix 17		
Miscellaneous	18th Bn. Machine Gun Corps No. S.25.To: Recipients of BAttalion Order No. 13	08/04/1918	08/04/1918
Miscellaneous	Reference 18th Bn. Machine Gun Corps. Order No. 13.		
Miscellaneous	Battery Chart For "A" Battery		
Miscellaneous	Battery Chart For "B" Battery		
Diagram etc	Office Copy		
Miscellaneous	18th Bn. Machine Gun Corps No. S. 28.	08/04/1918	08/04/1918
Operation(al) Order(s)	18th Battalion Machine Gun Corps (Cancelling Battalion Order No. 13.) Appendix 18		
Miscellaneous	Battery Chart For "A" Battery.		
Miscellaneous	Battery Chart For "B" Battery.		
Diagram etc	German Trenches		
Miscellaneous	Appendix 19.		
Operation(al) Order(s)	18th Battalion Machine Gun Corps. Order No. 15. Appendix 20	13/04/1918	13/04/1918
Operation(al) Order(s)	18th Battalion M.G.C. Corp Order No. 16. Appendix 21	17/04/1918	17/04/1918
Miscellaneous	Warning Order Appendix 22	21/04/1918	21/04/1918
Operation(al) Order(s)	18th Battalion Machine Gun Corps Order No. 17. Appendix 23	20/04/1918	20/04/1918
Operation(al) Order(s)	18th Battalion Machine Gun Corps, Order No. 18. Appendix 24	23/04/1918	23/04/1918
Miscellaneous	Changes In Establishment And Strength of Battalion During Month of April 1918. Appendix 25		
Heading	War Diary of 18th Bn Machine Gun Corps. From 1st May 1918 To 31st May 1918 (Volume IV)		
War Diary	Allery	01/05/1918	05/05/1918
War Diary	Ebart Farm Nr Beaucourt	06/05/1918	07/05/1918
War Diary	Baizieux	08/05/1918	25/05/1918

War Diary	Molliens-Au-Bois	26/05/1918	31/05/1918
Miscellaneous	List of Decoration Gained by Officers N.C.Os, And Men of The 18th Battalion Machine Gun Corps During Recent Fighting Appendix 26		
Operation(al) Order(s)	18th Battn. Machine Gun Corps Order No. 20. Appendix 27	03/05/1918	03/05/1918
Operation(al) Order(s)	18th Battn. B.G.C. Order No. 21. Appendix 28	04/05/1918	04/05/1918
Diagram etc	Disposition of M Gs on A/N Front		
Diagram etc	Disposition of M Gs A/N Front		
Diagram etc	Identification Trace for		
Diagram etc	Use with Artillery Maps.		
Miscellaneous	Legend Appendix 29		
Operation(al) Order(s)	18 Bn M.G. 6 Order No. 23. Appendix 30	08/05/1918	08/05/1918
Operation(al) Order(s)	18th Bn In Corporate Order No. 24 Appendix 31	12/05/1918	12/05/1918
Operation(al) Order(s)	18th Inf G.B. Order No. 25. Appendix 32	14/05/1918	14/05/1918
Operation(al) Order(s)	18th Inf 6 Order No. 26. Appendix 33	17/05/1918	17/05/1918
Operation(al) Order(s)	18th Inf G.B. Order No. 27. Appendix 34	17/05/1918	17/05/1918
Operation(al) Order(s)	18th Bn In G Order No. GK. 178 Appendix 35	19/05/1918	19/05/1918
Operation(al) Order(s)	18th Bn. G.B. Order No. 28 Appendix 36	21/05/1918	21/05/1918
Miscellaneous			
Operation(al) Order(s)	18th Inf G.B. Order No. 28A Appendix 37.		
Diagram etc			
Operation(al) Order(s)	18th Battn M.G.C. Order No. 29. Appendix 38	22/05/1918	22/05/1918
Miscellaneous	18th Battalion Machine Gun Corps.		
Miscellaneous	18th Battalion Machine Gun Corps. Appendix 39	29/05/1918	29/05/1918
Diagram etc	Sheet Senlis 1/2000		
Miscellaneous	18th Battalion Machine Gun Corps Warning Order Appendix 40	30/05/1918	30/05/1918
Operation(al) Order(s)	18th Battalion M.G.C. Order No. 30 Appendix 41		
Miscellaneous	18th Battalion Machine Gun Corps. Relief Table		
Diagram etc	Corps Boundary		
Miscellaneous	Casualties Incurred by The Battalion During The Month of May 1918. Appendix 42		
Miscellaneous	Changes In Establishment And Strength Changes In Officers, Drafts Etc. Received by The Battalion During The Month of May. Appendix 43		
Heading	War Diary of 18th Battn Machine Gun Corps. From 1st June 1918 To 30th June 1918 (Volume. V)		
War Diary	Molliens-Au-Bois	01/06/1918	02/06/1918
War Diary	Contay	03/06/1918	30/06/1918
Miscellaneous	Administrative Instructions In Connection With 18th Bn. M.G.C. Order No. 30. Appendix 44	03/06/1918	03/06/1918
Operation(al) Order(s)	18th Bn. M.G.C. Order No. 31. App 45		
Operation(al) Order(s)	18th Bn. M.G.C. Order No. 32. Appendix 46	08/06/1918	08/06/1918
Miscellaneous	Water Points.		
Operation(al) Order(s)	18th Battn. B.G.C. Order No 30. Appendix 47	09/06/1918	09/06/1918
Miscellaneous	Appendix "A"		
Diagram etc	Identification Trace for use with Artillery Maps.		
Operation(al) Order(s)	18th Bn. M.G.C. Order No. 33. Appendix 48	10/06/1918	10/06/1918
Operation(al) Order(s)	18th Battn. M.G.C. Order No. 34. Appendix 49	14/06/1918	14/06/1918
Diagram etc	Use with Artillery Maps		
Operation(al) Order(s)	18th Battn. M.G.C. Order No. 36. Appendix 50	26/06/1918	26/06/1918
Miscellaneous	Time And Base of Fire. Appendix "A"		
Diagram etc	(38 Guns Employed on A/N Front)		
Operation(al) Order(s)	18th Battn M.G.C. Order No. 35. Appendix 51	29/06/1918	29/06/1918

Miscellaneous	Casualties Incurred by The Battalion-During The Month-of-June 1918 Appendix 52	20/06/1918	20/06/1918
Miscellaneous	Changes In Establishment And Strength, Increases & Decreases Officers, Drafts Received Etc., By The Bn. During June. Appendix 53	20/06/1918	20/06/1918
Heading	War Diary. of 18th Battn Machine Gun Corps From 1st July 1918 To 31st July 1918 (Volume VI)		
War Diary	Contay	01/07/1918	13/07/1918
War Diary	Fourdrinoy	14/07/1918	30/07/1918
War Diary	Le Houssoye	31/07/1918	31/07/1918
Miscellaneous	18th M.G.C. M.G. 152 F. Appendix 54		
Miscellaneous	Report On Action of 18th Battalion M.G. Corps In Minor Operation Carried Out by The 54th Infantry Brigade on 30th June-3rd July 1918. Appendix 54A	05/07/1918	05/07/1918
Miscellaneous	A.B.C.D Coy Appendix 55	03/07/1918	03/07/1918
Miscellaneous	Battery Lines		
Operation(al) Order(s)	18th Battn M.G.C. Order No. 36. Appendix 56.	10/07/1918	10/07/1918
Miscellaneous	Embussing Table Appendix "B"	11/07/1918	11/07/1918
Miscellaneous	18th Battn M.G.C. No F. 56 Appendix 57	12/07/1918	12/07/1918
Miscellaneous	Amendment To Relief Table Issued With Order No. 36.	12/07/1918	12/07/1918
Operation(al) Order(s)	18th Battalion Machine Gun Corps Order No. 39. Appendix 64	31/07/1918	31/07/1918
Operation(al) Order(s)	18th Battn M.G.C. Order No. 38. Appendix 63	30/07/1918	30/07/1918
Miscellaneous	Administrative Instructions In Connection With Order 37.		
Miscellaneous	Embussing Table.		
Miscellaneous	March Table	28/07/1918	28/07/1918
Miscellaneous	18th Battalion Machine Gun Corps. Appendix 59		
Miscellaneous	18th Battn. M.G.C. No. S.56. Entrainment of Div. At 9 Hours Notice Appendix 60		
Miscellaneous	18th Battalion M.G.C. No. L.3/201. Tactical Lessons Learnt During The Past Monte Appendix 61	22/07/1918	22/07/1918
Miscellaneous	Entraining Table Appendix "A"	17/07/1918	17/07/1918
Miscellaneous	18th Battalion Machine Gun Corps.	14/07/1918	14/07/1918
Operation(al) Order(s)	18th Battn. M.G.C. Order No. 37. Appendix 62	28/07/1918	28/07/1918
Map	Trenches Corrected From Information Received Up To 18-5-18		
Miscellaneous			
Miscellaneous	Casualties Incurred by The Battalion During The Month of July 1918. Appendix 66		
Map	Appendix 65		
Miscellaneous	Changes In Establishment & Strength Changes In Officers-Drafts Received Etc. In Battn. During Month of July 1918. Appendix 67		
Heading	18th Division Divl. Troops. 18th Battalion Machine Gun Corps. August 1918		
War Diary	La Houssoye	01/08/1918	05/08/1918
War Diary	Valley C21c	06/08/1918	12/08/1918
War Diary	Warloy	12/08/1918	21/08/1918
War Diary	W. 25b 2.7	22/08/1918	24/08/1918
Operation(al) Order(s)	18th Battalion M.G.C. Order No. 40. Appendix 68	04/08/1918	04/08/1918
Miscellaneous	Fire Organistation Order		
Diagram etc	Identification Trace for use with Artillery Maps.		
Operation(al) Order(s)	18th Battn. M.G.C. Order No. 41. Appendix 69	06/08/1918	06/08/1918
Diagram etc	Use with Artillery Maps		

Miscellaneous	Narrative of Operation Showing The Part Played by The 18th Battalion M.G. Corps And "D" Company, 50th Bn. M.G.O. (Attached) During The Period 7th to 10th August 1918 Appendix 70	15/08/1918	15/08/1918
Miscellaneous	Casualties Incurred During The Period 8th to 10th August 1918. Appendix 'B'		
Diagram etc	Identification Trace for		
Operation(al) Order(s)	18th Battn. M.G.C. Order No. 42. Appendix 71	11/08/1918	11/08/1918
Miscellaneous	18th Battn. M.G.C. No. S.83. Amendment To 18th Bn. M.G.C. No. S.81 Appendix 72.	15/08/1918	15/08/1918
Operation(al) Order(s)	18th Bn. M.G.C. Order No. 43. Appendix 73	19/08/1918	19/08/1918
Operation(al) Order(s)	18th Battalion M.G.C. Order No. 44. Appendix 74	20/08/1918	20/08/1918
Diagram etc	Identification Trace for use with Artillery Maps.		
Operation(al) Order(s)	18th Battn. M.G.C. Order No. 45. Appendix 76	20/08/1918	20/08/1918
Miscellaneous	Fire Organization Chart.		
Miscellaneous	Fire Organisation Chart.		
Diagram etc	18th Bn Machine Gun Corps		
Diagram etc	Some Proposed Position After Consolidation.		
Diagram etc	Identification Trace for use with Artillery Maps.		
Miscellaneous	18th Battn. M.G.C. No. S. 124. Appendix 77	22/08/1918	22/08/1918
Miscellaneous	III Corps. No. E.13218 18th Div. No. 14/31/1"Q" 18th Battn. M.G.C. No. S.121 Appendix 78	23/08/1918	23/08/1918
Miscellaneous	Appendix 79	24/08/1918	24/08/1918
Miscellaneous	18th' Battalion Machine Gun Corps. Narrative of Operation Appendix 80		
Miscellaneous	18th Battalion Machine Gun Corps. Narrative of Operation 22nd August-5th September 1918	12/09/1918	12/09/1918
Miscellaneous	Key to Divisional Lines Appendix "A"	04/09/1918	04/09/1918
Miscellaneous	Summary of Lessons Learnt During Operations. Appendix 81		
Miscellaneous	Casualties Incurred by the 18th Battn. M.G. Corps During The Month of Aug. 1918 Appendix 82		
Miscellaneous	Changes In Establishment And Strength of Battn. Drafts Etc. During Month of Aug. 1918 Appendix 83		
Heading	War Diary of 18th Battn. Machine. Gun. Corps. From 1st Sept. 1918. To 30th Sept. 1918. Vol. VIII		
War Diary	Trones Wood	02/09/1918	02/09/1918
War Diary	Montauban Station	06/09/1918	14/09/1918
War Diary	Saulcourt	15/09/1918	16/09/1918
War Diary	Ronnsoy	17/09/1918	30/09/1918
Miscellaneous	Summary of Lessons Learnt During Recent Operations	18/09/1918	18/09/1918
Diagram etc			
Operation(al) Order(s)	18th Battn M.G.C. Order No. 47. Appendix 84	14/09/1918	14/09/1918
Operation(al) Order(s)	18th Battn. M.G.C. Order No. 48. Appendix 85	15/09/1918	15/09/1918
Operation(al) Order(s)	18th Battn. M.G.C. Order No. 49. Appendix 86	16/09/1918	16/09/1918
Miscellaneous	Commanded by O.C. "C" Coy. 100th Bn. M.G.C		
Miscellaneous			
Miscellaneous	Group Organization Chart.		
Miscellaneous	Medical Arrangements. Appendix "D"		
Diagram etc	Combined Tracing A B		
Operation(al) Order(s)	18th Battn. M.G.C. Order No. 50. Appendix 87	20/09/1918	20/09/1918
Diagram etc	Use with Artillery Maps.		
Miscellaneous	18th Battn. M.G.C. No. S.133. Appendix 89	27/09/1918	27/09/1918
Operation(al) Order(s)	18th Battn. M.G.C. Order No.32. Appendix 88	24/09/1918	24/09/1918
Operation(al) Order(s)	18th Battalion M.G.C. Order No. 53. Appendix 90	28/09/1918	28/09/1918

Miscellaneous	Casualties Incurred by The 18th Battn. M.G.Corps. During The Month of September 1918 Appendix 91		
Miscellaneous	Changes In Establishment And Strength of Battalion Drafts Received Changes In Officers Etc During Month of September Appendix 92	30/09/1918	30/09/1918
Heading	War Diary of 18th Battalion Machine Gun Corps From 1st October 1918 To 31st October 1918 Volume IX		
War Diary	Ronssoy Wood	01/10/1918	02/10/1918
War Diary	Montigny	03/10/1918	03/10/1918
War Diary	Warloy	04/10/1918	16/10/1918
War Diary	Le Cateau	17/10/1918	23/10/1918
War Diary	Bousies	24/10/1918	31/10/1918
Operation(al) Order(s)	18th Battn. M.G.C. Order No. 54. Appendix 93	01/10/1918	01/10/1918
Operation(al) Order(s)	18th Battn. Machine Gun Corps. Order No. 55. Appendix 94	01/10/1918	01/10/1918
Diagram etc	All Batteries 8 Guns 15		
Miscellaneous	Group "Z"		
Miscellaneous	Group "Y"		
Miscellaneous	Group "W"		
Operation(al) Order(s)	18th Battalion Machine Gun Corps Order No. 59. Appendix 99	21/10/1918	21/10/1918
Miscellaneous	A Form. Messages And Signals.		
Miscellaneous			
Miscellaneous	Barrage Guns		
Operation(al) Order(s)	18th Battalion Machine Gun Corps. Order No. 58 Appendix 98	20/10/1918	20/10/1918
Miscellaneous	Reference 18th M.G Battn Order No. 58 Para		
Miscellaneous	Group No. 3 Commanded by Coy. Comdr. 100th Bn. Battery "E"		
Miscellaneous	Group No. 4 Commanded by Lieut Leite Battery "D"		
Miscellaneous	Group No. 3 Commanded by Capt Llewellyn. Cattery "C"		
Miscellaneous	Group No. 2 Commander: Lieut. G. Young. Battery "B"		
Miscellaneous	Fire Organisation Chart.		
Miscellaneous	Medical Arrangements (To Accompany 18th Bn. M.G.C. Order No. 64)		
Operation(al) Order(s)	18th Battn. M.G.C. Order No. 64.	01/11/1918	01/11/1918
Miscellaneous	18th Battalion Machine Gun Corps. Warning Order Appendix 97	15/10/1918	15/10/1918
Operation(al) Order(s)	18th Batt Machine Gun Corps. Order No. 57 Appendix 96	18/10/1918	18/10/1918
Miscellaneous	Addenda To 18th Battn Machine Gun Corps Order No. 56.	15/10/1918	15/10/1918
Operation(al) Order(s)	18th Battn Machine Gun Corps. Order No. 56. Appendix 95	15/10/1918	15/10/1918
Operation(al) Order(s)	18th Battalion Machine Gun Corps Order No. 60. Appendix 100	22/10/1918	22/10/1918
Miscellaneous	Narrative Describing The Part Played by The 18th Battn. Machine Gun Corps During The Operations Leading Up To The Capture of Bousies & Robersart Appendix 102.		
Operation(al) Order(s)	18th Machine Gun Battn Order No. 61 Appendix 101	22/10/1918	22/10/1918
Miscellaneous			
Diagram etc	15 "A"		

Miscellaneous	Statement of Casualties Incurred by The 18th Battalion Machine Gun Corps For Period 22.10.18-24.10.1918 Appendix "C"	22/10/1918	22/10/1918
Operation(al) Order(s)	18th Battalion Machine Gun Corps. Order No. 62 Appendix 103.	24/10/1918	24/10/1918
Operation(al) Order(s)	18th Battalion Machine Gun Corps. Order No. 63. Appendix 104.	25/10/1918	25/10/1918
Miscellaneous	Casualties Incurred by The 18th Battn: M.G.Corps During The Month Of October 1918 Appendix 105.		
Miscellaneous	Changes In Establishment and Strength of Battalion Drafts Received, Changes In Officers Etc. During Month of October 1918 Appendix 106	01/10/1918	01/10/1918
Heading	War Diary of 18th Battn. Machine Gun Corps. From 1st November, 1918. To 30th November. 1918. (Volume X)		
War Diary	Bousies	01/11/1918	04/11/1918
War Diary	Preux Au Bois	05/11/1918	07/11/1918
War Diary	Lecateau	08/11/1918	17/11/1918
War Diary	Premont	18/11/1918	31/11/1918
Operation(al) Order(s)	18th Battn. M.G.C. Order No. 64. Appendix 108	01/11/1918	01/11/1918
Miscellaneous	Medical Arrangements. (To accompany 18th Bn. M.G.C. Order No. 64)	02/11/1918	02/11/1918
Miscellaneous	Fire Organisation Chart.		
Miscellaneous	18th Bn. M.G.C. No. S. 133 Recipients of Order No. 64	02/11/1918	02/11/1918
Heading	2 Lieut Regt Vol XX		
Miscellaneous	Narrative of Operations Carried Out by The 18th Battalion Machine Gun Corps Between The 25th October 1918 And 7th November 1918 Appendix 107.		
Miscellaneous	Summary of Lessons Learnt. Appendix. 'A'		
Miscellaneous	Changes In Establishment And Strength of Battalion, Drafts Received, Changes In Officers. Etc. During Month of November 1918. Appendix 109	01/11/1918	01/11/1918
Heading	War Diary of 18th Battalion Machine Gun Corps. From 1st December 1918 To 31st December 1918. Volume XI		
War Diary	Premont	01/12/1918	31/12/1918
Miscellaneous	Changes In Establishment And Strength of Battalion Drafts Received, Changes In Officers, Etc. During Month of December 1918. Appendix 110	01/12/1918	01/12/1918
Heading	War Diary of 18th Battalion Machine Gun Corps. From 1st January 1919. To 31st January 1919. (Volume XII)		
War Diary	Premont	01/01/1919	31/01/1919
Miscellaneous	Changes In Establishment And Strength of 18th Bn. M.G.C. Changes In Officers During The Month of January 1919. Appendix 111	31/01/1919	31/01/1919
Heading	War Diary of 18th Battalion Machine Gun Corps. From 1st February 1919. To 28th February 1919. (Volume XIII)		
War Diary	Elincourt	01/02/1919	28/02/1919
Miscellaneous	Changes In Establishment & Strength of 18th Battn. Machine Gun Corps Changes In Officers , During The Month of February 1919 Appendix 112		
Heading	War Diary of 18th Battalion Machine Gun Corps. From 1st March 1919. To 31st March 1919. (Volume XIV)		
War Diary	Elincourt	01/03/1919	31/03/1919

Miscellaneous	Changes In Establishment And Strength of 18th Battalion Machine Gun Corps Changes In Officers, During The Month of March 1919 Appendix 113

W095/2028(2)

18TH DIVISION

18TH BN MACHINE GUN CORPS

FEB 1918-MAR 1919

CONFIDENTIAL

7

War Diary.

Vol 1

~ of ~

18th BN. MACHINE GUN CORPS.

From:- 19th Feby 1918 — APPENDICES 1 &

To:- 28th Feby 1918. — 1a ATTACHED.

(VOLUME I)

18th Bn Machine Gun Corps **WAR DIARY** or **INTELLIGENCE SUMMARY.** February 1918.

Army Form C. 2118.

Instructions regarding War Diaries and Intelligence Summaries are contained in F. S. Regs., Part II. and the Staff Manual respectively. Title pages will be prepared in manuscript.

(*Erase heading not required.*)

Place	Date	Hour	Summary of Events and Information	Remarks and references to Appendices
		Ref.	ST QUENTIN SHEET 1/100000	
			On 16th February 1918 53rd (A) 54th (B) 55th (C) Machine Gun Companies moved from their respective billets to MONDESCOURT to form the 18th Battalion Machine Gun Corps.	JWW
MONDESCOURT	19/2/18		Battalion officially formed under LT-Colonel E. M. MINET DSO MC MGC Adjutant Captain J. W. K. WERNHAM MC (late 6th R Berks Regt) Training carried out in vicinity of Billets - Officers and NCOs reconnoitred lines in forward area	JWW
"	20/2-22/2		Training in vicinity of billets - parties of Officers & NCOs reconnoitring forward lines	JWW
"	23rd		"C" Coy proceeded by Route March to camp at FRIERES WOOD, parading 8 am arrived 1.0 pm A & B Coy & Bn HQ remained at Mondescourt - training	APPENDIX. I. JWW
	24th		"C" Coy moved from FRIERES CAMP to relieve 215 Coy 58 Bn MGC in line on FORT LIEZ Sector - Relief complete 12.20 am 25/2/18 Coy HQ. FORT LIEZ. "A" Coy moved to FRIERES CAMP. B Coy & HQ at MONDESCOURT	JWW

D. D. & L., London, E.C. (A7883) Wt. W809/M1672 350,000 4/17 Sch. 52a Forms/C/2118/14

18th Battn M.G. Corps

WAR DIARY or ~~INTELLIGENCE SUMMARY.~~

(Erase heading not required.)

February 1918

Army Form C. 2118.

Instructions regarding War Diaries and Intelligence Summaries are contained in F. S. Regs., Part II. and the Staff Manual respectively. Title pages will be prepared in manuscript.

Place	Date	Hour	Summary of Events and Information	Remarks and references to Appendices
MONDESCOURT	25th		"C" Coy in line - situation very quiet — A. Coy relieved 43rd Coy 14th Bn MGC in line in sector FORT VENDEUIL - E. of BENAY - HQ. at Quarry "B" Coy moved at 9.45 am to VILLEQUIER AUMONT arriving at 1.30 pm Bn HQ remained at MONDESCOURT	JWR
do	26th		Bn HQ moved from MONDESCOURT to VILLEQUIER AUMONT arriving 11.30 am. A & C Coys in line - situation quiet. B. Coy moved into Corps line (as per attached map) during early evening - positions taken up without casualties HQ. - REMIGNY	JWR
VILLEQUIER-AUMONT	27th		Situation very quiet - operations in line nil	JWR
"	28		Operations in line nil - situation very quiet - 5 Guns B Coy + 3 guns and teams from Battalions of 54th Infy Bde withdrawn from line into Corps Reserve. Corps Reserve - 54th Infy Bde at CAILLOUEL - 5 teams staged night at ROUEZ CAMP — Bn HQ moved to 18th DIV. HQ. ROUEZ	JWR

J W R Wernham
Capt & Adjt
18 Bn M.G. Corps

D. D. & L., London, E.C. (A7883) Wt W809/M1672 350,000 4/17 Sch. 52a Forms/C/2118/14

C O P Y

APPENDIX. 1.

18th Div. M.G. Battalion Order 1.

MOVE. 55th M.G.Coy. will move to-morrow 23rd February 1918 by Route March to FRIERES CAMP, S.9. Sheet 66.c.

ROUTE. CHAUNY - VILLEQUIER AUMONT - CAMP.

STARTING POINT. Road Junction K.11.c.2.3.

HOUR OF STARTING. To pass S.P. at 9 a.m.

BILLETING. 2nd Lt. BATCHELOR, 54th M.G.Coy will precede the party by lorry and billet for the Company at FRIERES CAMP. O.C. 55th M.G.C will detail 1 N.C.O. and 2 signallers to assist 2nd Lieut. BATCHELOR.

TRANSPORT. One lorry will report at Battn. H.Q. at 9 a.m. 55th M.G.C. will detail 1 O.R. to be at Bn.H.Q. at this Hour to guide it to Coy. Stores.

RATIONS. Rations for 23rd and 24th will be carried. 18th Div. Train will deliver rations for 25th inst. to the Company on the afternoon of 24th inst.

GUIDES. 2nd Lieut. BATCHELOR will send 1 signaller from FRIERES CAMP to meet 55th M.G.Company at Cross Roads S.8.c.1.5. to guide Company to Camp.

ORDERS FOR MOVE ON 24th INST. Orders for move on the 24th inst. and details of reliefs in the line will be issued to-morrow.

A C K N O W L E D G E.

(Signed) J.W.K.WERNHAM, Capt for
Lt-Colonel,
Commanding 18th Div. M. Gun. Battalion.

Copies to:-
No.1. to 53rd M.G.Coy.
No.2. to 54th M.G.Coy.
No.3. to 55th M.G.Coy.
No.4. to Battn. H.Q.

18th Div.

WAR DIARY

18th BATTALION, MACHINE GUN CORPS.

M A R C H

1 9 1 8

Attached:-

Narrative of Operations 21st/26th March.

Appendices 2 to 14a.

CONFIDENTIAL.

7

War Diary.

Vol 2

~ of ~

18th Battn Machine Gun Corps.

From:~ 1st March 1918

To:~ 31st March 1918.

Appendices 2 to 14A (inclusive) Attached.

(Volume II)

Instructions regarding War Diaries and Intelligence Summaries are contained in F. S. Regs., Part II. and the Staff Manual respectively. Title pages will be prepared in manuscript.

18th Battalion Machine Gun Corps

WAR DIARY or ~~INTELLIGENCE~~ SUMMARY.

(Erase heading not required.)

March 1918

Army Form C. 2118.

Place	Date	Hour	Summary of Events and Information	Remarks and references to Appendices
				Defence Scheme issued. see APPENDIX. 2.
ROUEZ	1st		Headquarters at ROUEZ – A. B (less 5 guns in Corps Reserve) & C Coys in	
	/9th		line – situation very quiet – operations nil	JWD (Appendix 3 & 4 issued on 2.3.1918)
"	10th		do 14th Division on left carried out raid at 10.15 pm	
			A. Coy supported attack by MG fire on ALAINCOURT	JWD (Appendix 5 issued 4.3.1918)
"	11/19		do Special conference of Company Commanders at	
			REMIGNY at 8 pm. on precautions against gas	JWD (Appendix 6 issued 13.3.1918)
"	20		do (Appendix 8 issued). Order to Prepare for attack received at 2.45 pm	JWD (Appendix 7 – 13.3.18)
	21/26		German Offensive – narrative of operations attached (Appendix 12)	JWD App 12.
	21st		Battalion HQ – ROUEZ Appendix 9 issued.	JWD App 9
	22nd		do	JWD
	23	12 noon	From ROUEZ to 800yds E. of VILLEQUIER AUMONT CHURCH and	JWD
			at 4.30 pm to UGNY-LE-GAY and redirected to BETHANCOURT	JWD
	24	10.30am	BN HQ moved to E 18 d 5 0 and at 3 pm to MONDESCOURT.	
			Later at 4.30 pm. to BABOEUF and at 11.30 pm to VARESNES	JWD
	25th	3 pm	Bn HQ moved to BOIS DE CARLEPONT where it bivouaced for night	JWD
	26th	9.30am	" CAIGNES where whole Battalion concentrated & reorganised	Appendix 10 issued JWD
			Losses in Machine Guns (Appendix 11)	App. 11

D. D. & L., London, E.C. (A7883) Wt. W809/M1672 350,000 4/17 Sch. 52a Forms/C/2118/14

18th Battalion Machine Gun Corps

WAR DIARY or INTELLIGENCE SUMMARY.

(Erase heading not required.)

March, 1918 (cont)

Army Form C. 2118.

Instructions regarding War Diaries and Intelligence Summaries are contained in F. S. Regs., Part II. and the Staff Manual respectively. Title pages will be prepared in manuscript.

Place	Date	Hour	Summary of Events and Information	Remarks and references to Appendices
CAGNES	26th	5.45 pm	Companies & HQ moved to NAMPCEL and AUDIGNICOURT – owing to NAMPCEL being allotted to 58th Div – and lack of billets at AUDIGNICOURT, companies marched on to LE MESNIL, arriving at 11 pm – Bn HQ AUDIGNICOURT	JW
AUDIGNICOURT	27th		Coys resting and cleaning up – Battalion guns pooled and 8 allotted to B Coy	
		2.30 pm	8 teams & guns under 2/Lt Brinkman B Coy proceeded to ST. AUBIN to join 54th Infy Bde who were in reserve to 58th Division in line	JW
..	28		Coys resting and cleaning up – Division warned units to stand by to move	JW
	29		8 teams attached 54th Inf Bde embussed 4 am with 54th Inf Bde B Coy (less 8 teams) & C Coy left LE MESNIL at 6 am to embuss at Cross Roads 1 miles W of NAMPCEL for HEBECOURT (near AMIENS). Owing to lack of lorries and being late, they were stopped at NAMPCEL to await further orders. The weather being very wet, troops were got under cover in NAMPCEL. Move Orders issued 6.25 am	App. 13/14
		4 pm	Battalion Transport moved to CHOISY and came under orders of O.C 18th Div. Train. All transport moved to new area under Divisional arrangements	JW

D. D. & L., London, E.C. (A7883) Wt. W809/M1672 350,000 4/17 Sch. 52a Forms/C/2118/14

Instructions regarding War Diaries and Intelligence Summaries are contained in F. S. Regs., Part II. and the Staff Manual respectively. Title pages will be prepared in manuscript.

Army Form C. 2118.

WAR DIARY or ~~INTELLIGENCE SUMMARY.~~

(Erase heading not required.)

18th Battalion Machine Gun Corps

March 1918 (cont)

Place	Date	Hour	Summary of Events and Information	Remarks and references to Appendices
			Reference Sheet 62D S.W. 1/20000	
AUDIGNICOURT.	30th		Weather very wet - Battalion moved as follows - A Coy from LE MESNIL B & C Coy from NAMPCEL - HQ from AUDIGNICOURT arriving at embussing point at 7 am - Embussing point Cross Roads 1 mile W of NAMPCEL. Embussed at 11 am in FRENCH lorries - proceeded to BOVES by route VIC-SUR-AISNE - ATTICHY - COMPIEGNE - CLERMONT - ST. JUST - BRETEUIL - FLERS-SUR-NOYE - ST SAUFLIEU - HEBECOURT - BOVES arriving ~~11 pm~~ 3 am. 31st and placed in rough billets for night - DIVISION ordered to take over line at once.	[initials]
	31st		During afternoon B Coy moved to billets in GENTELLES - A & C Coys to COPSE T.11.b.8.0 - Owing to transport moving by road and consequently not having arrived, no guns, material etc available. 15 new guns and parts sent up from Ordnance - 5 guns allotted each Coy - Coys moved into line on Divisional Front between HANGARD and VILLERS BRETONNEUX - A Coy on right B centre - C on left. HQuarters Bn HQ BOVES - A Coy DOMART, B Coy GENTELLES - C Coy MONUMENT (S of VILLERS-BRETONNEUX). Surplus personnel returned to billets in BOVES	For changes in strength see Appendix 14 [initials]

J.W.K. Wernham [?] Capt & Adjt 18th Bn M.G. Corps

D. D. & L., London, E.C. (A7883) Wt W809/M1672 350,000 4/17 Sch. 52a. Forms/C/2118/14

SECRET.

APPENDIX 2

COPY NO ..10.......

18TH DIVISION MACHINE GUN BATTALION.

DEFENCE SCHEME.

---

f. Maps -
ANCE, Sheet 66c.N.W., 1/20,000.
" " 66c.S.W., 1/20,000.

RONT.

1. The 18th Division holds the centre of the 3 Sectors of the III Corps front, the 58th Division being on the right and holding the Southern Sector, and the 14th Division being on the left and holding the Northern Sector.

2.(a). The boundary between the right of the 18th Division and the left of the58th Division is:-

O.32.a.4.0 - N.36.central - T.5.b.8.8 - cross roads T.4.a.6.1 (exclusive) - T.3.c.6.2 - T.8.d.4.2 - T.14.b.4.0 - T.19.c.6.8 - T.25.c.6.3 - F.28.c.4.6.

(b). The boundary between the left of the 18th Division and the right of the 14th Division is:-

I.13.d.6.9 - H.27.c.0.0 - H.32.b.4.7 (HINACOURT inclusive) - H.32.c.0.0 - N.1.d.0.0 - N.7.c.3.0 - M.30.b.5.8 to Railway M.30.c.0.0 - S.2.d.0.0 - X.15.c.6.4 (see attached map).

(c). Map "A", attached, shews the M.G. positions of the neighbouring divisions on the immediate flanks of the 18th Division (marked Green).

NES OF DEFENCE.

The defences of the 18th Divisional Area are organised in two Zones of Defence -

(a) The Forward Zone.
(b) The Battle Zone.

RINCIPLES OF DEFENCE.

The main principles of machine gun defence of the Divisional Sector are -

1. Organisation in depth.
2. Enfilade and cross fire.

P.T.O.

GUNS AVAILABLE FOR DEFENCE OFDIVISIONAL SECTOR.

43 Machine Guns are available for defence of the Divisional Sector.

Additional Guns.

In addition 8 guns have been allotted to the Brigade held in Corps Reserve.

Those guns are found as follows:-

(1) 5 guns from 54th M.G.Company.
(2) 3 guns already in possession of 54th Inf. Bde.

O.C. 54th M.G. Company will detail 2 officers to be in charge of these guns.

Distribution of Machine Guns in Divisional Sector.

24 guns have been allotted for defence of Forward Zone (marked Red on attached map).

14 guns have been allotted for defence of Battle Zone (marked Black).

5 guns have been allotted for defence of LY-FONTAINE SWITCH (marked Blue).

Gun positions are marked with a small round dot and the arrow indicates the normal direction of fire.

Gun positions have been numbored as per Map "A" attached.

A.1. - 13.)
B.~~1~~.3 - ~~5~~.4) Manned by 55th M.G.Coy.
C.7.)

B.5.)
C.1. - 6.) Manned by 54th M.G.Coy.
C.8. - 11.)

A.14 - 24 (to include 20a).)
B.1 - 2.) manned by 53rd M.G.Coy.
C.12 - 13.)

Guns will be grouped and each group placed under the command of an officer.

Battn. H.Q. is at S.27.a.3.3.
Coy. H.Q. of 53rd M.G.Coy. is at QUARRY H.28.d.3.3.
Coy. H.Q. of 54th M.G.Coy. is at REMIGNY N.14.c.3.5.
Coy. H.Q. of 55th M.G.Coy. is at LIEZ FORT N.34.c.

DETAILS OF DEFENCE.

Protection.

A garrison of infantry to each gun position has been detailed for the protection of that position. Group Commanders will report at once through the O.C., Coy. to Battn. H.Q. if these garrisons are not provided.

Cover.

Cover for guns and teams must be provided and belt filling shelters erected, These belt filling shelters MUST be protected from wet.

The C.R.E. 18th Division is arranging to provide accommodation for all gun teams but in the meantime M.G. emplacements must be constructed. Elephant shelters may now be obtained from R.E. Dump LIEZ. Special attention must be paid to CAMOUFLAGE and the prevention of movement around gun positions during the day.

Fighting Maps.

O.C., Coys. will ensure that every gun position is in possession of an Indirect Fire Sheet and a Fighting Map, showing indirect and direct targets. Copies of these maps and fire sheets will be forwarded to Battn. H.Q. for checking purposes.

Ammunition.

Ammunition as under will be dumped with each gun.

14 Belt Boxes.
15,000 rounds S.A.A. in boxes.

The ammunition will be placed at gun positions from Mobile Reserve and indents will be submitted to H.Q. to replenish the Mobile Reserve.

V.P. Ammunition at the rate of 6 cartridges per pistol will be maintained with each gun team.

Ammunition dumps have been formed as follows :-

Divisional Bomb Stores - S.16.c.4.4. (Sheet 66c).
Brigade Dumps - LA GUINGETTE, N.24.c.1.8.
Brigade Dumps LIEZ.

P.T.O.

These Brigade Dumps will be kept intact except in case of emergency, all trench requirements being indented for through Battn. H.Q.

Oil, Water, etc.

Two petrol tins of water will be kept with each gun, also a sufficient supply of flannelette, oil, etc. Care will be taken to ensure that spare parts are available at a moment's notice and ready for immediate use. Old petrol tins will be used as condensors.

Functions.

No gun will be moved or its function altered without first obtaining sanction of Battn. H.Q.

Group Commanders will be responsible for

(1) Elevation and direction of fire of the guns under their command.
(2) Cleanliness and efficiency of their guns.
(3) Compilation of Indirect Fire Sheet and Battle Maps.
(4) Precautions against gas.

GAS.

Group Commanders will take steps to see that gas blankets or anti-gas material is available for the protection of guns, ammunition, etc., from the effects of enemy gas. Daily inspections of S.B.R. will also be made. Dugouts must also be protected with blankets.

ACTION ON S.O.S.

Guns in the front line ONLY will fire short bursts on the normal lines of fire. If the signal is not repeated firing will cease after 10 minutes. No other gun will fire unless a direct target presents itself until proper belt filling positions have been provided.

ACTION IN THE EVENT OF ATTACK.

(1) In the event of attack, or the probability of attack, the following will be the procedure.

The message PREPARE FOR ATTACK will be sent out on receipt of which -

(a) All defences in the FORWARD ZONE will be manned and the utmost state of vigilance will exist.
(b) All O.Ps. will be manned instantly.
(c) All troops will be got ready to move at 15 minutes notice to their Battle Positions.

(2) The message MAN BATTLE POSITIONS will be sent out on receipt of which

(a) All troops detailed for defence of BATTLE ZONE will move into position.

(b) Artillery will commence a regular and heavy bombardment of the enemy front zone,

3. Any officer will carry out any of the instructions mentioned above, without waiting for either of the two telegrams, if, in his opinion, a situation arises necessitating such action.

(4) During the actual fighting, only those men actually required will be kept at the guns, the remainder being kept under cover in the vicinity ready to replace casualties and to fill belts.

(5) Every gun team will fight to the last and on no account will any gun be withdrawn from its present position without direct orders from Battn. H.Q.

LIAISON.

O.C., 54th M.G.Coy. will maintain close touch with O.Cs. 53rd and 55th M.G.Coy. Both LIAISON officers will be in a position to explain any part of the whole Divisional M.G. Defence and advise Brigades the role each gun can perform.

COMMUNICATION.

Battn. H.Q. WILL BE IN TELEPHONIC AND MESSENGER COMMUNICATION with Brigades in the line through 18th Divl. H.Q. O.C., 53rd M.G.Coy. will maintain close touch with 53rd Inf.Bde. by wire and runner.

O.C., 55th M.G.Coy. will maintain close touch with 55th Inf. Bde. by wire and runner.

O.C., 54th M.G.Coy. will maintain close touch with 18th Divl. Signal Exchange Office REMIGNY by wire and runner.

In case the communication breaks down between Divl. H.Q. and Brigades in the line, O.C. Coys. will ensure that personnel at their Transport Lines know the routes both from Coy. H.Q. in the line to Transport Lines and from Transport Lines to Battn. H.Q.

On receipt of message OCCUPY BATTLE ZONE or any notification to say that the enemy is attacking, each Coy. will immediately send a Mounted Orderly to Battn.H.Q. to await orders.

P.T.O.

MEDICAL ARRANGEMENTS.

Location of Medical Posts.

(1) For defence of BLUE Line.

R.A.P. (a) VENDEUIL N.13.d.9.5.
(b) GUINGETTE FARM H.24.c.1.5.
(c) MOY T.25.b.2.1.

Advanced Dressing Station - REMIGNY N.14.c.2.6.

(2) For defence of RED Line.

(a) LIEZ QUARRY N.31.b.4.1.
(b) REMIGNY N.14.c.2.6.

These posts would also serve as collecting posts for the Field Ambulance Bearers.

Advanced Dressing Station - RAILWAY CUTTING M.36.a.9.0.

J.W.K. Wenham

Captain & Adjutant,
18th Divisional Machine Gun Battalion.

March 1st 1918

Copies to - 1. Hd.Qrs.
2. 53rd M.G. Company.
3. 54th M.G. Company.
4. 55th M.G. Company.
5. 53rd Inf.Bde.
6. 54th Inf.Bde.
7. 55th Inf.Bde.
8. 18th Division G.
9. 18th Division Q.
10/11. War Diary.
12. III Corps M.G.Officer.
13. D.M.G.O., 14th Division.
14. D.M.G.O., 58th Division.

APPENDIX. 3.

SECRET COPY No. 3/6

18th. BATTN. MACHINE GUN CORPS ORDER No 2

MOVE.

Five gus and teams and 2 Officers of 54th M.G.Coy. will move from ROUEZ CAMP tomorrow 3rd inst. to join 54th Infy. Bde. at CAILLOUEL. On arrival they will come under direct orders of G.O.C. 54th Infy. Bde.

(These guns are intended to combine wit h 3 guns already in possession of 54th Infy Bde. to form a battery of 8 guns at disposal of G.O.C. 54th Infy. Bde.

TIME OF STARTING.

Party will leave ROUEZ CAMP at 10 a.m. arriving at CAILLOUEL about 12.15.p.m.

ROUTE

VILLEQUIER-AUMONT -- COMMENCHON -- BETHENCOURT -- CAILLOUEL

COMPOSITION OF PARTY

Party will be composed as under ;-

2 Officers
2 Batmen
5 Gun Teams
4 Limbers
4 Drivers
14 Mules
1 Officers Charger

(54th Infy Bde will detail 2 Limbers 1 four mule 1 two mule to complete transport of the 8 gun battery)

AMMUNITION EQUIPMENT ETC

The following equipment ammunition etc. will be taken,

5Guns complete
100 Belt Boxes (20 per gun)
48 Ertra Belt Boxes (To complete to 20 per gun of 3 guns already with 54th Infy Bde.)
18,000 Rds S.A.A.

Note:- 54th Infy. Bde will provide 18,000 rds S.A.A. to complete establishment of S.A.A. required for battery of 8 guns. 12 belt boxes are already in possession of 54th Infy. Bde.

RATIONS

Party will be rationed up to and including 4th inst from which date it will be rationed by 54th Infy Bde.

BILLETS

Billets have been arranged by Staff Captain 54th Infy. Bde.

REPORTS ETC.

Completion of move will be notified to Battn.H.Q.

ACKNOWLEDGE 2.3.18

J.W.K. Warren
Capt. and Adjt.
18th Battn Machine Gun Corps

APPENDIX 4.

SECRET

Copy No. 1

18th Battn. MACHINE GUN CORPS, ORDER No 3.

RELIEFS

The following changes in dispositions of Machine Guns will take place tomorrow 3rd March 1918.

2 Guns positions of 53rd M.G.Coy. at BERRY CEMETERY H.b.3.7. will be taken over by 224 M.G.Coy.(14th Division)

1 Gun position of 224M.G.Coy. at H.27.d.55.30. will be taken over by 53rd M.G.Coy.

TIME

Reliefs will take place at 7 a.m. 3rdinst. Other details of relief will be arranged between Officers concerned Completion of reliefs will be notified to Battn.H.Q.

ACKNOWLEDGE

J.A.K. Wemberg[illegible] Capt and Adjt.
18th Battn. M.G.C.

Copies to

No 1 - Batt HQ
2 - 53 MGC
3 - ~~224 MGC~~ 14th Batt. M.G.C.
4 - War Diary

APPENDIX 5

SECRET. Copy No ..8...

Reference Maps:-
66.C.N.W. & 66.C.S.W. 1/20,000. 4th March 1918.

18TH BATTALION MACHINE GUN CORPS ORDER NO. 4.

1. To allow Companies to arrange reliefs between themselves, the following reallotment of positions will take place:-

54th M.G.Company will take over Gun Positions 1 and 2.
54th M.G.Company will hand over to 53rd M.G.Coy Gun Positions C.10. and 11.
54th M.G.Company will hand over to 55th M.G.Company Gun Positions C.1. to 6.
55th M.G.Company will hand over to 54th M.G.Company Gun Positions B.3 & 4, and A.10 - 13.

2. Reliefs will be carried out during the night 4th/5th March 1918. Details to be arranged between Os.C. Companies concerned.
Reliefs will be so timed as to ensure that the least possible number of guns are out of action during any one period.

3. On completion of reliefs Companies will be disposed as follows :-

A. 1 - 9)
C. 1 - 7) Manned by 55th M.G.Company.

A.10 - 13)
B. 1 - 5) Manned by 54th M.G.Company.
C. 8 - 9)

A.14 - 24)
C.10 - 12) Manned by 53rd M.G.Company.

4. Defence schemes will be amended accordingly.

5. Completion of reliefs will be reported to this Office by wire quoting the number of this order only.

6. A C K N O W L E D G E.

J W K Weaver [signature]
..................Capt & Adjt.
18th Battn. Machine Gun Corps.

Issued at 11:20 a.m. by D.R.L.S.

Copies to:-
No.1.Copy, C.O.
" 2 " 53rd M.G.Company.
" 3 " 54th M.G.Company.
" 4 " 55th M.G.Company.
" 5 " 18th Division "G".
" 6 " 53rd Infantry Brigade.
" 7 " 55th Infantry Brigade.
" 8 " War Diary.
" 9 " War Diary.
" 10 " File.

SECRET. APPENDIX 6. Copy No......
18th Bn. M.G.C.No.S.11.

WARNING ORDER.

1. In the event of the 18th Division being withdrawn from the line, a reserve Company of the 14th Div. M.G.Bn. will relieve "A" Company and part of "B" Company. A reserve Company of the 58th Div. M. G. Battalion will relieve "C" Company and remainder of "B" Company.

2. Guns attached to 53rd and 55th Infantry Brigades will be relieved on night of "Z" plus 1/"Z" plus 2.

3. (a) Positions to be taken over by the relieving Company of the 14th Div. M. G. Battn. from "A" and "B" Companies, will be:-

A.21. A.22. A.23. A.24. A.19. A.18. A.20. A.20.a.
A.17. A.15. A.10. C.11. C.12. C.13. A.10. B. 5.

(b) Positions to be taken over from "C" and "B" Coys by the relieving reserve Company of the 58th Div. M.G. Battn. will be:-

B.1. B.2. B.3. B.4. A.8. A.5. A.1. A.3.
C.1. C.2. C.3. C.4. C.5. C.6. C.8. C.9.

Guns not included in above relief will withdraw after Infantry Brigades have completed their reliefs.

4. On "Z" day, 8 guns now at CAILLOUEL will proceed direct to MONDESCOURT.

5. "A" Company will stage the night at ROUEZ, "B" and "C" Companies at NOUREUIL and will proceed to MONDESCOURT next day.

6. Transports will be situated as follows:-

"A" Company:- VILLEQUIER AUMONT.
"B" Company:- ROUEZ CAMP.
"C" Company:- NOUREUIL.

7. A representative of each Company should report to Battalion Headquarters on "Z" day and their billets will be indicated.

8. Companies will take over same billets in MONDESCOURT as those previously occupied by them.

....................Capt & Adjt.,
18th Battalion Machine Gun Corps.

13th March 1918.

No.1.Copy, 18th Div. "G"
" 2 " 18th Div. "Q"
" 3 " 14th D.M.G.Bn.
" 4 " 58th D.M.G.Bn.
" 5 " 18th Divl. Train.
" 6 " 53rd Inf. Bde.
" 7 " 54th Inf. Bde.
" 8 " 55th Inf. Bde.
" 9 " "A" Company.
" 10 " "B" Company.
" 11 " "C" Company.
" 12 " Qr.Mr.
" 13 " War Diary.
" 14 " War Diary.
" 15 " File.

S E C R E T. APPENDIX 7.

1E'TH Div. G.918.
18th Battn. M.G.C. No.S.14.

To:- O.C. "A" Company.
"B" Company.
"C" Company.

Reference 18th Div. G.902 (attached) dated 13th inst.

The system laid down for Communication of Hour for Counter Attack will be employed for any class of Counter-Attack which is being carried out with Artillery support.

In the case of the immediate counter-attack Companies there will not always be time to arrahge for artillery support and for the presence of an aeroplane, but should such time be available the system referred to will be used so as to have only one form of signal for this purpose.

....................Capt & Adjt.,
18th Battn. Machine Gun Corps.

15th March 1918.

S E C R E T.

18th Battn. M. G. C. No. S.15.
18th Division No. G. 902.

III Corps Defence Scheme.

APPENDIX VIII.

F. - Communication of Hour for Counter Attack.

The following method will be adopted in communicating the hour of the counter-attack to all concerned.

1. The Brigadier conducting the Counter-attack will settle, so far as he be able, zero hour for the counter attack (say 2 p.m.) and communicate it to all concerned. The hour selected will always be the clock-hour or half-hour.

2. The Battalion Commander or Commanders carrying out the attack will establish their Headquarters to-gether and as near to the zone of deployment of their troops as feasible, and mark their Headquarters with the senior Battn. Commanders aeroplane strips.

3. Should the Battn. Commanders realise that they cannot get their troops into position in time for the assault at the hour fixed (i.e. 2p.m.) they will fire two clusters of Red Very Lights (at a short interval, the first cluster at a quarter of an hour before zero, i.e., at 1:45 p,m.) as a signal to the Artillery that Zero hour has been postponed half-an-hour. They will also, if possible, communicate the postponement in B.A.B. Code by 'phone to their Brigade H.Q. and the Artillery and to the Division for communication to the R.F.C. (via Corps Hd.Qrs).

4. The Artillery (Both Field and Heavy) will then reduce their fire, as much as possible, for 10 minutes before and after the zero hour fixed (i.e., from 1:50 p.m. to 2.10 p.m.) so as not to mislead the Infantry into thinking that the Barrage has commenced.

5. Should, on the other hand, the Battn. Commanders consider that the attack can proceed at the zero hour fixed, they will display, at their combined Headquarters, awwhite cross (made of white strips 10' x 2') five minutes before zero hour (i.e. 1.55 p.m.)

6. Two contact aeroplanes will leave the ground together half an hour before zero (i.e. 1.30 p,m.) and on seeing the strips, the leading 'plane (to be nominated by the 82nd Squadron R.F.C.) will fire a succession of White Very Lights. These lights will be the signal to the infantry for the assault to commence.

7. Each postponement will always be for 30 minutes.

8. A second postponement (i.e. to 3 p.m. instead of 2.30.p.m.) can, if necessary, be made by the same means, i.e. by firing Red Very Lights again at 2.15 p.m. A third postponement (i.e. to 3.30 p.m.) can also be made, but a fourth postponement will indicate that the operation is cancelled for the time being.

9. The artillery will always reduce their fire for 10 minutes before zero, so as to emphasize the moment for the attack, when the barrage falls.

SECRET APPENDIX.8. 18th Battn. M.G.C. No. S.22.

WD

To:- Os.C. "A", "B", "C" Coys.
Div."G", C.R.E. 18th Div.
53rd, 54th, 55th Inf. Bdes.
14th Bn. M.G.C.
58th Bn. M.G.C.
III Corps M.G.O.

Machine Guns in 18th Divisional Sector have been re-numbered/ in depth as follows:-

Old Number.	New Number.	Old Number.	New Number.
A.22.	A.1.	B.1.	B.7.
A.21.	A.2.	C.9.	B.8.
A.24.	A.3.	C.8.	B.9.
A.23.	A.4.	B.4.	B.10.
A.20.	A.5.	B.3.	B.11.
A.20a.	A.6.	A.8.	C.1.
A.19.	A.7.	A.7.	C.2.
A.18.	A.8.	A.6.	C.3.
A.17.	A.9.	A.5.	C.4.
A.16.	A.10.	A.3.	C.5.
A.15.	A.11.	A.2.	C.6.
A.14.	A.12.	A.1.	C.7.
(C)A.12.	A.13.	A.1a.	C.8.
C.11.	A.14.	C.6.	C.9.
C.10.	A.15.	C.5.	C.10.
A.13.	B. 1.	C.7.	C.11.
A.12.	B.2.	C.4.	C.12.
A.11.	B.3.	C.3.	C.13.
A.10.	B.4.	C.2.	C.14.
B. 5.	B.5.	C.1.	C.15.
B. 2.	B.6.		

[signature]
Lieut-Colonel,
Commanding 18th Battn. Machine Gun Corps.

20th March 1918.

COPY.

SECRET. APPENDIX. 9. Copy No.4....

18th BATTN. MACHINE GUN CORPS ORDER No.6.

21st March 1918.

1. Owing to the Division having been ordered to fall back on to the GREEN LINE, Transports of Coys. will also withdraw from their present Camps as follows:-

"A" Coy, from VILLEQUIER AUMONT to GUYENCOURT.
"B" Coy. from ROUEZ CAMP to CAILLOUEL.
"C" Coy. from NOURIEUL to LE PLESSIER.

2. Coys. will at once take steps to remove all stores etc. to their new locations.

3. Sites for Camps will be selected by Coys. themselves.

4. Corps Headquarters have advised that all troops should avoid villages as much as possible and transport, therefore, should be directed to fields etc.,

5. Bn. H.Qrs. will remain at ROUEZ for the present. Coys. will send one mounted Orderly to Battn. H.Qrs giving location of Camp.

(Signed) J.W.K.WERNHAM, Capt & ADjt.,
18th Battalion Machine Gun Corps.

Issued at 9.20 p.m.

Copies to:-

No.1.Transport Officer, "A" Company.
" 2 do., "B" Company.
" 3 do., "C" Company.
" 4 War Diary.
War Diary.
" 5 File.

Prefix............Code..............m | Words. | Charge.

Office of Origin and Service Instructions.

APPENDIX. 10.

Sent At..........m. To.......... By..........

This message is on a/c of: ....Service. (Signature of "Franking Officer.")

Recd. at..........m. Date.......... From.......... By..........

TO 18th Bn M.G. Corps Order No. 8.

Sender's Number.	Day of Month.	In reply to Number.	AAA
—	26.3.18	-	

Ref Map 70 E. N.W. EUROPE Sheet 10

1/ The 18th Bn M.G. Corps will move this afternoon at 5.45pm to the NOMPOEL ANDIGNICOURT PASSENS MORSAIN area

2/ Route to be taken by Coys is as follows:- Cross Roads Q25d 1.8 - The mill Q32a 2.7 - junction of tracks Q32a 9.4 - to junction of roads Q33a 99.70 - junction of roads W3c 0.0

3/ Coys will march at 5 minutes interval in the following order "A" - "B" - "C"

4/ All transport will move with their Coys

From Issued at 4pm
Place Copies to A.B.C.
Time Coys & QM

The above may be forwarded as now corrected. (Z)

Censor. Signature of Addressor or person authorised to telegraph in his name. [signature] Lt Col

* This line should be erased if not required.

(3198.) Wt W1295?/M1294. 375,000 Pads. 1/17. H. W. & V., Ld. (E. 818.)

APPENDIX. 11.

LOSSES OF MACHINE GUNS

during operations from 21st to 26th March 1918.

Number of M.G.'s captured by the Enemy	28	(Includes 6 Guns surrounded by Enemy and nothing further known. (8 Guns and Teams "Missing". (4 Guns probably destroyed by shell fire before capture. (5 rendered useless before capture. (Nothing known of 5.
Destroyed by enemy fire.	11.	

All guns have been replaced by Ordnance.

28th March 1918.

A P P E N D I X   1 2 .

Narrative relating to the part played during the Operations from the 21st to 26th March 1918 by the 18th Battalion Machine Gun Corps.

(**Note:** This Appendix precedes the War Diary.)

APPENDIX 12

Reference Maps:-

S E C R E T.

FRANCE, Sheet 66.c.N.W.1/20,000.
Sheet 66.c.S.W.1/20,000.
Sheet 70.d. 1/40,000.
Map Attached (Appendix "A")

N A R R A T I V E

RELATING TO THE PART PLAYED

DURING THE OPERATIONS FROM THE 21ST TO 28TH MARCH 1918.

--- by the ---

18TH BATTALION MACHINE GUN CORPS.

-----ooo-----

APPENDICES "A", "B", and "C" ATTACHED.

22.4.18.

NARRATIVE RELATING TO
THE PART PLAYED DURING THE OPERATIONS
FROM THE 21st TO 26th MARCH 1918
- by the -
18TH BATTALION MACHINE GUN CORPS.

The period 21/26th March 1918 represents the time the Battalion was engaged in actual operations with the enemy, commencing with the opening of the German Offensive on the morning on the 21st March until the Battalion was withdrawn from the line on the 26th March 1918.

On the 20th March the 18th Division was holding a sector of the British Front from roughly 2,000 yards South of VENDEUIL to just West of ALAINCOURT. This Divisional Sector was divided into two, the 55th Infantry Brigade holding the South or right sub-sector, the 53rd Infantry Brigade holding the North or left sub-sector. The 58th Division being on our right or Southern Boundary and the 14th Division on our left or Northern Boundary. All three Companies of the 18th Battalion Machine Gun Corps were in the line with the exception of 8 guns of "B" Company which were at disposal of G.O.C. 54th Infantry Brigade in Corps Reserve. Each Company was organised in depth and the guns disposed mutually supporting each other

DISPOSITIONS.

The Dispositions of Guns, sites of Company H.Qrs and Divisional and Brigade boundaries on the night of the 20th are shown on the attached Map.

"A" Company's guns were as follows:-
A.14, 15, 16, 17, 18, 19, 20, 20a, 21, 22, 23, 24.
C.10, 10a, 11, 12.
Company Headquarters at Quarry H.28.d.1.5.

"B" Company's Guns:-
A.10, 11, 12, 13, XX
B.1, 2, 3, 4, 5.
C.8, 9.
Company Headquarters at REMIGNY N.14.c.3.8.

"C" Company's Guns:-
A.1, 1a, 2, 3, 5, 6, 7, 8.
C.1, 2, 3, 4, 5, 6, 7.
1 Gun in reserve at VENDEUIL FORT.
Company Headquarters:- FORT DE LIEZ.

Battalion Headquarters were with Divisional Headquarters at ROUEZ S.27.a.4.5.

OPERATIONS.

At 2.45 p.m. on the 20th March 1918, a telegram was received from 18th Division as follows:-

"PREPARE FOR ATTACK"

This warning did not apply to us as all positions were continually manned.

On 21st March 1918, the German barrage opened at 4.30 a.m. and seems to have been more severe and intense on the Northern Sector than on the Southern Sector. At this time it was nearly dark and a very thick mist hung over the ground.

At 6.25 a.m. O.C. "C" Company reported everything fairly quiet in his sector and that most of the shelling was ours.

The main German attack seems to have been delivered against the 14th Division on our left where the enemy quickly penetrated the forward defences and started to work South and South-West.

Owing to the very thick mist he was able to work right up to our gun positions and there is little doubt that the 12 forward guns of "A" Company were very quickly destroyed or captured.

Of the 4 guns of "B" Company at LE VERT CHASSEUR in N.6. very little is known except that a few belts were got off into the mist on S.O.S. lines. A Corporal and private were taken prisoners, but managed to escape and report that 2nd Lieut. J. H. COLLINSON who was with these guns was last seen fighting to the last and firing his revolver from behind the gas blankets at the entrance of the dugouts until he was finally killed or wounded by enemy bombs.

Nothing is known of the guns in positions B.1. and 5.

B.2. position. This gun was withdrawn to a position 150 yds. to the S.W. and secured many good targets, inflicting severe losses on the enemy.

B.3. and 4 guns remained intact during the morning and later when the mist cleared performed excellent work including the beating off of an enemy attack near VENDEUIL FORT.

C.8 and 9 positions did not come into action.

The enemy appears to have worked through VENDEUIL VILLAGE and made their way South along the main ST QUENTIN Road to the Western slope of the ridge in N.36.b.

No information was received of guns at A.7, 8, C,7, and reserve gun in VENDEUIL FORT.

Only one message was received from 2nd Lieut. DALZELL, Commanding the guns A.2. and 3. This was timed 10 a.m. and stated:- "Enemy through, numbers unknown, am knocking hell out of them"

No further information was received from any of these guns.

The fog lifted about 1 p.m. but by this time it was impossible to get any communication through to the forward area with the exception of A.1, 1a, 5, and 6.

"A" Company was being heavily attacked from the North where the enemy had succeeded in capturing BENAY.

At 11.30 a.m. Company Headquarters had moved to an Infantry Strong Point about H.33.b.5.8 and had also brought in the gun C.12. to this point. This gun caused heavy casualties to the enemy who again and again were beaten off after attempting to capture the position. This gun remained in action until 7 p.m. that night when it was knocked out by shell fire. The No.1 and No.2. of this gun (Pte. LUCAS. and Pte. SHILLCOCK) rendered particularly gallant service in keeping this gun in action continuously for 7 hours under heavy fire.

Meanwhile the enemy was attempting to work further South from VENDEUIL.

Corporal J. LIVESAY who was with one of the forward guns of "C" Company was taken prisoner but managed to escape. He reports that he was made to carry German wounded and that later while with a large party of Germans was heavily shelled by our guns. The enemy scattered and he hid himself under a bank. At night he saw a light approaching along the road and found it was a German on a bicycle. He shot the Boche with his revolver, took his bicycle and made his way through the enemy's lines to his Company Headquarters.

At 1 p.m. the enemy was engaged in N.30 b and d. by our guns at N.36.a.(A.1. and 1a.) and driven East over the ST QUENTIN ROAD, casualties being inflicted.

The guns(C.5. and 6) North of RONQUENET FARM under 2nd Lieut. HORTON engaged the enemy throughout the afternoon and inflicted many casualties. The enemy was many times forced to retire although at one time he got to within 150 yards of the guns

Between 4 and 6 p.m. there was a slight lull in the operations on our Divisional front, but on the 58th Divisional Front on our right the enemy advanced rapidly thus exposing our right flank. Two guns of this Division were used to protect this flank as the enemy were seen massing for an attack on FORT LIEZ. This attack was beaten off.

During the day the 54th Brigade were ordered forward together with the 8 guns of 18th Battalion Machine Gun Corps, ("B" Company) to take up positions in **LY FONTAINE SWITCH.**

At night orders were received to withdraw over the Canal. "B" Company aided the 8th East Surrey Regiment in covering the withdrawal of the 53rd Infantry Brigade. This was completed about 1 a.m. 22nd March.

<u>22nd March 1918.</u>

"A" and "B" Companies concentrated at **FRIERES - FAILLOUEL** which village was reached at 3 a.m.

"C" Company concentrated at S.18.c. with Company Headquarters at ROUEZ.

Battalion Headquarters at ROUEZ.

The 8 guns were still with 54th Infantry Brigade and were dug in along the West bank of the **CROLAT CANAL**, which was our front line.

At 5 a.m. orders were issued to "A" and "B" Coys by G.O.C. 53rd Infantry Brigade to reconnoitre positions in front of **FRIERES WOOD** and **FRIERES FAILLOUEL.**

No. of guns available for defence were as follows:-

"A" Company,	3
"B" Company,	5 (1 without tripod) plus 8 guns with 54th Infantry Brigade.
"C" Company,	10.

and positions taken up were as follows:-

<u>"A" Company.</u>	1 gun, S.4.d.9.8.
	1 gun, S.4.d.95.60.
	1 gun, S.5.a.3.2.
<u>"B" Company.</u>	2 guns, S.10.b.8.5.
	2 guns, S.10.d.7.5.
	8 guns along Canal Bank from M.30.b. - M.18.a.
<u>"C" Company.</u>	2 guns in S.17.a.
	2 guns in S.24.a.
	2 guns in S.23.d.
	2 guns in S.24.c.
	2 guns in S.29.a.

During the morning no Infantry operations were undertaken by the enemy on our front. The 8 guns with 54th Infantry Brigade successfully engaged hostile cavalry and Infantry on the East side of the Canal.

In the afternoon the enemy succeeded in capturing **TERGNIER** and **VOEL** and later he twice massed for an attack between **VOEL** and the **BUTTE DE VOEL** but was each time dispersed and heavy casualties inflicted by the 8 guns in S.24.c. and S.24.a. During one of these attacks it was clearly observed that with one burst of fire from these 4 guns a whole Company was wiped out with the exception of three men.

In the evening the enemy attacked the 54th Infantry Brigade in M.23.b. and two of the 8 forward guns of "B" Company were put out of action.

About 6 p.m. the 4 guns of "B" Company in S.10. b. and d. and the three guns of "A" Company in S.4.d and 5a, who up untill now had been under the orders of G.O.C. 53rd Infantry Brigade were told to withdraw from their positions - "A" Company to proceed to ROUEZ CAMP S.27.b.2.4., "B" Company to proceed to **FRIERES FAILLOUEL** and report to G.O.C. 54th Infantry Brigade. Later these 4 guns of "B" Company were sent forward to the West Bank of the **CANAL** to reinforce the 8 guns attacked to 54th Infantry Brigade and were dug in in the forward system by early morning of the 23rd March.

23rd MARCH 1918.

On the early morning of the 23rd March, under cover of a thick mist the enemy again attacked along the whole Divisional Front; his barrage being very heavy on edge of wood in S.17.c. and d and S.23.a.

The guns available for defence were now:-

"A" Company.

3 guns at ROUEZ CAMP which were later put into positions:-

S.21.c.3.0.
S.27.a.0.6.
S.27.a.3.4.

"B" Company.

10 guns along the Canal Bank in M.30.b. - S.16.a.

"C" Company.

10 guns as disposed during 22nd.

Early in the renewed attack, "B" Company had two guns knocked out by hostile shell and T.M. fire. Orders having been received to withdraw to the line of the Railway, the remaining 8 guns covered the withdrawal of the Infantry.

In the subsequent withdrawal to the FAILLOUEL LINE two more guns were placed out of action.

On reaching FAILLOUEL VILLAGE orders were received from G.O.C. 54th Infantry Brigade for these 6 guns to go into Brigade Reserve near VILLEQUIER AUMONT. During this withdrawal the guns and teams again suffered very severely, only 2 guns under 2nd Lieut. WILSON reaching VILLEQUIER AUMONT in the evening.

Meanwhile the guns of "C" Company had been heavily engaged throughout the day. The enemy during the morning attacked from the direction of TERGNIER and forced our Infantry back.

The guns in S.17.a. and S.24.a. remained in position until almost surrounded before they withdrew and incurred several casualties amongst the gun teams while getting the guns away, two guns were rendered useless by hostile Machine Gun fire.

The position of "C" Coys. guns at 12 noon was:-

4 guns at S.28.Central.
4 guns extended from S.22.c. to S.28.a.

At about 1 p.m. the enemy having advanced through FRIERES WOOD worked South from S.22.d. to S.28.b. where he was immediately engaged by the 4 guns at S.28.Central under 2nd Lieut. HORTON and the four guns S.22.c. - S.28.a. under 2nd Lieut. BURDEN. He was held up and forced to retire back to the wood.

At this time 3 Machine Gun teams of 6th Cavalry M.G. Squadron were re-organised and placed in position in small trench just West of KEEPERS HOUSE, S.22.c.6.5. by 2nd Lieut. BURDEN.

Great difficulty was experienced in obtaining sufficient S.A.A. for refilling belts but this was overcome by collecting spare bandoliers from the Infantry whilst 2nd Lieut. FRIEND and signallers (7th Battn. (Queens) Royal West Surrey Regt) gave valuable aid by filling between 40 and 50 belts during the afternoon.

Between 6 p.m. and 7 p.m. these positions were subjected to heavy artillery bombardment after which the enemy attacked in close formation. Enemy Machine Gun Fire was exceptionally heavy and our Infantry and Machine Guns were forced to withdraw. During this attack 4 out of the 7 guns under 2nd Lieut BURDEN were put out of action and later the remaining three were also knocked out.

During the above operations quite 50, to 60,000 rounds were fired direct at the enemy and several casualties inflicted.

Colonel A. L. RANSOME, D.S.O., M.C. Comdg 7th Buffs, speaks very highly of the conduct of 2nd Lieut. BURDEN . He states that without this Officers valuable assistence he would not have been able to hold his positions for 8 hours as was the case and that it was due to 2nd Lieut. BURDEN's remarkable gallantry and supervision of the guns under his Command.

The 4 guns under 2nd Lieut. HORTON were kept in action untill the enemy advanced through the long grass to within 50 yards of his position. He was unable to get his guns away but they were put out of action before he withdrew.

Battalion Headquarters had remained at ROUEZ until about 12 noon 23rd inst, when with "C" Company's H.Q. moved to the small light railway embankment about S.26.a.5.6.. 8 Complete guns now arrived and belts were filled and positions taken up. As however it was found that the Infantry were taking up positions on the high ground further to the West, these positions were abondoned and the guns withdrawn to 53rd Brigade Headquarters on road S.25.d.1.4. and there dug in.

At 6 p.m. 3 guns of "A" Company were ordered by G.O.C. 53rd Infantry Brigade to take up positions in A.8.a. and c. to protect the left flank of the French Army as the enemy were reported to have got possession of NOUREUIL and VIRY NOUREUIL. However neither "C" not "A" Coys guns fired that night.

Orders having been received from Division for the Battalion to concentrate in MONDESCOURT, orders were accordingly issued by Battalion Headquarters.

"B" Company from VILLEQUIER AUMONT to MONDESCOURT.

"A" Company withdrew from its positions in A.8.a. and c. at 1 a.m. 24th and proceeded to GOMMENCHON AND later to BETHANCOURT

"C" Company withdrew from its positions in S.25.d. at 1 a.m. 24th and proceeded to BETHENCOURT en route for MONDESCOURT and on the way back handed over 1 gun to the Cavalry Corps who was going forward.

<u>24th MARCH 1918.</u>

At 9 a.m. just as Bn.H.Q. "C" Company and "A" Company were preparing to move back to MONDESCOURT, orders were received for all available guns to take up positions for the defence of BETHANCOURT and were placed at disposal of G.O.C. 55th Inf. Bde.

The 3 guns of "A" Company took up positions on the NEUFLIEUX - BETHANCOURT Road about F.14.d.4.0 and the 2 guns of "C" Company positions about F.14.Central

At about noon orders were received for a general withdrawal to the high ground East of CAILLOUEL.

The guns were accordingly withdrawn to their new positions. "B" Company had by this time arrived at CAILLOUEL from MONDESCOURT and reported to G.O.C. 54th Infantry Brigade.

At 3 p.m. dispositions of guns were as follows:-

"A" Coy. 2 guns about E.2[illegible]
"C" Coy. 2 " about E.24.b.2.2.
"B" Coy. 2 " E.7.[illegible], E.[illegible].a.
1 " E.2[illegible]

At 3.30 p.m. Battn. H.Q. moved to MONDESCOURT and at 4.30 p.m. moved to BABOEUF, and later at 11.30 p.m. proceeded to VARESNES.

No enemy attack developed against this CAILLOUEL Line but "A" and "C" Coys guns were in action against small parties of the enemy who were working forward S.E. and N.W. of BETHANCOURT which were dispersed.

<u>25th MARCH 1918.</u>

Orders to withdraw to the CREPIGNY LINE were received about 3 a.m. and new positions taken up by 6 a.m. Dispositions on this line were as follows:- (P.T.O)

"A" Company, 3 guns about K.3.a.
"C" Company, 2 guns about E.2[illegible].b.5.8.
"B" Company, 3 guns E.22.d.5.7 - E.1[illegible] - E.15.b.7.5.

2nd Lieut, BRINKMAN with his gun secured a good target of enemy transport moving in E.[illegible].b. which he completely dispersed.

At about 10 a.m. a further withdrawal being ordered a line was taken up along high ground in K.10.c. - K.[illegible].Central - K.[illegible].
The 3 guns of "A" Company were ordered to withdraw across the canal at APILLY and accordingly proceeded to CUTS as touch had been lost with 53rd Infantry Brigade.
The two guns of "C" Company took up positions, one about K.[illegible].Central and the other in K.3.c. Between 3.30 p.m. and 5 p.m. these two guns inflicted heavy casualties on the enemy who was coming on in masses and all available ammunition was exhausted on these targets whereupon the guns were withdrawn across the Canal to VARESNES AT WHICH PLACE THE NIGHT was spent.
Of the 3 guns of "B" Company originally with 54th Inf. Bde. only 2 now remained, 1 having been destroyed by shell fire. The 54th Brigade holding the high ground in K.3. counter-attacked the village of BABOEUF during the early evening and was completely successful. Two guns of "B" Company assisted the attack by overhead fire and then went forward to help in the consolidation but one was put out of action by enemy shrapnel.
About 8 p.m. Orders were received for all troops to withdraw South of the Canal. The withdrawal of the 54th Inf. Bde. began at 2 a.m. on 26th. 2nd Lieut. BRINKMAN with the one remaining gun of "B" Company brought up the rear of the Infantry and covered the withdrawal.
At 3.30 p.m. Battn. H.Q. had moved from VARESNES to wood P.16.a,6.5.

<u>26th MARCH 1918.</u>
Orders were issued early in the morning for the Battalion to concentrate at CAIGNES. This was accomplished by 12 noon.
At 5.45 p.m. the Battalion proceeded to NAMPCEL and was re-directed to ANDIGNICOURT. As billets could not be found here for the whole Battalion. "A", "B", and "C" Coys marched on to LE MESNIL where they were accommodated.

-ßßßßßßßßßßßßßßßßßßß-

<u>A P P E N D I C E S.</u>

APPENDIX "A" Map showing dispositions of Guns on night 20th/21st March 1918.

APPENDIX "B" List of Casualties incurred during above operations.

APPENDIX "C" Lessons Learnt from Operations.

--------oOo--------

Lieut-Colonel,
Commanding 18th Battalion Machine Gun Corps.

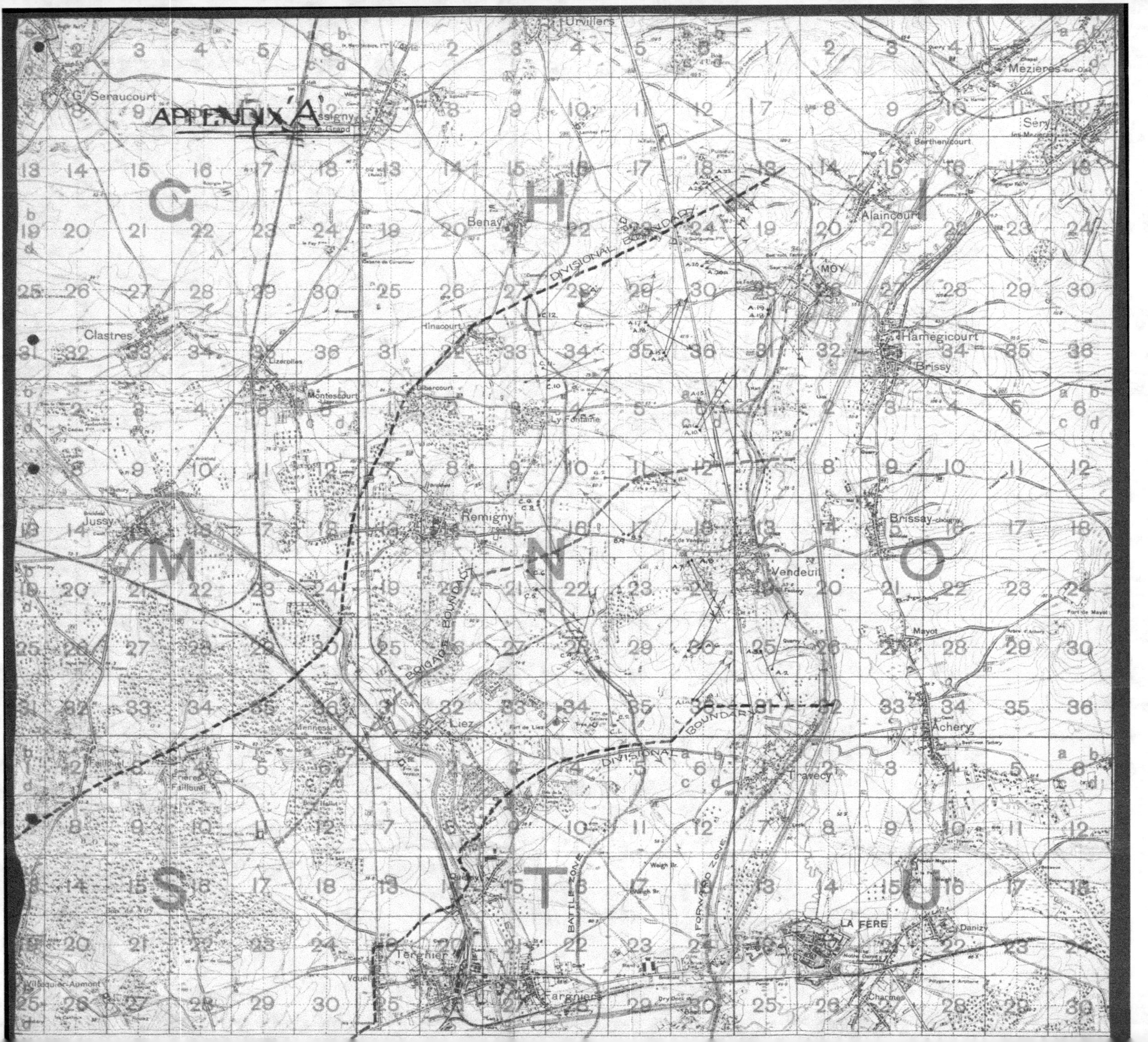

APPENDIX 'A'
G
H
I
M
N
O
S
T
U
DIVISIONAL BOUNDARY
BRIGADE BOUNDARY
BATTLE ZONE
FORWARD ZONE
Urvillers
Mezieres-sur-Oise
Séry
Seraucourt
Berthenicourt
Alaincourt
Benay
Moy
Hinacourt
Clastres
Hamégicourt
Brissy
Lizerolles
Montescourt
Ly-Fontaine
Remigny
Jussy
Brissay-Choigny
Vendeuil
Mayot
Liez
Achery
Mennessis
Travecy
Frières-Faillouël
La Fère
Danizy
Tergnier
Vouel
Fargniers
Charmes
Villequier-Aumont

APPENDIX "B".

CASUALTIES INCURRED DURING THE OPERATIONS from 21ST TO 26TH MARCH 1918, by the 18TH BATTALION MACHINE GUN CORPS.

OFFICERS.

Killed in Action
Lieut. Percy COOPER.

Wounded in Action.
Capt. Ernest Leslie WALLACE, M.C.
2nd Lieut. Ainsworth Frederick NEED.

Wounded at Duty.
2nd Lieut. Cyril HORTON.

Wounded and Missing.
2nd Lieut. J. H. COLLINSON.

Missing.
Lieut. Archibald Basil JONES.
2nd Lieut. Harold Isherman KAY.
2nd Lieut. Frederick Charles CHEESEMAN.
2nd Lieut. Robert Forbes GALBRAITH.
2nd Lieut. Thomas Frost DALZELL.

-----ooo-----

OTHER RANKS.

"A" COMPANY.

Killed	Nil.		
Wounded,	10.		
Missing.	54.	Total:-	64

"B" COMPANY.

Killed,	2.		
Wounded,	27.		
Missing,	27.	Total:-	56

"C" COMPANY.

Killed,	1.		
Wounded,	20.		
Missing,	51.	Total:-	72
		TOTAL CASUALTIES:-	192

ooo------

18TH BATTALION MACHINE GUN CORPS.

LESSONS LEARNT FROM THE RECENT OPERATIONS FROM
March 21st to 28th. 1918.

---

1. Insufficient use of fighting limbers in a war of movement. Owing to the long duration of stationary warfare, all M.G. Transport began to be considered 1st Line only, and the fighting limbers left with the rest far behind. If more use had been made of them, much fatigue would have been saved, for the men and sections become more mobile.

2. Guns should always be grouped in pairs or in sections of four, and always under the control of an Officer, the importance of this was brought out continually and too much stress cannot be laid on it, particularly in operations such as at the present time.

3. The ammunition supply for barrage and covering fire from behind the first line of defence was most difficult, if not impossible, to cope with. This was due to the length of time needed to fill belts, the lack of personnel to fill them owing to casualties, and the large amount of S.A.A. required. In addition to this a reserve of filled belts must always be kept for emergency, and the close defence of battle lines.

4. A clearer understanding appears to be required amongst Machine Gunners as to their role in defensive tactics, several instances having occurred when the Infantry retired through M.G. positions and the machine gunners joined in the backward movement, whereas they should remain at their positions to obtain short range enemy targets and only retire when ammunition is exhausted

5. Owing to the seeming lack of co-ordination of the Battalion Lewis Guns it is next to impossible to obtain full value out of both weapons, i.e., Lewis and Machine Guns, each has its distinctive role assisting one another; the Lewis Gun covering ground impossible to be taken on by Machine Guns, this has frequently led to misunderstanding and a solution of the difficulty seems very necessary. A suggestion has been made that Lewis Guns should be grouped in one platoon per Company under an Officer and co-ordinated in conjunction with the Officer i/c Forward Machine Guns, in theory this should always be done, in practice owing to many obvious reasons it very often is not.

6. Owing to the great attention paid recently to the Training of Machine Gunners in indirect and barrage fire a large number of Officers, N.C.Os. and men appear to have lost sight of the greatest value of Machine Gun fire, i.e., direct shooting up to a range of 800 yards, in operations like the recent and present ones. Whereas targets are engaged from ranges 1,000 yards to 2,000 yards, where visibility, accuracy of fire, and the killing power of the gun is not at its best, not enough consideration has been paid to the obvious fact that by husbanding ammunition supply, which in open warfare is inevitably difficult to obtain, and awaiting the approach of the enemy to a distance of 800 yards to 1000 yards away, far more killing is done, visibility and accuracy of fire correspondingly better and less ammunition wasted, furthermore more accurate results are seen and appreciated by the gunners themselves.

7. During the first 3 days of fighting it was proved conclusively that the Machine Gun defence and siting of guns was sound, but when it came to a battle of movement it was extremely difficult to co-ordinate guns or to obtain any system of communication.

8. The most frequent cause of putting a gun out of action was shrapnel holes in the barrel casing, at least 10 of the guns of this Battalion were temporarily out of action by this means. If some sort of light armour could be supplied for protection, or a very quick method of repair suggested it would be a very good thing. The system of supplying all guns with strips of corrugation to fit over the puncture and be rivetted on, is an idea.

9. After the first three days of fighting when all ranks were very tired, and many casualties had occurred amongst Officers and men, wild and exaggerated rumours flew about everywhere which certainly did not help the Machine Gunners to remain at their positions after the Infantry had retired past them and distinctly lowered their morale

10. In siting the machine guns in depth in open warfare the greatest difficulty is found in firing the rear guns over the heads of our front line troops with safety owing to the exact location of our line being often obscure, and further if the forward troops retired through our rear guns, great difficulty was again experienced owing to our own troops retiring right across the line of fire of these guns.

11. The importance of having the very best type of Officers and men in the Machine Gun Corps to ensure the principles set out in para 4 of these notes being carried out. Furthermore the importance of Machine Guns being boldly and skillfully handled in open warfare cannot be overrated and great initiative and resolution on behalf of the Officer in charge is essential.

12. A certain number of N.C.Os. and men, highly trained Machine Gunners were left behind at Reinforcement Camps. These men instead of being used to take the place of casualties in their M.G. Units were utilised as Infantrymen in composite detachments, this would appear to be utterly wrong.

Lieut-Colonel,
Commanding 18th Battalion, Machine Gun Corps.

20th April 1918.

SECRET. APPENDIX 13 Copy No.......

18th BATTN. M.G.CORPS ORDER NO. 9.

Reference Map:-
French Maps SOISSONS
and LAON and FRANCE
AMIENS,17, 1/100,000

29th March 1918.

1. Orders have been received for the Division to proceed to an area for re-organisation.

2. Dismounted personnel will proceed by lorry. Orders as to move of Transport will be issued later.

3. The following Units will embus forthwith and will proceed to embussing points at once:-

53rd Brigade (less Transport)
55th Brigade (less Transport)
"B" Coy, 18th Bn.M.G.C. (less transport, guns and personnel with 54th Inf. Bde)
"C" Coy, 18th Bn.M.G.C. (less Transport)

"B" and "C" Companies will move in same group of lorries as 55th Brigade.

4. Embussing point is as follows:-

TRACY.- NAMPCEL and CARLPONT - VIC-SUR-AISNE Cross Roads.

5. Lorries will hold 20 men.

6. Destination HEBECOURT (7 miles S. of AMIENS).

7. Troops will be formed up in groups of 20 men. Each group 15 yards apart, Officers in proportion.

8. Head of 55th Brigade will be at TRACY - NAMPCEL - and CARLPONT - VIC-SUR-AISNE Cross Roads. Remainder on road towards VIC-SUR-AISNE.

9. Troops will carry 1 blanket per man, packs and rations for 29th.

10. Officers valises will be dumped and collected by Coy Transport Officers under arrangements to be made by Companies.

11. Orders as to move of "A" Company will be issued later.

12. Capt. G. W. H. NICOLSON, will proceed with "B" and "C" Companies and billet for the Battalion.

13. ACKNOWLEDGE.

J.C.K. Wernham
.....................Capt & Adjt.,
18th Battalion Machine Gun Corps.

Issued at 6.25 a.m.
Copies to recipients of Operation Orders.

"A" Form.

Army Form C. 2121.
(In pads of 100.)

MESSAGES AND SIGNALS.

No. of Message......

Prefix........ Code........ m | Words. | Charge.

Office of Origin and Service Instructions.

Sent
At.............m.
To...............
By...............

This message is on a/c of:
APPENDIX "A"
................Service.
(Signature of "Franking Officer.")

Recd. at .... m.
Date..............
From..............
By................

TO: Recipients of Operation Orders

Sender's Number.	Day of Month.	In reply to Number.	AAA
*	29th		

18th Bn M G C Order No 10.
Ref French Sheet Soissons Sheet 33

1/ All transport of the 18th Div (less Arty) to move to CHOISY (2 miles NE of COMPEIGNE)

2/ Route for transport of M G Corps – NAMPCELL – QUENNEVIER – ECAFAUT FARM – BERNEUIL-SUR-AISNE – RETHONDES – LE FRANC PORT – CHOISY.

3/ Rations are being delivered by 18th Div Train to transport lines and will then be distributed to Coys.

Rations for the man must be carried on the man and rations for transport on the

From
Place
Time

The above may be forwarded as now corrected. (Z)
Censor. Signature of Addressor or person authorised to telegraph in his name.

* This line should be erased if not required.

(3198.) Wt. W 12952/M1294. 375,000 Pads. 1/17. H. W. & V., Ld. (E. 818.)

"A" Form.

MESSAGES AND SIGNALS.

Army Form C. 2121.
(In pads of 100.)

No. of Message..............

Prefix.......... Code.......... m.	Words.	Charge.	This message is on a/c of:	Recd. at ....m.
Office of Origin and Service Instructions.	Sent		..................Service.	Date..........
	At..........m.			From ....
	To..........			
	By..........		(Signature of "Franking Officer.")	By..........

TO { -2-

Sender's Number.	Day of Month.	In reply to Number.	AAA
*			

Transport.

4/ As soon as rations are distributed. Transport will get on the move at once as per above route

5/ All Bn transport will move together today under orders from HQ Transport On concentrating in CHOISY area all transport will come under Command of 18th Div Train who will make arrangements regarding Billets. bivouacs. Wagon lines etc.

6/ Further orders re move of Transport from CHOISY will

From

Place

Time

The above may be forwarded as now corrected. (Z)

Censor. Signature of Addressor or person authorised to telegraph in his name.

* This line should be erased if not required.

(3198.) Wt. W 1295/M1294. 375,000 Pads. 1/17. H. W. & V., Ld. (E. 818.)

"A" Form.

Army Form C. 2121.
(In pads of 100.)

MESSAGES AND SIGNALS.

No. of Message..............

Prefix...........Code...........m	Words.	Charge.	This message is on a/c of:	Recd. at.........m.
Office of Origin and Service Instructions.	Sent		..................Service.	Date..........
	At...............m.			From ....
	To..............			By..........
	By..............		(Signature of "Franking Officer.")	

TO

* Sender's Number.	Day of Month.	In reply to Number.	AAA

be issued by O.C. 18th Div Train.

7/ The above orders do not apply to detachment of "B" Coy attached to 54th Inf Bde. This detachment will move under orders of 54th Bde.

8/ Acknowledge.

From 18th Bn M.G.C.

Place

Time

The above may be forwarded as now corrected. (Z) (Sgd) [illegible] Capt & Adjt

..................Censor. Signature of Addressor or person authorised to telegraph in his name.

* This line should be erased if not required.

(3198.) Wt. W 12952/M1294. 375,000 Pads. 1/17. H. W. & V., Ld. (E. 818.)

APPENDIX 14.a.

CHANGES IN ESTABLISHMENT AND
STRENGTH OF BATTALION DURING
THE MONTH OF MARSH 1918.

Paper Strength (excluding attached):-

1st March:-	37 Officers	510 Other Ranks.
31st March:-	27 Officers.	460 Other Ranks.

DRAFTS RECEIVED.

1 Warrant Officer Class II joined Battn. from 8th Norfolk Regt, (Disbanded) 2.3.18.

60 O.Rs. Joined Bn. from 12th Middlesex Regt. (Disbanded) 23.2.18.

83 O.Rs. Joined Battn. from Infantry Units pending transfer to Machine Gun Corps. 5.3.18.

16 O.Rs. Joined Battn. from Divisional Depot Battn. 13.3.18

CHANGES IN OFFICERS.

Lieut. & QrMr. W. McKINLEY, M.C. Joined Battn. from 8th Norfolk Regiment, 1.3.1918.

Casualties to Officers during the month of March attached. (See Appendix 12.)

-------000-------

18th BATTALION, MACHINE GUN CORPS.

A P R I L

1 9 1 8

Attached:

1. App. 19. Narrative of Operations 31st March/ 13th April, 1918.
2. War Diary.
3. Apps. 15 to 18 and 20 to 25.

CONFIDENTIAL

7

War Diary.

Vol 3

— of —

18th Bn MACHINE GUN CORPS

From:- 1st APRIL 1918

To:- 30th APRIL 1918

APPENDICES 15

to 25 (INCLUSIVE)

ATTACHED.

(VOLUME III)

12

Army Form C. 2118.

Instructions regarding War Diaries and Intelligence Summaries are contained in F. S. Regs., Part II. and the Staff Manual respectively. Title pages will be prepared in manuscript.

18th Battalion, Machine Gun Corps

WAR DIARY or INTELLIGENCE SUMMARY.

(Erase heading not required.)

April 1918

Place	Date	Hour	Summary of Events and Information	Remarks and references to Appendices
			Ref Sheet 62D S W 1/20000 . AMIENS, DIEPPE, LENS ABBEVILLE 1/100000	
BOVES	1st		5 teams & guns A B & C Coys in line – 20 extra guns arrived in afternoon and allotted to Coys as follows 8 · A Coy – 8 · B Coy 4 C Coy. Guns cleaned and belts filled but owing to tripods not having been sent forward, guns and teams were kept in billets in BOVES to await their arrival	[initials]
"	2nd		20 guns in Boves moved to Gentelles to await orders – operations in line nil. Orders for move issued 10.20 am see Appendix 15	[initials] App 15
"	3rd		Tripods for 20 guns at Gentelles arrived from Ordnance – Transport which had been moving from CHOISY by road arrived at LOEUILLY	[initials]
"	4th		Transport divided into A & B Echelons – A Echelon to BOVES B Echelon to SALEUX – German attack on VILLERS-BRETONNEUX narrative of operations ~~[illegible]~~ 31/3 – 13/4/18 attached (see Appendix 19)	App 16 issued [initials] App 19.
"	5th		Coys came out of line to billets in BOVES with the exception of 5 Guns B Coy under Lieut STRANG & 3 guns A Coy under LT. COATES	[initials]
"	6th		8 Guns still in line – operations nil – Companies at BOVES resorting and overhauling equipment	[initials]

D. D. & L., London, E.C. (A7883) Wt. W809/M1672 350,000 4/17 Sch. 52a Forms/C/2118/14

18th Battalion Machine Gun Corps

WAR DIARY
or
INTELLIGENCE SUMMARY.

(Erase heading not required.)

April (cont)

Army Form C. 2118.

Instructions regarding War Diaries and Intelligence Summaries are contained in F. S. Regs., Part II. and the Staff Manual respectively. Title pages will be prepared in manuscript.

Place	Date	Hour	Summary of Events and Information	Remarks and references to Appendices
BOVES	7th		8 Guns still in line - operations nil - Companies at BOVES refitting and reorganising under Company Commanders - Orders issued for operation due to take place on 9th April	JWD
"	8th		8 guns in line operations nil - Preparations made for operation on 9th - positions reconnoitred by Company Officers etc.	App. 17 issued JWD
			Operations for 9th cancelled (Proposed operations given in Orders Nos 12, 13 & 14)	App 18
"	9th		8 guns in line - operations nil - Intercompany relief at night -	
		1 pm	278 Company arrived to join Battalion as 4th Company and named D Coy.	JWD
"	10th		8 guns in line - Enemy attacked HANGARD 7 pm but was repulsed - our guns did not come into action - Companies in BOVES training under Company arrangements - Inspection by C.O. of D Coy 10 am - A Coy 3 pm	JWD
	11th		8 guns in line operations nil - companies at BOVES training	JWD
"	12th		2 guns of A Coy in line cooperated in successful attempt to clear HANGARD Village - companies at BOVES training	JWD

D. D. & L., London, E.C. (A7883) Wt. W809/M1672 350,000 4/17 Sch. 52a Forms/C/2118/14

Instructions regarding War Diaries and Intelligence Summaries are contained in F. S. Regs., Part II. and the Staff Manual respectively. Title pages will be prepared in manuscript.

18th Battalion Machine Gun Corps

WAR DIARY
or
~~INTELLIGENCE SUMMARY~~.
(*Erase heading not required.*)

April (cont)

Army Form C. 2118.

Place	Date	Hour	Summary of Events and Information	Remarks and references to Appendices
BOVES	13th		8 Guns in line - Valley N & E of DOMART heavily gas shelled (see narrative)	
			These guns relieved at night & proceeded to billets in BOVES	
		1.30pm	Battalion (less 8 guns in line) moved to AMIENS and billeted in	
			ECOLE NORMALE - billets very good Orders for move attached see	app 20
AMIENS	14th		Companies resting and cleaning up - 8 guns & teams joined Battalion	
			from BOVES 10.30 am - 11 am. Battalion Church parade in	
			College square	
"	15		Training in vicinity of billets.	
"	16		do	
"	17	11.15am	Battalion moved to CAMP on HEBECOURT-DURY Road, 1 mile	
			N. of HEBECOURT - arrived in camp 1 pm — Billets - tents - accommodation	
			very limited Orders for move issued under Order No.16 (attached)	app 21
CAMP	18		Training in vicinity of camp	
"	19		do 265 Coy arrived as reinforcements -	
"	20	9am	Orders received to place 2 Sections of the Battalion at disposal of	
			58th Division for Reserve line. Orders issued to Coys attached see Appendix 23	

D. D. & L., London, E.C. (A7883) Wt. W203/M1672 350,000 2/17 Sch. 52a. Forms/C.2118/14

18th Battalion Machine Gun Corps

Instructions regarding War Diaries and Intelligence Summaries are contained in F. S. Regs., Part II, and the Staff Manual respectively. Title pages will be prepared in manuscript.

WAR DIARY

or

~~INTELLIGENCE SUMMARY.~~

(*Erase heading not required.*)

April (cont)

Army Form C. 2118.

Place	Date	Hour	Summary of Events and Information	Remarks and references to Appendices
CAMP	20th (cont)	9.45am	Orders issued to D Coy	
		1 pm	2 Sections D Coy moved into forward area by motor lorries under orders of 58th Division – Placed in position near Gentelles but later returned to billets in BOVES	
		1 pm	Orders issued to 2 Sections A Coy & 2 Secs B Coy to stand by ready to move at 15 mins notice (Issued under 537)	[illegible] App 22
"	21st		2 secs D Coy in forward area – remainder of Battalion Church parade at 11.30 am – Troops warned to stand by. Stood to at 4.30 am	[illegible]
"	22nd		Limited training in vicinity of camp	[illegible]
"	23rd		do	
		5 pm	8 guns B Coy proceeded to join 54th Infy Bde at CAGNY	
		6 pm	8 guns A Coy proceeded to join 53rd Infy Bde at ST FUSCIEN	
			8 guns D Coy ordered to be ready to move forward on morning of 24th April. Orders issued under Order No 18 (attached)	[illegible] App 24
"	24th		Hostile bombardment opened 3 am – First news of enemy attack 6.15 am. – 8 guns of D Coy which had been placed at	

D. D. & L., London, E.C. (A7883) Wt. W593/M1672 350,000 4/17 Sch. 52a Forms/C/2118/14

Instructions regarding War Diaries and Intelligence Summaries are contained in F. S. Regs., Part II. and the Staff Manual respectively. Title pages will be prepared in manuscript.

18th Battalion Machine Gun Corps

WAR DIARY
or
INTELLIGENCE SUMMARY.
(Erase heading not required.)

Army Form C. 2118.

April 1918 (cont)

Place	Date	Hour	Summary of Events and Information	Remarks and references to Appendices
	24th		disposal of 58th Division on 20th April rejoined Battalion 4 am.	
		6.30am	8 Guns D Coy left Camp to take up positions in railway bank at T 14 d 9.5	
		9am	Remainder of Battalion "Standing To" ready to move	
		1pm	C Coy moved to Chateau S 4 b 0.2	
		5.20pm	Remaining 8 guns A Coy moved to Chateau S 4 b 0.2	
			During day 53rd & 54th Infy Bdes moved forward accompanied by their respective allotment of guns	
			8 Guns of A Coy att 53 Infy Bde in shelters at N 33 b 9.1 with Coy HQ at N 32 d 2.9	
			8 Guns of B Coy att 54th Infy Bde were alloted by Bde to Battalions as follows 2 guns - 7th Bedfords, 2 guns 8th Northants Regt, 2 Guns 11th Rl Fusiliers - 2 Guns Bde HQ Reserve	
		11pm	54th Infy Bde cooperated in counterattack S. of Bois L'Abbé Guns accompanied their Battalions and aided in consolidation	JW

D. D. & L., London, E.C. (A7853) Wt. W5091/M1672 350,000 4/17 Sch. 52a Forms/C/2118/14

Instructions regarding War Diaries and Intelligence Summaries are contained in F. S. Regs., Part II. and the Staff Manual respectively. Title pages will be prepared in manuscript.

18th Battalion Machine Gun Corps

WAR DIARY or ~~INTELLIGENCE SUMMARY.~~

(Erase heading not required.)

April 1918 (cont)

Army Form C. 2118.

Place	Date	Hour	Summary of Events and Information	Remarks and references to Appendices
CAMP N of HEBECOURT	25th		Desposition of guns was as follows	
			A Coy 8 guns N 33 b 9.1 8 guns S 4 b 0.2	
			B " 1 Gun U 5 c 3.0	
			2 Guns U 10 a 5.5	
			2 " U 3 c 6.3	
			2 " U 9 a 3.5	
			1 " with Coy H.Q. at T 5 a 9.3 } Only 8 guns could be manned by B Coy	
			C " 16 guns S 4 b 0.2	
			D " 4 guns T 4 a	
			4 guns T 14 d 9.5 8 guns at CAMP. N of HEBECOURT	
		8.30am	Advanced Bn H.Q. moved to camp ~~T 1 a~~ M 35 d 9.0 arrived 12 noon	
			Signallers from 18th Division joined Battalion	
			On night 25/26th 53rd Inf Bde relieved 54th Infy Bde – 8 guns A Coy relieving the 8 guns of B Coy & taking over similar dispositions. 8 guns of B Coy moving to billets in BOVES.	JW
	26th	9.30am	C Coy + 8 guns of A Coy at S 4 b 0.2 and Rear Bn H.Q. + 8 guns D Coy moved to OISSY but redirected to REINCOURT	
			Operations in line – nil	JW

D. D. & L., London, E.C. (A7833) Wt. W5o3/M1672 350,000 4/17 Sch. 52a Forms/C/2118/14

Instructions regarding War Diaries and Intelligence Summaries are contained in F. S. Regs., Part II, and the Staff Manual respectively. Title pages will be prepared in manuscript.

18th Battalion Machine Gun Corps

WAR DIARY
or
~~INTELLIGENCE SUMMARY.~~
(Erase heading not required.)

April 1918 (cont)

Army Form C. 2118.

Place	Date	Hour	Summary of Events and Information	Remarks and references to Appendices
CAMP M.35d9.0	27th		Operations in line - nil	
		3 pm	Advanced Bn HQ + 8 guns D Coy + 8 guns B Coy at Boves - moved to	
			SALEUX arrived in billets 5.30 pm.	
			8 guns A Coy attached 53rd Bde still in line	
			During day portion of Battalion at REINCOURT moved to billets	
			in ALLERY	
			On night 27/28th 53 Inf Bde withdrawn from the line - 8 attached	
			guns moved to La Bouvillerie Amiens arriving 2 am 28th	JWS
SALEUX	28th		Troops at ALLERY resting and cleaning up	
		10 am ~~9.30 am~~	Troops of Batt at SALEUX moved to CAVILLON arriving 2 pm.	
			Detachment of A Coy attd 53rd Inf Bde moved by lorry from AMIENS	
			to AIRAINES and marched to ALLERY arriving 6 pm.	JWS
CAVILLON	29th	9.30 am	Advd Bn HQ + 8 guns B Coy + 8 guns D Coy marched from CAVILLON	For change in strength see appendix
			to ALLERY arriving 1.30 pm.	
		1.30 pm	Whole Battalion in billets at ALLERY - very comfortable	25.
ALLERY	30th		Companies resting reorganising and refitting	JWS

J W Wanton
Capt & Adjt 18th B M G C.

D. D. & L., London, E.C.
(A7883) Wt. W803/M1672 350,000 4/17 Sch. 52a Forms/C/2118/14

1

appendix 19.

NARRATIVE OF OPERATIONS

DESCRIBING THE PART PLAYED

- by the -

18TH BATTALION MACHINE GUN CORPS.

--- DURING THE ---

OPERATIONS NEAR VILLERS BRETONNEUX

From:- 31st March 1918.

To:- 13th April 1918.

Reference Map:- FRANCE. 62.D., S.E. and S.W.

NARRATIVE OF OPERATIONS
SHOWING THE PART PLAYED BY
-THE-
18TH BATTN.MACHINE GUN CORPS
DURING THE PERIOD, 31st
March 1918 - 13th April 1918.

Reference Map:- FRANCE. 62.D., S.E. and S.W.

MARCH 31st.

At 3 a.m. the Battalion arrived in lorries at BOVES from COMPIEGNE district, a matter of 65 miles. After a short rest in BOVES, orders were received for Companies to move forward.

In afternoon "A" and "C" Companies moved to Copse T.11.b.8.0., "B" Company to GENTELLES; Battalion H.Q. remaining at BOVES.

Owing to Transport having proceeded from COMPIEGNE district by road and not yet having arrived, gun teams were without guns, ammunition etc.,

However at 3 p.m. 15 guns complete arrived by lorry from Ordnance and were immediately overhauled and belts filled. Five guns were allotted to each Company. (Battalion was then only 3 Coys. strong)

It was impossible to take over any dispositions from Machine Guns in the line as these were composed of the remnants of several Machine Gun Battalions, without any co-ordination or general plan of defence. Our guns were therefore disposed to meet the situation and the Units to be relieved were ordered to withdraw to their concentrated areas.

In the evening at about 7 p.m. "A" Company moved to positions immediately West of DOMART U.26.d.5.9. with H.Qrs in cellars in DOMART. "B" Coy. remained in billets in GENTELLES; "C" Company moved to VILLERS BRETONNEUX with H.Q. at MONUMENT in U.6.a. All surplus personnel above 5 gun teams per Company were left in BOVES.

APRIL 1st.

"A" Company no change.

"B" Company. During the day positions were dug and guns placed in the GENTELLES Line. At 7 p.m. one gun was ordered to take up position South of HANGARD to enfilade enemy trench in U.24.b.

At about 3 p.m. 20 extra guns arrived at BOVES from Ordnance. These were allotted:- 8 guns "A" Coy; 8 Guns "B" Coy; 4 Guns "C" Coy. Belts were filled and arrangements completed for guns to move forward at a moments notice.

APRIL 2nd.

"A" Company no change. "B" Company - No change during day - Gun South of HANGARD did not obtain a target.

At 6.45 p.m. 54th Infantry Brigade attacked enemy positions North of HANGARD. (Four Guns - 1 from South of HANGARD and 3 from GENTELLES LINE - under 2nd Lieut. W. J. BRINKMAN, M.C. were detailed to consolidate and hold ground captured. Attack was unsuccessful and original line occupied. These 4 guns accordingly took up positions - 2 at U.23.b.3.7. and 2 in Cellars in HANGARD VILLAGE.

The same evening the 5 guns of "C" Company took up positions 2 under Lieut. D. W. ADAM in U.18a. and 3 under 2nd Lieut. CAREY in V.7.a.

Meanwhile the 20 guns at BOVES moved forward as follows:-

8 Guns "A" Coy. to GENTELLES and HAMGARD.
8 Guns "B" Coy. to GENTELLES.
4 Guns "C" Coy. to GENTELLES.

APRIL 3rd.

No changes or operations during day.

On night 3rd/4th April, the following dispositions were made:-

"A" Company. 3 Guns from U.26.d.5.9. to U.26.b.8.5.
2 Guns from U.26.d.5.9. to U.21.d.65.85.
4 Guns from GENTELLES to U.9.d.
2 Guns from GENTELLES to U.21.d.65.85.
"B" Company. 2 Guns U.23.b.)
2 Guns U.22.d.) Under 2nd Lt. C. A. WILSON.
4 Guns U.11.a. under Sergt. RIDLEY.
3 Guns in DOMART under 2nd Lieut. BRINKMAN, M.C.
"C" Company. 2 Guns from GENTELLES to Railway Embankment in V.1.b. under 2nd Lieut. H. W. BURDEN, M.C.
3 Guns under Lieut.D.W.ADAM in Quarry V.13.a..
3 Guns under 2nd Lieut CAREY in V.7.a.

The remaining guns could not be used owing to shortage of Gun Teams.

APRIL 4th.

At about 4.30 a.m. the enemy heavily Bombarded our lines and later attacked along the Divisional Front, mainly towards VILLERS BRETONNEUX and our troops were forced to withdraw slightly.

Two of "B" Coys. guns at U.23.b. were put out of action by artillery fire

The guns of "C" Company under Lieut. D. W. ADAM and 2nd Lieut. CAREY inflicted severe casualties on the enemy.

During the morning our line was restored, but later, at about 4.30 p.m. a second hostile attack developed.

The Bombardment which preceded this attack knocked out 2 Guns of "C" Company - 1 at V.7.a. and 1 at V.13.a. O.C. "B" Company brought up the three guns from DOMART to Advanced Brigade H.Qrs. at U.21.d. and sent them forward to support the front line. During the attack the 4 guns at U.11.a. under Sergt. RIDLEY were heavily engaged. All the ammunition was expended with excellent results. Late in the day 2 of the guns were buried and put out of action by shell fire. Sergt RIDLEY immediately got up extra guns and ammunition and fresh teams. "A" Company also sent forward 2 Guns under 2nd Lieut. LYTHGOE to support the 54rd Inf. Brigade. One of these were knocked out by shell fire and the other with remaining two guns at U.21.d.65.85 were put in position in U.28.b. Our line which had been driven in by the enemy attack was again re-established by the 54th Infantry Brigade before dark.

The guns and teams of "C" Company were withdrawn and concentrated at GENTELLES where they remained in billets for the night.

<u>APRIL 5th.</u>

No action by Battalion Machine Guns. Dispositions were as given below:-

"A" Company, 4 Guns at U.9.d.
3 Guns in U.28.b.
3 Guns in U.26.b.8.5.
"B" Company, 1 Gun at U.22.c.3.4.
1 Gun at U.22.a.3.1.
3 Guns at U.21.a.
4 Guns at U.11.a.
"C" Company, in GENTELLES.

During night of 5th April, 58th Division took over the line and all guns were withdrawn to billets in BOVES with the exception of:-

3 Guns "A" Company at U.26.b.8.5. under Lieut. C.M.COATES.
5 Guns "B" Company - 1 Gun U.22.c.)
1 Gun U.22.a.) Under Lieut. T. E. STRANG.
3 Guns U.21.a.)

"C" Company arrived in billets at BOVES about 9 p.m. "A" and "B" Coys. arrived in billets at BOVES at about 3 a.m. April 6th.

<u>APRIL 6th/8th.</u>

3 Guns of "A" Company and 5 Guns "B" Company still in line under 58th Division. Operations - Nil.

<u>APRIL 9th.</u>

Inter-Company relief for Teams in line.
2nd Lieut. H. J. LYTHGOE relieved Lieut. C. M. COATES, "A" Company.
2nd Lieut. A. E. FERGUSON relieved Lieut T. E. STRANG, "B" Company.

<u>APRIL 10th/11th.</u>

No Change.

<u>APRIL 12th.</u>

2 Guns of "A" Company co-operated in successful attempt to clear HANGARD Village.

<u>APRIL 13th.</u>

Valley to North and East of DOMART heavily shelled with Gas causing heavy casualties to teams of "B" Company and a considerable number to "A" Company.

2nd Lieut. H. W. BRINKMAN, M.C. and fresh teams were sent forward to replace 2nd Lieut A. E. FERGUSON and men of "B" Company who had been evacuated.

At night the 3 Guns of "A" Company and 5 Guns of "B" Company were relieved by 58th Division and proceeded to billets in BOVES.

Lieut-Colonel,
Commanding 18th Battalion Machine Gun Corps.

18th May 1918.

APPENDIX "A".

CASUALTIES INCURRED BY THE 18TH BATTN. MACHINE GUN CORPS DURING THE OPERATIONS COVERING THE PERIOD 31.3.18 to 13.4.18.

OFFICERS.

Capt Gerald Percy Humfrey, Wounded 4.4.18.

Lieut. Douglas Walter Adam, Died of Wounds, 4.4.18.

2nd Lieut. Charles Alfred Wilson, Wounded, 5.4.18.

2nd Lieut. Alexander Edward Ferguson, Wounded, 13.4.18. (Gas)

2nd Lieut. John Matthew Harold Lythgoe, Wounded, 13.4.18. (Gas)

OTHER RANKS.

Date.	Killed.	Wounded.	Wounded (Gas)	W.@ Duty.	TOTAL.
31st.	-	7	-	1	8
1st.	-	3	-	-	3
2nd.	-	-	-	1	1
3rd.	-	2	-	-	2
4th.	1	4	-	-	5
5th.	1	5	-	-	6
6th.	-	2	-	-	2
9th.	-	1	-	-	1
11th.	-	1	-	-	1
12th.	2	6	-	-	8
13th.	-	-	27	11	38
TOTAL:-	4	31	27	13	75

A P P E N D I C E S

15
16
17
18

20
21
22
23
24
25

COPY.

SECRET. *Appendix 15.* 2nd April 1918.

18th BATTN. M. G. C. ORDER No. 11.

1. The 20 Guns ("A" Coy 8, "B" Coy 8; "C" Coy, 4) with teams will move to GENTELLES This morning. Transport has been asked to report to Battn. H.Qrs at 11 a.m.

2. Guns will be ready for action and all available belt boxes filled. Belt boxes which are not filled by the time teams move off will be filled on arrival at GENTELLES.

3. Coys. will report Bn. H.Q. number of Officers and O.Rs. sent forward.

4. Gun teams will be composed of 4 ~~guns~~ men. All Officers will be sent forward except 2nd-in-Commands' who will remain at BOVES.

5. A dump of 40,000 has been formed at 61st Divl. H.Q. GENTELLES. Detachment of "B" Coy. will report to Capt. BURNS at 54th Bde. H.Q. GENTELLES. "C" Company will make own arrangements as regards billets in GENTELLES. Teams of "A" Coy. will report Lt.POCOCK at 53rd Bde. H.Q.

6. One Officer per Company should be sent on at once to arrange accommodation.

(Signed) J. W. K. WERNHAM. Capt & A/Adjt.,
18th Battalion Machine Gun Corps.

Issued at 10.20 a.m.

S E C R E T. appendix 16 Copy No. 17

18th Bn. Machine Gun Corps.

Operation Order No. 17

Reference Map. Sheet 66 c 1/40,000. 4th April 1918.

---

1. An operation in connection with the French on our right will take place on a date to be notified later.

2. General Idea.

The 53rd and 54th Inf. Bdes. will advance their line approximately from the copse in V13 a, and copse U29 b 9 7 to copse in V19 a and copse to V19 c 5 0, where they will consolidate and join up with the French who will capture DEMUIN.

3. Action on M.G's

"A" Coy.

2 guns of "A" Coy. at present in U 26 c will move forward to-night to copse at U24 b 1 8 near present Lewis gun post of 6th Northants Regt. These guns will fire direct on to ridge in V 1. c and engage any targets presenting themselves. Should the enemy fire power be great nuetralising fire will be employed. The guns at present in U 26 b will move at once to U 27 a 5 .

"B" Coy.

2 guns at present in reserve at GENTELLES will be sent forward tonight to cellar in HANGUARD to be used as Consolidating guns for 54th Inf. Bde. O.C. "B" Coy. will report to G.O.C. 54th Inf Bde regarding the rôle of the guns.

"C" Coy.

2 guns at present at U 18 d 2 5 will take up a position tonight at V 7 d 6 5 to form a battery of 4 guns . This battery will fire into valley at V 1. b and d from Zero to Zero plus 15 . Barrage chart is attached (App. "A")

O's C.Coys will report as soon as guns are in position as shown on attached map.

3. Ammunition Supply.

"A" Co.

6,000 rounds will be sent to DOMART tonight on limber detailed for conveyance of rations.

"B" Co.

"B" Co. will make own arrangements.

"C" Co.

6,000 rounds will be sent tonight to the Monument for use of battery in V 7 d. by means of ration limber.

4. Transport

The limber which is bringing up rations to-night to GENTELLES will be retained by O.C. "B" Coy. and be used to convey the guns of "B" Coy to HANGARD.

5. ACKNOWLEDGE.

Capt and Adjt.
18th Bn. Machine Gun Corps.

Issued at. 3.15 pm
Copies to.

1. C.O.
2. 2nd i/c.
3. Adjutant
4. "A" Co.
5. "B" Co.
6. "C" Co.
7. 18th Div. "G"
8. 53rd Inf. Bde.
9. 54th Inf Bde.
10. 55th Inf Bde.
11, 12, and 13. War Diary and File.

Appendix "A".

Composition of 4 guns of "[illegible]" Coy. Zero line V7 d 6.8, through V 13. d 6 [illegible].

Location of directing gun V 7 [illegible] Grid bearing Zero line 18[illegible]

No. of directing gun - 4. Commanded by.-

No. of barrage	No of guns	Targets.	[illegible] Zero time.	Range	[illegible]	Rate of fire.	Remarks.
1.	4	[illegible] to [illegible]		[illegible] yds. to [illegible] yds [illegible]	[illegible] [illegible] [illegible]	[illegible]	[illegible]

SECRET   appendix 17.   Copy No.

Reference Map
Sheet 62 d 1/40,000

18th Battalion Machine Gun Corps Order No.13.

1. General Plan.

(a) The 5th Australian Brigade and the 175th Inf. Bde (58th Division) will carry out an operation on the morning of the 9th April with a veiw to advancing the present line to the general line.
The CEMETARY in U 20 b (exclusive) - U24 b. - V 13 central thence along our present front line.

(b) It is intended to support this operation with Machine Guns. (i) During the attack, firing on to selected targets and (ii) after the attack providing S O S barrage fire

(c) Guns available for this operation
16 guns 18th Battalion M.G.C.
16 guns 58th Battalion M.G.C.

2. Organisation & Disposition of the Guns

(a) Guns will be grouped in batteries of 8 guns.
(b) 2 batteries known as A & B Batteries under the command of an officer to be detailed by O.C, 58th Bn. M.G.C. will be situated in U 28 d.
2 batteries to be known as C. and D. batteries under the command of Capt. Burns 18th Bn. M.G.C. will be situated in U 5 a
"C" and "D" Batteries will be composed of 5 guns of "A" Coy and 11 guns of "B" Coy 18th Bn. M.G.C.
Exact locations of batteries are shown on attached map "A" (issued to all concerned)
(c) Batteries will be divided into 2 sections each under the command of an officer.

3. Tasks of Batteries

A. and B. Batteries will barrage approximately the valley in U 24 a. to U 18.c. from Zero to Zero plus 10. These guns will then take up their final S.O.S barrage on a line running from V 25 c 5.8. to V 19.c.0.0.
C. and D. batteries will barrage the valley in U 18 c and.d. from U 18 c.0.0. to U 18.d.1.4. to Zero plus 10. and will then switch on to the wood on a line running U 18 central to V 7.c.5.1. until Zero plus 35 when they will come on to their S O S line V 8.c.1.9.-V 2.c.[illegible].0. V 2 a. central.
All guns will cease firing at Zero plus 1 hour 20. unless S O S barrage fore is called for.

4. Zero Hour

Will be notified later.

5. Ammunition.

20 belt boxes per gun will be provided at each battery position. 10,000 rounds S A A will beplaced at -
(i) Cellars in HANGARD at U28 d 8.5. for re-filling belts for A&B. Batteries.
(ii) At "C" and "D" Battery positions in U 5 a for refilling belts of these batteries.

6. Transport

Guns and material should be taken to their positions tomorrow night 8th inst.
Transport for "A" and B" Batteries shouod proceed via the DOMART-AMIENS Road and on to HANGARD.
Transport for C and D Batteries via the GENTELLES-CACHY-MARCELCAVE Road.
Transport should not move until dusk.

7. CONSTRUCTION OF GUN POSITIONS

Gun positions will be constructed during the night of 8/9th April.
Reconnaisance should be made and positions marked out during the daylight og the 8th inst.

8. GUIDES

Guides for gun teams will be detailed and arrangements made for getting guns into position by Group Commanders. Capt. GAMMON 58th Bn. Machine Gun Corps (now at GENTELLES) will provide guides for A and B Batteries. Capt BURNS will make his own arrangements.

9. Reports

All guns will be in position by 3 a.m. 9th inst and reports to this effect will be made to H.Q. 18th Division.

10. SYNCHRONISATION OF WATCHES

All watches will be synchronised at an hour to be notified later.

11. FUTURE ARRANGEMENTS

Unlessorders are issued to the contrary Batteries will remain in position dirung the day and will provide S O S barrages as called for. They will withdraw at Dusk without waiting for further orders.

12. A C K N O W L E D G E.

Capt and Adjt.
18th Battalion Machine Gun Corps.

Issued at 1 am. 8th inst.

Copies to.-
1. C.O.
2. Group commander A and B Battery.
3. Group commander C. and D. Battery.
4. 18th Division. "G"
5. 58th Bn. Machine Gun Corps.
6. 175th Inf Bde.
7. 5th Aust. Inf Bde.
8. C R A 61st Division.
9. 5th Australian Division.
10. 29th French Division.
11. War Diary.
12 War Diary.
13. File.

18th Bn. Machine Gun Corp
No. S.25.

To:- Recipients of Battalion Order No. 13.

With reference to the above order. Herewith Appendices A and B with amendments.

Please acknowledge receipt.

Capt. and Adjt.

8th April 1918. 18th Bn. Machine Gun Corps.

Reference 18th Bn. Machine Gun Corps Order No. 13.

Appendix "A".

Light Signals.
The following light signals will be employed.
S.O.S. Red over Red over Red. parachute flares.
Sucess Signal.
These will be used to denote success.
When Blue line has been captured. --2 Green Very Lights.
When Red line has been captured. -- 2 Red Very Lights.

Note.
Blue line-- U 23 c 8.2. -- U 12 d 7 8
Red Line. U 30 a 1.8.-- U 24 b. 5.0. --V 13 central--
V7 d 0.2.

Appendix "B"

Medical arrangements

1. 3 bearer Officers with four squads each (more if necessary) will maintain touch with the R.M.O's of Battalions and be responsible for the evacuation of cases to the Ford car waiting post at U 21 a 6.9.
2. 2 Ford cars(more if possible) will be kept running between the SUNKEN ROAD at U 21 a 5.9. and the car relaypost at the eastern end of CACHY U8 a.9.9.
3. 6 large cars (3 or 4 more if possible) will run in a continous circuit between eastern end of CACHY and Adv Dressing station N 25 d. 3.6.
4. Two Horse ambulances(if possible 3 or more) will work continuously between eastern end of GENTELLES and adv . dressing station N25d 3.6.
5. All walking cases will be directed to eastern end of GENTELLES for conveyance by horse ambulance(they will be directed through CACHY or across the fields) direct.

Reference 18th Bn. Machine Gun Corps Order No. 13.

Corragenda para 3 Tasks of batteries

Tasks of C and D batteries should read .- C and D batteries will barrage the valley in U 18 c and d from U18 c.0.0. to U 18 d 1.4. to Zero plus 10. and will then switch on to the east edge of the wood U 18 d 4.6. to V13 a 8.9. until Zero plus 37 when they will come on theirS.O.S. lines V 8 c 1.9. -- V 2 c 4.0. to V 2 a central.

ADDENDA.

Add after para 3.
Rates of fire during the operation will be ---
Zero to zero plus 10. Rapid-- 250 rds per min.
Zero plus 10 to zero plus 1 hour 2?.-- slow-- 75 rds per min.
All guns will traverse 1° right and left

Add to para 5.
The 5th Australian Bde have formed dumps of S.A.A as follows
50,000 rounds at U 16 c 6 7
50,000 rounds at CACHY U 8 a 6.0.55
100000 rounds on limbers at Bde H.Q. T12 a 9.8.

System of Supply

The system of supply will bwby limbers to U 16.c.6.7.
and thence by carrying party to the required destination
These dumps will not be used by the 18th and 58th
Battalions M.G.C. unless in case of urgent necessity.

BATTERY CHART for "A" Battery

Place

Date

Composition 8 Guns 58th Bn.

Commanded by

Location of Directing Gun. V 28 d 40.40. V 28 d 50.20.

No. of Directing Guns

[illegible] Bearing 40°

Zero Line 40°

Grid Bearing of Zero Line

TASK.
A. Enfilade Barrage
B. Frontal Barrage.

No. of Barrage	No. of Guns	Clock Time	Zero Line	Angle of Switch	Distribution angle	Range	[illegible]	[illegible]	Range to [illegible] Barrage lifts	Rate of Fire
A	8		40°	-	-	2300x to 2600	+22x	6° 30' 30' [illegible]		Rapid 250 rds per minute
B	8			4° Right.		2400x	—	6° 40'		Rapid.
C										

BATTERY CHART for "B" Batty

Place:

Date:

Composition 8 Guns 58 Batty M.G.C

Commanded by

Location of Directing Gun V28 d 2.0. to V28d 25 Grid Bearing 44°

Zero Line 44°.

No of Directing Guns. Grid. Bear. of Zero Line

TASK.

No of Barrage.	No of Guns.	Clock Time.	Zero Line.	Angle of Switch.	Distribution Angle.	Range.	V. I.	Q. E.	Range to F. T. when Barrage lifts.	Rate of Fire.
A.	8		44°			2000x to 2400x	+ 11x	4° 40' 20' diff		Rapid 1 to 150 [illegible]
B.	8			32° Right	40°.	2500	+ 22x	8°		Rapid.

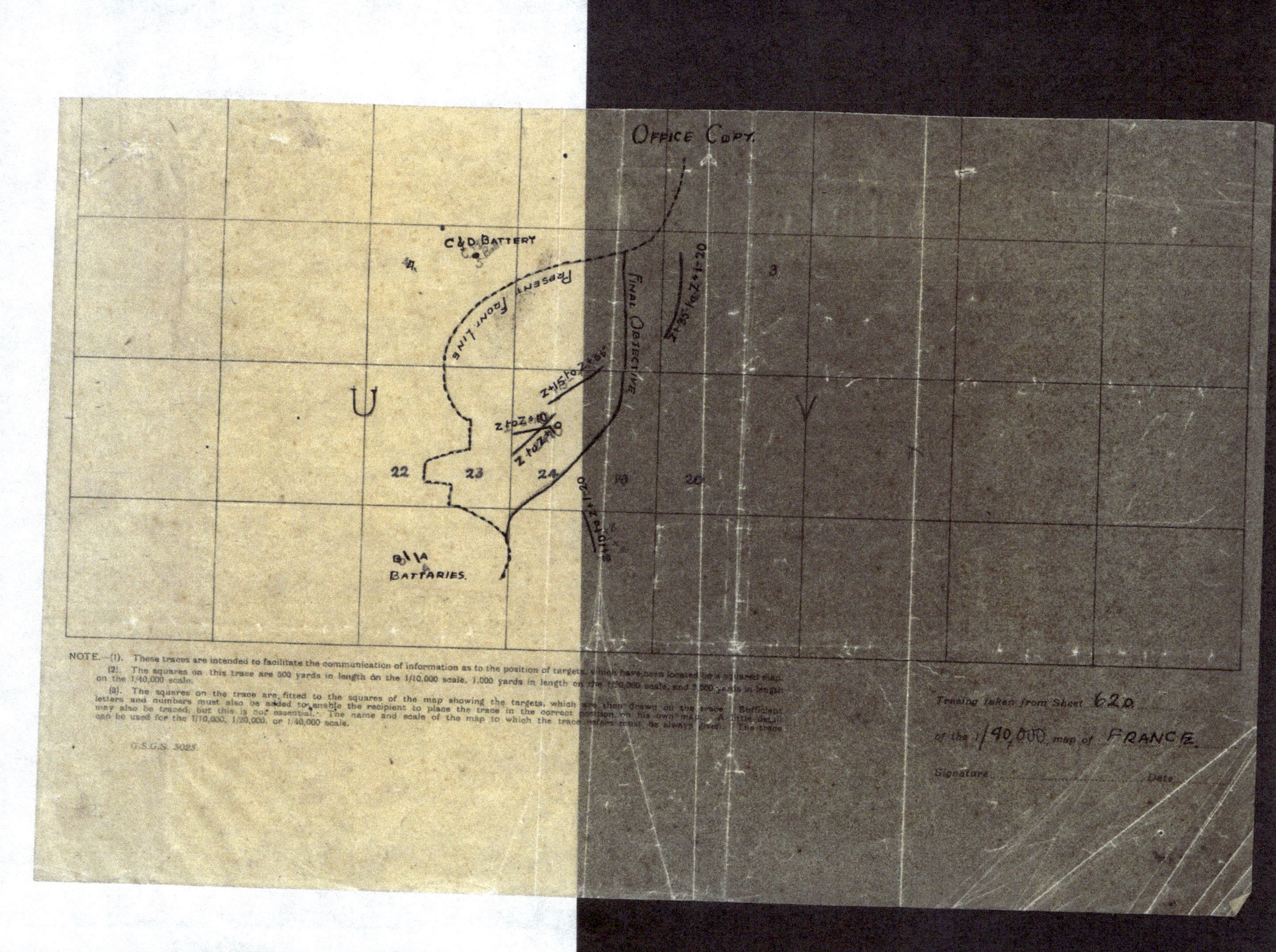
OFFICE COPY.
C & D BATTERY
PRESENT FRONT LINE
FINAL OBJECTIVE
Z+35 to Z+1-20
Z+15 to Z+35
Z to Z+10
Z to Z+10
U
V
3
22
23
24
19
20
Z+10 to Z+1-20
B & A
BATTARIES.
NOTE.—(1). These traces are intended to facilitate the communication of information as to the position of targets which have been located on a squared map.
(2). The squares on this trace are 500 yards in length on the 1/10,000 scale, 1,000 yards in length on the 1/20,000 scale, and 2,000 yards in length on the 1/40,000 scale.
(3). The squares on the trace are fitted to the squares of the map showing the targets, which are then drawn on the trace. Sufficient letters and numbers must also be added to enable the recipient to place the trace in the correct position on his own map. A little detail may also be traced, but this is not essential. The name and scale of the map to which the trace refers must be always given. The trace can be used for the 1/10,000, 1/20,000, or 1/40,000 scale.
G.S.G.S. 3025.
Tracing taken from Sheet 62D
of the 1/40,000 map of FRANCE.
Signature
Date

SECRET

18th Bn. Machine Gun Corps No. S. 28.

TO:- O's.C. "A" Coy.
"B" Coy.
"C" Coy.
"D" Coy.

Copies to C.O., War Diary and File.

Ref 0013

The following amendments will be made to Para 2(b) sub-para 3 which should now read:-

"C" and "D" Batteries will be composed of --- 2 guns "A" Coy 6 guns "B" Coy and 8 guns "D" Coy.

O.C." D " Coy will get in to touch with and obtain all information from O.C."B" Coy. as to the role and requirements of these guns.

ACKNOWLEDGE.

8th April 1918.

Capt and Adjt.
18th Bn. Machine Gun Corps.

SECRET   Appendix 18.   Copy No. 3

18th Battalion Machine Gun Corps
No. 14.
(Cancelling Battalion Order No, 13.)

Reference map-
Sheet 62 D. 1/40000

1. GENERAL
AREA.

(a) The 5th Australian Brigade and 175th Inf. Bde (58th Division) will carry out an operation at a date to be notified later with a view to advancing the present line to the general line.
The CEMETERY in U 29.b (exclusive) --U24 central -- V 13 central--V7 d [illegible] 3.[illegible] -- V 1 b. 8.0.
joining our present line at P 31.d.8.0.

(b) The operation will be supported with Machine Guns (i) during the attack , firing on selected areas and (ii) after the attack providing S.O.S. barrage fire.

(c) Guns available for this operation----
24 guns 18th Battalion M.G.C.
16 guns 58th Battalion M.G.C.

2. ORGANISATION
AND DISPOSITION
OF GUNS.

(a) Guns will be grouped in batteries of 8.

(b) 2 batteries known as "A" and "B" batteries.

~~[illegible]~~ under the command of an officer to be detailed by O.C. 58th Battn. M.G.C. will be situated in U 28 d.
1 battery known as "C" Battery under command of Capt. H.S.PATERSON 18th Bn. M.G.C. will be situated at U5a.9.2.
2 batteries known as "D" and "E" Batteries under the command of Capt. W.Burns 18th Bn. M.G.C. will be situated at O. 36 c.0.0.

(c)
"A" and "B" Batteries will be found by 58th Bn. M.G.C.
"C" Battery will be found by "D" Coy 18th Bn. M.G.C.
"D" and "E" Batteries will be found by 18th Bn. M.G.C and composed as follows:-
8 guns "D" Coy.
2 guns "A" Coy.
6 guns "B" Coy.

(d) Batteries will be divided into 2 sections each under the command of an officer.

(e) Exact locations of batteries are shown on attached map "a" (issued to all concerned).

3. TASKS OF
BATTERIES.

(a) "A" and "B" batteries will barrage approximately the valley in U 24 a. -V. 19 c. from Zero to Zero plus 15. These guns will then take up their final S O S barrage on a line running from V 25 c 5.8. to V 19 c.0.0.

(b) "C" battery will barrage the trenches in U. 18 c and a. on a line approximately U 18 c 3.2. --U18 a 6.8. from Zero to Zero plus 15. and will then switch on to east end of wood U 18 d 4.6. to V 13 a 8.9. until Zero plus 40 when they will cease fire .

(c) "D" and "E" Batteries will barrage east end of wood U 18 d.4.6. to V 13 a 8.9. from Zero to Zero plus 40 when they will come on their ~~barrage line~~ S.O.S. line running from V 8 a.1.1. to V 2 b. 0.1.

(d) "A","B","D" and "E" batteries will cease fire at Zero plus 90 unless S.O.S. barrage fire is called for.

(e)

(e) Rates of fire during the operation will be --
Zero to Zero plus 10 to plus 40 and plus 40 to 50
Rapid-- 250 rounds per minute.

Zero plus 10 to Zero plus 40. and Zero plus 50 to Zero plus 90. --Slow-- 75 rounds per minute.

All guns will traverse 1 ° right and left.

4. ZERO HOUR. Will be notified later.

5. AMMUNITION.
20 belt boxes per gun will be provided at each battery position. In addition S.A.A for filling belts will be provided as follows:-
(a) 80,000 rounds at Cellars in HANGARD (U28 d8.5.) for A & B Bty's.
(b) 40,000 rounds S.A A at U 5 a 9.2. for "E" Battery
(c) 80,000 " in O.36. c.O.O. for "D" and "E" Battery.
(d) 5th Australian Bde have formed dumps of S.A.A. as follows:-
50.000 rds at U 16 c 6.7.
50,000 rds at CACHY U 8a60.55.
100,000 rds on limbers at Bde H.Q. T12c.9.8.

The system of supply will be by limbers to U 16 c 6.7.and thence by carrying parties to the required destination.
These dumps will not be used by the 18th and 58th M.G.Bttns except in cases of urgent necessity.

6.REPORTS AND ORDERS
All guns will proceed to take up positions on night of "Y" day and be ready for operations by 10 p.m.same night. A report to this effect will be sent to H.Q. 18th Division.
Batteries will remain in position during the day of the operation and will provide S O S barrages as called for.
They will only withdraw on receipt of orders to do so.

7. CONSTRUCTION OF GUN POSITIONS
Gun positions will be constructed on night of "Y" day.
Reconnaisance should be made and positions marked out during daylight, beforehand.

8. GUIDES
Guides for gun-teams will be detailed and arrangements made for getting guns into position by Group Commanders concerned.

9. TRANSPORT.
Transport for A and B Batteries should proceed via the DOMART-AMIENS Road and on to HANGARD.
Transport for C ,D and E,batteries via the VILLERS-BRETONNEUX LONGEAU)AMIENS Road. Transport should not move until dusk.

10. Synchronization of watches
All watches will be synchronized at an hour to be notified later. and under no circumstances by telephone.

11. ACKNOWLEDGE.

J.W.K.Wernham
Capt. and Adjt.
18th Bn. Machine Gun Corps.

Issued at......
Copies to :-
1. C.O.
2. Second i/c.
3. Adjutant.
4. "A" Coy.
5 "B" Coy.
6. "C" Coy.
7. "D" Coy.
8. 18th Div. "G".
9. 58th Bn. M.G.C.
10. War Diary
11. War Diary.
12. File.

BATTERY CHART for "A" Battery.

Place:

Date:

Composition 8 Guns 58th Battalion

Commanded by — Grid Bearing 40°

Location of Directing Gun. U,28,d,40.40 to U28,d,50,20 — Zero Line 40°

No of Directing Guns — Grid. Bear. of Zero Line 40°

TASK.

A. Enfilade Barrage

B. Frontal Barrage

No. of Barrage.	No of Guns.	Clock Time.	Zero Line.	Angle of Switch.	Distribution Angle	Range.	V. I.	Q. E.	Range to F. E. when Barrage lifts.	Rate of Fire
A.	8		40°	—	—	2300x to 2800x	+22x	6°–20′ 30′ difference	—	Rapid 250 rds P.M.
B.	8			40° Right	50′	2400x	—	6°–40′	—	Rapid
C.										

BATTERY CHART. for "B" Battery

Place:

Date:

Composition 8 Guns of 58th Battn

Commanded by

Location of Directing Gun U,28,d,2.6 to U28,d,25.40.

No of Directing Guns..

Grid Bearing 44°

Zero Line 44°

Grid. Bear: of Zero Line 44°

TASK

No. of Barrage.	No of Guns.	Clock Time.	Zero Line.	Angle of Switch.	Distribution Angle.	Range.	V. I.	Q. E.	Range to F. L. when Barrage lifts	Rate of Fire
A.	8		44°	—	—	2000ˣ to 2400ˣ	+11ˣ	4°, 40' 20' difference	—	Rapid 250 Rds P.M.
B.	8			32° Right	40'	2500ˣ	+22ˣ	8°	—	Rapid
C.										

D & E Batteries
C. Battery
3.
4.
ORIGINAL FRONT LINE
U.
V.
Z to Z+15
Z to Z+15
C. Batt. Z+15 to Z+40.
D & B Batt. Z to Z+90.
Z+40 to Z+90
FINAL OBJECTIVE.
21.
22
20.
21.
German Trenches
Z+15 to Z+90.
B A Batteries.

...en located on a squared map. ...ale, and 2,000 yards in length

...n on the trace. Sufficient ... own map. A little detail ...be always given. The trace

Tracing taken from Sheet 62.D.

of the 1: 40.000 *map of* FRANCE

Signature WAR DIARY *Date*

A P P E N D I X 19.

(Note: This Appendix, Narrative of Operations, 31st March/ 13th April, 1918, precedes the War Diary.)

SECRET.

Appendix 20.

Copy No......

18th Battalion MMachine Gun Corps.
Order No. 15.

Reference Map.
Sheet. 62.d. 1/40,000.

13th April 1918.

1. The Battalion (less 8 gun teams in line) will move to-day from BOVES to ECOLE NORMALE. AMIENS.

2. (a) Hour of Start and Order of March:-

"A" Echelon Transport and H.Q. Coy.	1.30 p.m.
"A" Company.	1.45 p.m.
"B" Company.	2 p.m.
"C" Company.	2.15 p.m.
"D" Company.	2.30 p.m.

(b) Starting Point:- Road Junction S.12.b.3.8.
(c) Route:- CAGNY - BOUTILLERIE - AMIENS.
(d) Dress:- Full Marching Order; Steel Helmets to be worn.

3. Advance Party.
Capt. G. W. H. NICOLSON has preceded the Battn. and will arrange billets. C.Q.M.S's and a representative from Headquarters will report Orderly Room at 12.15 p.m. They should be provided with bicycles and will proceed to AMIENS to ascertain from Capt NICOLSON the billets allotted to Coys. They will meet their respective Companies at Cross Roads M.20.a.5.9.
Leading Company is expected to arrive at this point about 2.45 p.m.

4. Kits, Blankets, baggage etc., will be loaded under arrangements to be made by Companies during the morning and return all Transport ready to move to Transport Lines by 12 noon. Bulk S.A.A. will be dumped in old Quartermaster's stores next to H.Q. Mess and amounts notified to Bn.H.Q.

5. Billets will be inspected after the departure of Companies and must be left absolutely clean.

6. Marching out states to be handed to R.S.M. at 12 noon.

7. The relief of the 8 guns now in the forward area is being arranged. These teams will be billeted at BOVES on night of 13th/14th and will rejoin the Battn. on the morning of the 14th inst.,
O.C. "A" Company will arrange to set apart a billet for 1 Officer and 50 O.Rs. and Q.Mr. will leave behind 1 limber for bringing guns out of the line.

.....................Capt & Adjt.,
18th Battn. Machine Gun Corps.

Issued at 10.45 a.m. Copies to:-

No.1.Copy	C.O.
" 2 "	"A" Coy.
" 3 "	"B" Coy.
" 4 "	"C" Coy.
" 5 "	"D" Coy.
" 6 "	Quartermaster.
" 7 "	R.S.M.
" 8 "	War Diary.
" 9 "	War Diary.
" 10 "	File.

S E C R E T. appendix 21. Copy No........1

Reference Map:- [illegible] 1/100,000 17th April 1918.

18th BATTALION M.G.CORPS ORDER NO. 16.

1. The 18th Battalion M.G.C. will move to-day from [illegible], [illegible] to the Camp in vicinity of [illegible] on [illegible] side of the [illegible] Road 1 mile North of the "[illegible]" in [illegible].

2. (a) Starting point:- Cross Roads 1[illegible] yards East of [illegible].
   (b) Time of passing Starting Point:- Head of column will pass Starting Point at 11.15 a.m.
   (c) Order of March:- "A", "B", "C", "D", [illegible].
   (d) Route:- Cross Roads 1[illegible] yards East of [illegible] - [illegible] - Camp.
   (e) Dress:- Full Marching Order and Steel Helmets.
   (f) Distances of [illegible] yards will be maintained between Coys.

3. Transport will move under arrangements to be made by [illegible]. Usual distances will be kept to prevent congestion of traffic.

4. BAGGAGE, KITS, etc.

Transport Officer will detail necessary limbers to collect stores, blankets, Officers kits etc. These are to be dumped outside Quartermaster's Stores by 10.30 a.m.

5. [illegible].

[illegible]'s will report to Orderly Room at 10.[illegible] a.m. with bicycles ready to proceed to New Camp where they will report to Major. [illegible], D.S.O.

6. SYNCHRONISATION OF WATCHES.

Watches will be synchronised at Battn. H.Q. at 10.40 a.m.

7. MARCH DISCIPLINE.

Strict March discipline will be maintained throughout the march.

8. Marching Out States will be handed to the [illegible] at 10.45 a.m.

[signature]

........................Capt & Adjt.,
18th Battalion Machine Gun Corps.

Issued at 10 a.m. Copies to:-

No.1.Copy C.O.
" 2 " "A" Coy.
" 3 " "B" Coy.
" 4 " "C" Coy.
" 5 " "D" Coy.
" 6 " Quartermaster.
" 7 " Transport Officer.
" 8 " M.O.
" 9 " War Diary.
" 10 " War Diary.
" 11 " File.

SECRET. *appendix 22* 18th Bn. M.G.C. No. [illegible].37.

WARNING ORDER

Reference Map:-
Sheet 62.D.N.E. 1/20,000. 20th April 1918.

1. It has been found necessary that in case of an enemy attack, Brigades will have to move forward to be nearer the scene of action. The moves forward will be carried out in two stages.-
   1st Stage. 53rd Inf. Bde. will move from ST FUSCIEN to neighbourhood of [illegible].4.
   54th Inf. Bde. from billets to neighbourhood of [illegible].2.
   2nd Stage. 53rd Inf. Bde. from [illegible].4.area to [illegible].27. area.
   54th Inf. Bde. from [illegible].2.area to [illegible].11. area.

2. The 18th Battn. Machine Gun Corps will hold itself in readiness to move at a moments notice and will stand to in billets at daybreak (4.30 a.m.) on the 21st inst.

3. 8 Machine Guns of 18th Battn. M.G.C. have been placed at disposal of G.O.C. 53rd Infantry Brigade and 8 guns to G.O.C. 54th Inf. Bde.
   O.C. "A" Company will detail 8 guns for 53rd Infantry Brigade
   O.C. "B" Company will detail 8 guns for 54th Infantry Brigade.

4. (i) Move of 8 guns of "A" Company.
   On receipt of orders "Stand-by" these 8 guns will move off immediately to join 53rd Inf. Bde. by following route:-
   1st Stage. Track from present Camp to ST FUSCIEN - CAGNY - CAGNY-BOVES Road to about [illegible].4.b. from thence a scout will be sent forward to about [illegible].4.Central to find 53rd Infantry Brigade.
   2nd Stage. [illegible].4.Central on to CAGNY-BOVES Road to [illegible] via track and pontoon bridge to main LONGUEAU - VILLERS BRETONNEUX Road, [illegible].25.d.2.4. to [illegible].27.Central.
   (ii) Move of 8 guns of "B" Company.
   On receipt of orders "Stand-by" these 8 guns will move off immediately to join 54th Inf. Bde. by following route:-
   1st Stage. Camp - ST FUSCIEN to junction of CAGNY-BOVES Road [illegible] through [illegible] over river by new bridge - through Railway Bridge, thence by track to [illegible].2.
   2nd Stage. [illegible].2. by road to [illegible].11. on north edge of [illegible] WOOD.

5. TOOLS ETC.
   These 16 Gun Teams will each carry 2 shovels. Transport Officer will arrange to collect these from the Transport and hand 16 each to "A" and "B" Coys respectively.

6. BLANKETS, KITS, ETC.
   Overcoats will be worn. Blankets will be put in packs. All packs are to be properly labelled or marked and left in tents. In case of move they will be collected under arrangements to be made by Quartermaster.

7. HOT TEA, RATIONS ETC.
   Quartermaster will arrange for a supply of hot tea to be ready for the Battalion at 4 a.m. To-morrows rations are being issued and in the case of a move, will be carried on the man.

8. COMMUNICATIONS.
   2 Signallers will return to each Company in the event of the Battalion moving.
   C.O. has arranged a system of mounted orderlies but in case of operations proper orders for communication will be issued.

Issued at 11.10 p.m.

[signature] Capt. and Adjt.
18th Bn. Machine Gun Corps.

appendix 23

S E C R E T

Copy No.....5

Reference Map:-
Sheet 62.d.S.W. 1/20,000.

20th April 1918.

18TH BATTALION MACHINE GUN CORPS ORDER NO.17.

1. Two complete Machine Gun ~~Teams~~ sections of "D" Company, 18th Battn. M.G.C. are placed at the disposal of 58th Division for the purpose of manning the Reserve line on 58th Divsnl. front.

2. These sections will move by lorry under Company Commanders arrangements to be at Cross Roads T.10.a.0.0. at 12 noon to-day.

3. Guides will be provided by 58th Division and will be at Cross Roads T.10.a.0.0. at 12 noon to guide teams to gun positions.

4. Transport.
6 Limbers required for the above teams will move off at once and will meet the sections on Cross Roads at U.11.a.5.8. O.C. Detachment will arrange for a guide to meet this transport and to guide it to required destination. Transport will then return to BOVES where it will be accommodated in billets to be arranged by 58th Division. A Mounted Orderly should be sent on at once to 58th Divsnl H.Qrs, BOVES to find out the billets allotted.

5. RATIONS.
Rations will be delivered to the Transport Lines at BOVES under Battalion arrangements. O.C. Detachment will make his own arrangements as regards getting rations forward from BOVES.

6. 1 Mounted Orderly will be detailed by Transport Officer to accompany limbers proceeding to BOVES to-day to find and report to Battalion Headquarters exact location of Transport Lines in BOVES.

7. O.C. Detachment will render the usual daily reports to Battalion Headquarters. He will get into touch with the nearest H.Qrs in or around GENTELLES, from which H.Qrs he will be in telephonic communication to 58th Division, 18th Division and Battalion Headquarters.

8. Report will be forwarded showing gun positions as soon as possible.

9. A C K N O W L E D G E.

....................Capt & Adjt.,
18th Battn. Machine Gun Corps.

Issued at 10.25 a.m. Copies to:-

No.1. Copy C.O.
" 2 " "D" Company.
" 3 " Quartermaster.
" 4 " Transport Officer.
" 5 " War Diary.
" 6 " War Diary.
" 7 " File.

appendix 24

SECRET. Copy No. 5.

18th BATTALION MACHINE GUN CORPS, ORDER No. 18.

Reference Map:-
AMIENS, 1/100,000. 23rd April 1918.

1. The 8 guns of "A" Company and the 8 guns of "B" Company which are at present "standing by" will move to-day to join their respective Brigades.

This move has been ordered to enable Training to be carried out with Infantry and to have the Machine Guns nearer the scene of action in case of an enemy attack

2. Brigades are located as below:-
H.Q. 53rd Inf. Bde. ST FUSCIEN.
H.Q. 54th Inf. Bde. CAGNY.

3. Hour of start.
"B" Coys. Detachment to leave Camp by 5 p.m.
"A" Coys. Detachment to leave Camp by 6 p.m.

4. Arrangements for Move.
All arrangements for move will be carried out by the Company Commanders concerned.

5. Rations.
Both Detachments will be rationed by Bn. H.Q. Transport Officer will be responsible for delivery of same.

6. Communication.
All Communication, Reports etc., should be sent from Headquarters of the Brigades to which Coys are attached. Locations of Camps will be wired to Battalion Headquarters immediately on arrival.

J W K Wenham
Capt. and Adjt.,
18th Battn. Machine Gun Corps.

Issued at 3.25. Copies to:-

No.1.Copy "A" Company.
" 2 " "B" Company.
" 3 " Transport Officer.
" 4 " Quartermaster.
" 5 " War Diary.
" 6 " War Diary.
" 7 " File.

APPENDIX 25.

CHANGES IN ESTABLISHMENT AND
STRENGTH OF BATTALION DURING
MONTH OF APRIL 1918.

Paper Strength (excluding attached):-

1st April:-	27 Officers, 460 Other Ranks.
30th April:-	48 Officers. 731 Other Ranks.

DRAFTS RECEIVED.

10 O.Rs. joined Battn. from Div. Depot. Bn. 13.4.18.

278th Machine Gun Company joined Battn (Strength 10 Officers 177 Other Ranks) 9.4.18.

265th Machine Gun Company joined Battn (Strength 9 Officers, 170 Other Ranks) 19.4.18.

OFFICERS - DECREASE.

Casualties to Officers during the month shown in Appendix 19.

Lieut. V. D. Pilcher.) Struck off strength of Bn. having been
Lieut. G. E. Coleman.) evacuated out of Corps Area. 4.4.18.

Lieut. G. Young. Ditto., do., 28.4.18.

OFFICERS - INCREASE.

Lieut. G. H. BROWNRIGG-JAY.)
2nd Lieut. C. RICHARDSON.)
2nd Lieut. A. C. FERRIS.)
2nd Lieut. W. RAMAGE.)
2nd Lieut. G. E. T. SMITH.) Joined 18th Battn. as
2nd Lieut. C. P. L. WATTS.) Reinforcements. 12.4.18.
2nd Lieut. H. G. HARDING.)
2nd Lieut. C. FFOLLIOTT.)

-----------ooo-----------

18

Vol 4

CONFIDENTIAL

War Diary.

~ of ~

18th Bn MACHINE GUN CORPS.

From:- 1st May 1918.

To:- 31st May 1918.

APPENDICES ~ 26 to 43 ~ ATTACHED

(VOLUME IV)

Instructions regarding War Diaries and Intelligence Summaries are contained in F. S. Regs., Part II. and the Staff Manual respectively. Title pages will be prepared in manuscript.

18th Battalion Machine Gun Corps

WAR DIARY or ~~INTELLIGENCE SUMMARY.~~

(Erase heading not required.)

May 1918

Army Form C. 2118.

Place	Date	Hour	Summary of Events and Information	Remarks and references to Appendices
			Ref Sheets AMIENS, DIEPPE, LENS, ABBEVILLE 1/100000	
			List of Awards attached / Casualties / Changes in Estab + Strength	App 26 / App 42 / App 43
ALLERY	1st		Battalion in rest - training under Company arrangements	
"	2nd		do B Coy ordered to be ready to join Australian Corps in line	
"	3rd		do C Coy transport moved to join Australian Corps in BAIZIEUX sector - staged night at AMIENS - D Coy warned to be ready to move to join Australian Corps - 3 pm A and B Coys attended rehearsal parade at BELLOY for medal ribbon distribution by Corps Commander	Order No 20 issued see App. 24
Allery	4th		D Coy Transport moved at 1 pm to join Australian Corps - staged night at ECOLE NORMALE, AMIENS Order No 21 issued	See App 28
		7 am	Remainder of Battalion warned to be prepared to move to forward area - Battalion Transport moved at 3 pm to AMIENS. Corps Commanders parade cancelled.	
"	5th		HQ. A. B + D Coys moved by bus at 9.30 am from ALBERT to following destinations HQ - EBART FARM, 1 KM NE of BEAUCOURT - A Coy + D Coy - BEAUCOURT - B Coy WARLOY. All Coys in Billets by 3 pm - Transport joined Coys during the afternoon - C Coy in line in sector E of LAVIEVILLE	

D. D. & L., London, E.C. (A7853) Wt. W1031/M1672 350,000 4/17 Sch. 52a Forms/C/2118/14

Instructions regarding War Diaries and Intelligence Summaries are contained in F. S. Regs., Part II. and the Staff Manual respectively. Title pages will be prepared in manuscript.

18th Battalion Machine Gun Corps

WAR DIARY
or
~~INTELLIGENCE SUMMARY.~~

(Erase heading not required.)

May 1918 (cont)

Army Form C. 2118.

Place	Date	Hour	Summary of Events and Information	Remarks and references to Appendices
			For Dispositions of Machine Guns on 18th Div front see appendix 29	
EBART FARM Nr. BEAUCOURT	6th		Officers reconnoitring line – A Coy moved from BEAUCOURT to EBART FARM during evening. – B Coy moved into line under orders of 47th Division – D Coy moved into positions in rear of forward guns as selected by 18 Battalion Commander during day – C Coy in line.	
	7th		18th Division took over sector of front – C Coy on right – B Coy on left – D Coy in support – A Coy in EBART FARM. Dispositions are shown on attached Map A.	
			Forward Bn HQ moved to BAIZIEUX	JWS
BAIZIEUX	8th		B C & D Coy in line – situation quiet – operations nil – A Coy at Ebart Farm. – During evening A Coy relieved C Coy taking over exact dispositions – relief complete 11 pm. – C Coy returned to Ebart Farm Order No 23 issued.	JWS App. 30
	9th		A B & D Coys in line – situation quiet – operations nil – C Coy at Ebart Farm	JWS
	10th		do do Harassing fire carried out during night according to Divisional programme	JWS
	11th		do do	JWS

D. D. & L., London, E.C. (A7883) Wt. W603/M1672 350,000 4/17 Sch. 52a Forms/C/2118/14

Instructions regarding War Diaries and Intelligence Summaries are contained in F. S. Regs., Part II. and the Staff Manual respectively. Title pages will be prepared in manuscript.

18th Battalion Machine Gun Corps

WAR DIARY
or
INTELLIGENCE SUMMARY.
(Erase heading not required.)

May 1918 (cont)

Army Form C. 2118.

Place	Date	Hour	Summary of Events and Information	Remarks and references to Appendices
BAIZIEUX	12th		Same as for 11th Order No 24 issued	JB Appendix 31
	13th		do	JB 31
	14th	Night 14/15th	Order No 25 issued C Coy relieved B Coy in left Brigade Sector taking over similar dispositions – B Coy to [illegible] Farm – No [illegible]	Appendix 32 JB
	15		No change – operations nil	JB
	16		do do	JB
	17		Order No 26 issued 8 guns 34th Bn MG Corps took over 8 gun positions of this Battalion in [illegible] line during night – 2 guns D Coy brought back [illegible]	Appendix 33
			6 guns C Coy moved forward – dispositions shown on attached map	JB
	18		Order No 27 issued 54th & 55th Infy Bdes carried out raids [illegible] Australian Corps overnight – Zero 2 am 19th inst – [illegible] 2500 rds fired during MG Barrage	Appendix 34
			Evening 18th May B Coy relieved A Coy in Right Brigade [illegible] Complete 12 15 am 19th inst – Dispositions B Coy shown on attached map – A Coy returned to [illegible] FARM	JB
	19th	2am	Raids as above – otherwise operations nil – [illegible]	JB
			Circular letter issued respecting orders re Action of M.Gs	Appendix 35

D. D. & L., London, E.C. (A7883) Wt. W503/M1672 350,000 4/17 Sch. 52a Forms/C/2118/14

18th Battalion Machine Gun Corps

Instructions regarding War Diaries and Intelligence Summaries are contained in F. S. Regs., Part II. and the Staff Manual respectively. Title pages will be prepared in manuscript.

WAR DIARY
or
INTELLIGENCE SUMMARY.
(*Erase heading not required.*)

Army Form C. 2118.

May 1918 (cont)

Place	Date	Hour	Summary of Events and Information	Remarks and references to Appendices
BAIZIEUX	20th		No change - operations nil - Harassing fire during night	JJD
	21st	3.15am	Battalion standing to during a suspected enemy attack - this did not materialise - Battalion "stood down" 5 am - operations nil - Harassing fire during night. Order No 28 issued	JJD App 36
	22		No harassing fire during night - A Coy relieved C Coy in the Left Brigade Sector - relief complete 12.15 am 23rd - C Coy returned to billets at Ebart Farm. Order No 28a issued	JJD App 37
	23		No change - harassing fire at night. Order No 29 issued for Relief	JJD App 38
	24		Relief commenced of Battalion by 47th Bn M.G.C. - A Coy from Left Brigade Sector to Warloy relief complete 12 midnight - 6 guns D Coy (4 at D12a.c.1 - 2 in BAIZIEUX) to Ebart Farm - relief complete 1.30 am 25th	JJD
	25	10am	Adv. Bn H.Q. from BAIZIEUX to MOLLIENS-AU-BOIS	
		11am	Rear Bn H.Q. - C Coy - 6 guns D Coy at EBART FARM to MOLLIENS-AU-BOIS 6 guns D Coy redirected on to MIRVAUX	
			During night B Coy relieved in right Brigade Sector relief complete 2am 26th	JJD

D. D. & L., London, E.C. (A7833) Wt. W1023/M1672 350,000 1/17 Sch. 52a Forms/C/2118/14

Instructions regarding War Diaries and Intelligence Summaries are contained in F. S. Regs., Part II. and the Staff Manual respectively. Title pages will be prepared in manuscript.

Army Form C. 2118.

18th Bn Machine Gun Corps WAR DIARY or INTELLIGENCE SUMMARY. May 1918

(Erase heading not required.)

Place	Date	Hour	Summary of Events and Information	Remarks and references to Appendices
	25th (cont)		B Coy on relief to Wood C 20 b 8.0	
			10 guns of D Coy relieved – relief complete 2.30 am 26th and	
			proceeded to EBART FARM	JWD
MOLLIENS-AU-BOIS	26th	10 am	10 guns D Coy moved from Ebart Farm to MIRVAUX	
			– Dispositions A Coy – WARLOY	
			B " Wood C 20 b 8.0	
			C " MOLLIENS-AU-BOIS	
			D " MIRVAUX	
			HQ MOLLIENS-AU-BOIS	JWD
"	27		Resting – cleaning up & refitting	JWD
"	28		Training in vicinity of Billets	JWD App. 39
"	29		do M.G. Defence Scheme for Bn in Corps Reserve issued	JWD
"	30		do Warning Order to relieve 58th Div issued	JWD App 40
"	31	11 am	D Coy moved from MIRVAUX to MOLLIENS-AU-BOIS Order No. 30 issued	App 41
		5 pm	C Coy moved from MOLLIENS-AU-BOIS to WARLOY	
		5.30 pm	D " " " to CONTAY	[signature] Capt. 18th Bn M.G. Corps JWD

D. D. & L., London, E.C. (A7883) Wt. W593/M1672 350,000 4/17 Sch. 52a Forms/C/2118/14

APPENDIX 26.

LIST OF DECORATIONS GAINED BY OFFICERS, N.C.Os. AND MEN OF THE 18th BATTALION MACHINE GUN CORPS DURING RECENT FIGHTING.

MILITARY CROSS.

2nd Lieut. H. W. BURDEN.	"C" Company.
2nd Lieut. C. HORTON.	"C" Company.
2nd Lieut. W. J. BRINKMAN.	"B" Company.

DISTINGUISHED CONDUCT MEDAL.

4171 Cpl. A. W. FARR.	"C" Company.

BAR TO MILITARY MEDAL.

71087 Sgt. A. BARFORD, M.M.	"B" Company.
4079 Cpl. W. MARTIN, M.M.	"B" Company.

MILITARY MEDAL.

9465 Pte. W. W. LUCAS.	"A" Company.
36454 L/C. R. LEACH.	"B" Company.
114613 Pte. A. V. NORTON.	"C" Company.
73929 Pte. H. W. MOSSMAN.	"B" Company.
4177 L/S. R. G. HARDIMAN.	"C" Company.
4109 Pte. A. TREASURE.	"B" Company.
4123 Pte. H. HUNTER.	"B" Company.
84560 L/C. C. E. BUXTON.	"C" Company.
90174 L/C. W. BAIN.	"C" Company.
114462 Pte. T. Niddrie.	"C" Company.
27841 Sgt. D. Ridley.	"B" Company.

---------ooo---------

SECRET. APPENDIX 27 Copy No. 1 ....

Reference Maps,
DIEPPE, AMIENS, 1/100,000
and Sheet 62.E. 1/40,000.

3rd May 1918.

18TH BATTN. MACHINE GUN CORPS ORDER NO.20.

1. "C" and "D" Companies 18th Bn.M.G.C. complete will move to join 55th Infantry Brigade attached Australian Corps as follows:-

On 3rd inst.

Transport "C" Coy, will move to RIVERY.

On 4th inst.

Personnel "C" Coy. will move by bus to BAIZEUX.

Transport "C" Coy. will move from RIVERY to Australian Corps Area under orders of Australian Corps.

Transport "D" Coy. moves from ALLERY to RIVERY.

On 5th inst.

Personnel "D" Coy. moves by bus to BAIZEUX

Transport "D" Coy. moves from RIVERY to Australian Corps Area under orders of Australian Corps.

2. ORDERS FOR TRANSPORT.

(a) Route:- AIRAINES - SOUES - PICQUIGNY - AMIENS - RIVERY.

(b) Billets:-Will be obtained from Area Commandant RIVERY.

(c) Time:- (i) Transport of "C" Coy will move under orders given by Coy. Transport Officer at 11.30 a.m. 3rd inst.

(ii) Transport "D" Coy will move as above at 11 a.m. on 4th inst.

3. ORDERS FOR PERSONNEL.

Arrangements as regards busses will be notified later.

4. RATIONS. Rations for "C" Company have been arranged as follows:-
1 G.S.Wagon wi[illegible] be picked up by Transport at approximately B.24.d.00.10 On AIRAINES - SOUES ROAD ½ mile East of QHESNOY. This wagon will be loaded with
(i) Rations for Transport for 4th inst.
(ii) Rations for Transport and Coy. for 5th inst.

The same arrangements will apply to "D" Coy, except that 4th should be read as 5th, and 5th as 6th.

1 Water Cart will accompany Transport of "C" Coy and will be for use of both Coys. in the forward area.

5. KITS, BAGGAGE, ETC. Baggage will be loaded under arrangements to be made by Company Commanders. Officers valises should be sent forward by Transport to-day.

6. BILLETING CERTIFICATES.
"C" and "D" Coys. will render Billeting Certificates for this area, to reach Orderly Room by 6 p.m. to-night. Transport Officer will forward certificate for billets occupied by "C" and "D" Coys. Transport.

7. A C K N O W L E D G E.

..................Capt & Adjt.,
18th Bn. Machine Gun Corps.

Issued at 10.50 a.m.

Copies to recipients of Operations Orders.

SECRET.

Copy No..4...

APPENDIX 28

Ref Maps:- DIEPPE, ABBEVILLE,
AMIENS, LENS, 1/100,000.

4th May 1918.

18TH BATTN. M.G.C. ORDER NO. 21.

1. 18th Bn. M.G.C. (less "C" & "D" Coys) are transferred from the III Corps to the Australian Corps and will move as follows.

2. On the 4th inst (to-day) Transport will move by road to ECOLE NORMALE, AMIENS, and stage there the night of the 4th/5th. Orders for move to Australian Corps Area on the 5th inst. will be issued to Bn.T.O. at ECOLE NORMALE.

3. Route. Via PICQUIGNY.

4. Transport will move to-day under orders of B.T.O. Coy. Comndrs will make arrangements to have all necessary kit etc., loaded on limbers etc. at once.

5. On the 5th inst. Personnel of above will move by Busses to Australian Corps Area. Time of embussing and destination will be notified as soon as particulars are received from Div.

6. Dress. Full Marching Order. Blanket should be carried on the man.

7. Cooking arrangements. Cookers will proceed with Transport to-day. Arrangements will be made to leave sufficient dixies behind for cooking purposes during move. These will be carried on lorries to-morrow.

J.W.R. Wemb...
Capt & Adjt.,
18th Battalion Machine Gun Corps.

Issued at 11.15 a.m.
Copies to recipients of O.Os.

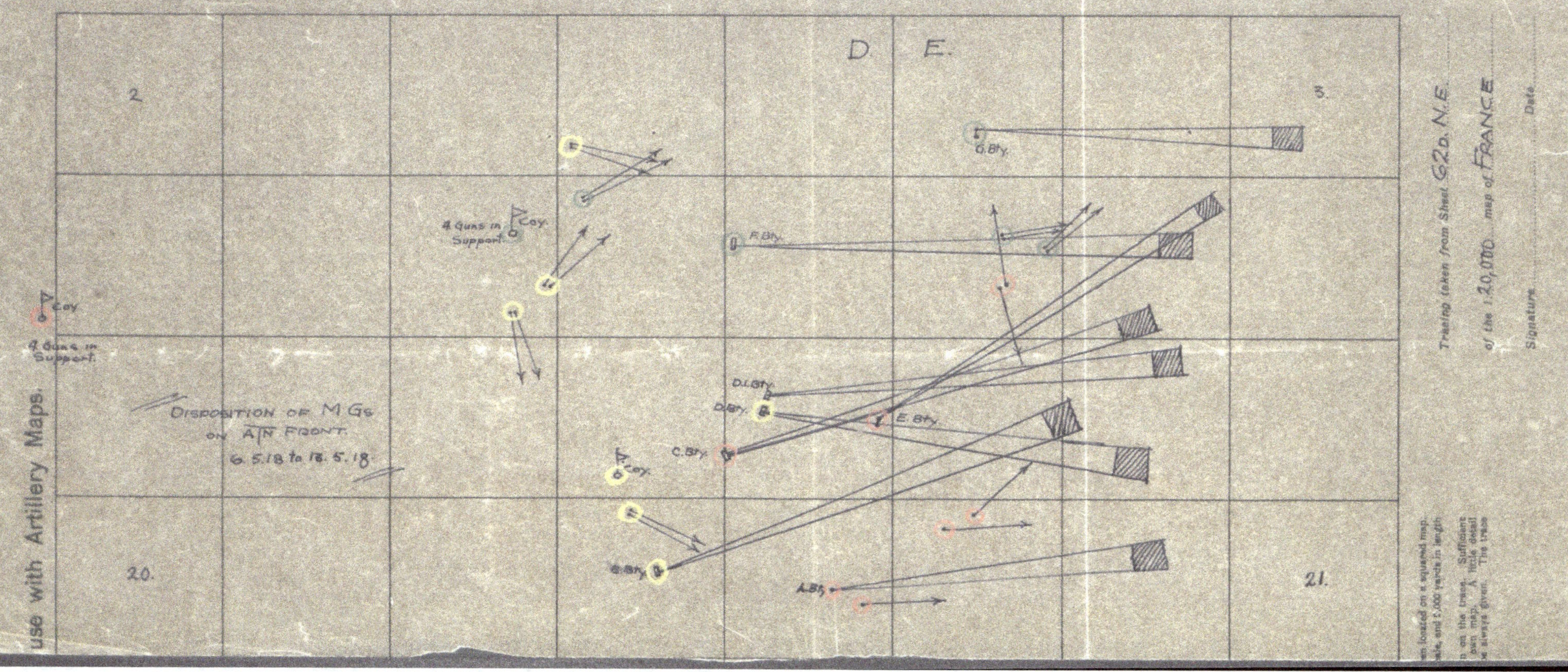

use with Artillery Maps.
D
E.
2
3.
20.
21.
DISPOSITION OF M.Gs
ON A/N FRONT
6.5.18 to 18.5.18
4 Guns in Support.
Coy.
G.Bty.
F.Bty.
D.1.Bty.
D.Bty.
E.Bty.
C.Bty.
B.Bty.
A.Bty.
Tracing taken from Sheet 62D. N.E.
of the 1:20,000 map of FRANCE
Signature
Date

Identification Trace for

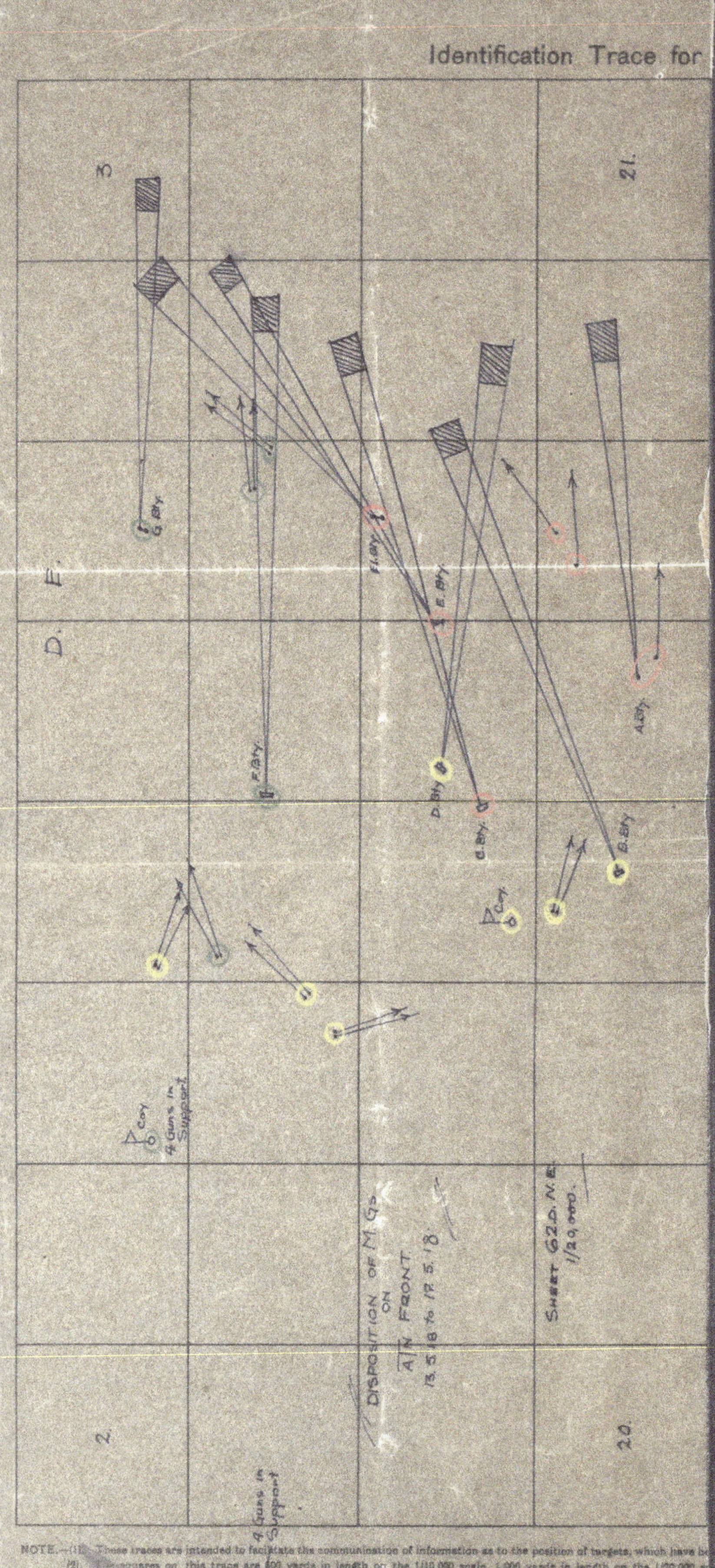

NOTE.—(1). These traces are intended to facilitate the communication of information as to the position of targets, which have be

(2). The squares on this trace are 500 yards in length on the 1/10,000 scale, 1,000 yards in length on the 1/20,000 s on the 1/40,000 scale.

(3). The squares on the trace are fitted to the squares of the map showing the targets, which are then draw letters and numbers must also be added to enable the recipient to place the trace in the correct position on his may also be traced, but this is not essential. The name and scale of the map to which the trace refers must can be used for the 1/10,000, 1/20,000, or 1/40,000 scale.

G.S.G.S. 2748

Identification Trace for

Sheet 62D NE. 1/20,000.

Disposition of M.Gs. on A/N front 18.5.18 to 22.5.18.

2

20.

NOTE.—(1). These traces are intended to facilitate the communication of information as to the position of targets, which have be

(2). The squares on this trace are 500 yards in length on the 1/10,000 scale, 1,000 yards in length on the 1/20,000 sc on the 1/40,000 scale.

(3). The squares on the trace are fitted to the squares of the map showing the targets, which are then draw letters and numbers must also be added to enable the recipient to place the trace in the correct position on his may also be traced, but this is not essential. The name and scale of the map to which the trace refers must b can be used for the 1/10,000, 1/20,000, or 1/40,000 scale.

G.S.G.S. 3023.

use with Artillery Maps.

DISPOSITION OF M. Gs.
ON A/N FRONT.
22.5.18 to 26.5.18.

2

3.

20.

21.

D. E

P Coy
4 Guns in Support.

P Coy
4 Guns in Support.

P Coy
2 Guns at Barzieux

34 Bn M.G.C.

47 M.G.C.

No 1.
No 2
No 3.
No 4
No 5
No 6
No 7
No 8
No 9
No 10
No 11

Tracing taken from Sheet 62D. N.E.

of the 1:20,000 map of FRANCE.

Signature .... Date ....

APPENDIX 29

LEGEND

Battery-of-4 Guns ... ...

Battery-of-2 Guns ... ...

Direct Fire ... ...

S.O.S. Area ... ...

Right Sector ... ...

Left Sector ... ...

Support Coy. ... ...

H. Q. Adv. ... ...

SECRET. Copy No 10

APPENDIX. 30

18 Bn M. G. C.

Order No 23.

1/ The 53rd Inf Bde will relieve the 55th Inf Bde in the Right Brigade Sector on the night 8/9th May

2/ "A" Coy 1st Bn M G C will accordingly relieve "C" Coy 18th Bn M G C in the above Sector

3/ All details of relief will be arranged between Coy Commanders concerned

4/ 12 Guns "A" Coy will take over the gun positions as now held by 12 guns "C" Coy. O/C A Coy will place 4 guns at disposal of G.O.C. 53 Inf Bde.

5/ On relief "C" Coy will be disposed of as follows
8 Guns in Bn reserve EBART Fm
8 Guns at disposal of G.O.C 55th Inf Bde (at EBART Fm

6/ All documents information etc. connected with sector will be handed over on relief.

7/ Completion of relief will be notified to Bn HQ using the name of Coy Commander as code word.

8/ Acknowledge

[signature]

Capt & Adjt

8/8/18 18th Bn M G Corps.

Copies to
1 C.O.
2 Adjt
3 O/c A Coy
4 O/c C Coy
5 T O
6 Q.M
7 O/c Signals
8 53 Inf Bde
9 55 " "
10/11/12 War Diary & File

SECRET. Copy No 1

18th Bn M G Corps APPENDIX. 31.

Order No 24

1/ The tactical situation permitting the 55th Inf Bde will relieve the 54th Inf Bde in the left sector 18th Divnl front on night May 13/14

2/ C Coy 18th Bn MGC will not relieve B Coy until night 14/15 May all details of relief will be arranged between Coy Commanders concerned

3/ O/C 8 guns of B Coy at present at disposal of GOC 54th Inf Bde for Counter attack purposes will report to GOC 55th Inf Bde as early as possible on morning of 14th inst These 8 guns are at disposal of GOC 55th Inf Bde until relieved by 8 guns of B Coy.

4/ Similarly the O/C 4 guns of B Coy now at the disposal of GOC 54th Inf Bde in line will report to GOC 55th Inf Bde when Brigade reliefs are complete.

5/ C Coy will take over same dispositions as now held by B Coy.

P.J.O

6/ O/c B Coy will arrange that his officers reconnoitre forward positions and get in touch with opposite numbers.

7/ All documents information etc connected with the sector will be handed over on relief

8/ Completion of relief will be advised to Bn (Adv) HQ using Coy Commanders name as code word and giving time

9/ Ack/

12.5.18.

Copies to
1. O/c B Coy
2. O/c C Coy
3. 54 Inf Bde
4. 55 ~

Capt R[illegible]
18 Bn MG Corps

SECRET. [illegible]

18th Bn M.G.C. [illegible] APPENDIX 32

Order No. 25.

1. On relief tonight the [illegible] of [illegible] will proceed to billets at [illegible]

2. [illegible] These guns will be in [illegible] reserve under orders of O.C. 18th Bn. M.G.C.

3. The remaining 8 guns are placed [illegible] for counter attack [illegible] O/C [illegible] 8 guns will report to [illegible] as soon as possible after relief.

4. 8 Guns placed at the disposal of [illegible] Inf. Bde. will be prepared to move within 1½ hours after notification [illegible] if the enemy attacks the front.

5. Acknowledge.

6. [illegible]

[illegible] Capt.

14.5.1918 Adjt. 18th Bn. M.G. Corps.

SECRET.

Copy No.

18th Bn M.G.C. APPENDIX 33

Order No 26.

1/ The tactical situation permitting the 54 Inf Bde will relieve the 53 Inf Bde on night 17/18th May

2/ B Coy 18th Bn M.G.C will relieve "A" Coy 18th Bn M.G.C on night 18/19 May.
All details of relief will be arranged between Coy Commanders concerned

3/ The 8 guns of B Coy at present at disposal of G.O.C 54th Inf Bd for counter attack purposes will report to G.O.C. 53 Inf Bde as early as possible on morning 19th inst
These guns are at disposal of 53 Inf Bde until relieved by A Coy.

4/ Similarly the 4 guns A Coy at present at disposal of G.O.C. 53 Inf Bde relieved will report will report to G.O.C 54 Inf Bde when the reliefs are completed.

5/ "B" Coy will take over same positions as now held by "A" Coy

6/. OC B Coy will arrange that his officers reconnoitre forward positions and get in touch with opposite numbers.

7/. All documents information etc connected with the sector will be handed over on relief.

8/. Completion of relief will be wired to Bn (adv) HQ using Coy Commanders name as Code Word & giving time.

9/ Acknowledge.

17/5/18.

Capt & Adjt
1st Bn M. G. C.

Copies TO.
1/. OC A Coy
2/. OC B Coy
3/. 53 Inf Bde
4/. 54 – –
5/.
6/. } War Diary & Files.
7/.

RCM I

APPENDIX 34

1st Bn MG
Orders no. 27.

1/ On relief the whole of your Coy will proceed to billets at [illegible]

2/ 8 guns will be in Btn reserve and under orders of C. O.

3/ The remaining 8 guns are placed at the disposal of G.O.C. 53 Inf Bde for counter attack purposes. These 8 guns will report to G.O.C. 53 Inf Bde as soon as possible after relief.

4/ The 8 guns at disposal of G.O.C. 53 Inf Bde will ~~get~~ prepare to move within 1½ hours ~~notice~~ of notification from Bn HQ of an Enemy attack

5/ acknowledge.

17/5
10/

O/C. [illegible]
53 Inf Bde [illegible]
Rear Bn HQ.

Capt [illegible]
1st Bn MGC.

18th Bn M.G. Corps No. JK.178/7

To/ A.B.C & D Coys 18th Bn M.G.C.
18th Division
53rd 54th & 55th Inf Bde
All Infy Battns of the Division } for information

APPENDIX 35

Certain orders have been issued by 54th Inf Bde regarding action of Machine Guns.

No notice will be taken of these orders and the 18th Bttn Machine Gun Corps standing orders as issued to all gun teams will be adhered to.

19-5-1918.

[signature] Lieut. Col
Commdg 18th Bn Machine Gun Corps

Copy No 1

[illegible]

[illegible]

APPENDIX. 36.

1 The tactical situation permitting the 5? Inf Bde will relieve the 5? Inf Bde [illegible] the [illegible] night [illegible].

2 Also 18 Bn M.G.C. will relieve C Coy night [illegible] May. All details of relief will be arranged between Coy Commanders concerned.

3 The 8 Guns of A Coy at present at disposal of G.O.C. 53 Inf Bde for counter attack purposes will report to G.O.C. 5? Inf Bde as early as possible on morning [illegible]. These guns are at disposal of G.O.C. 5? Inf Bde until relieved by C Coy

4 Similarly 4 Guns of C Coy at present at disposal of G.O.C. 5? Inf Bde in line will report to G.O.C. 5? Inf Bde when Bde reliefs are complete.

5 A Coy will take over line positions as now held by C Coy

6 O/C B Coy will arrange for his officers to reconnoitre forward positions & get in touch with opposite numbers.

7. All documents, information etc. connected with the sector will be handed over on relief.

8. Completion of relief will be notified to Bn HQ by wire using OC Commanders name as code word and giving time.

9. Acknowledge.

[illegible]
Capt/Adjt
18th Bn K G Corps

21.5.1918

Copies to
1/ OC A Coy
2/ " C Coy
3/ 52 Inf Bde
4/ 11 Inf Bde
5/6 War Diary.

Note.

Targets and Battery positions are shown on attached ~~map~~ tracing "A"

SECRET Copy No 7

18th Bn M G C

Order No 28A APPENDIX 37.

1/ On a date & hour to be notified separately the Division on our right is carrying out an operation with a view to capturing village of VILLE-SUR-ANCRE and high ground to the South.

2/ The 54 & 55 Inf Bdes 18th Division are assisting this attack by raiding enemy trenches as follows.

54 Inf Bde Trench E13d6.0 — E13d 3.5.
55 Inf Bde — E8c90.55 — E8a 9.0.

3/ Action of M.G's.

B D C & G Batty's 18th Bn M G C will cooperate in these raids and are allotted tasks as follows:

Batty	Coy	Target	Time
B	D	E	Zero to Zero + 35
D	D	B	do
C	B	A	do
G	D	D	" " " + 25

At Zero plus 25 G Batty will cease fire
At Zero plus 35 B C & D batteries will concentrate on C target for 10 minutes.
At Zero + 45 these batteries will

cease fire and all guns will lay on original SOS lines to be ready to reply to SOS if called upon

In addition to above O/c C Coy will arrange to fire on any suitable targets as directed by G.O.C. 55 Inf Bde

4 Rates of Fire

Zero to Zero plus 5 Rapid 250 rds per min
Zero plus 5 to Z plus 35 Slow 75 " " "
Z plus 35 to " 45 Rapid 250 " " "

5 Synchronization of Watches

Watches will be synchronized at Zero – 2 hours at the respective Bde HQ.

6 Spare Ammn

Every effort will be made to keep belts filled.

G. Norwood
Captain
18th Bn M G Corps

Copies To
1/2/3 B C & D Coys
4/5 54 & 55 Bdes
6 18 Div
7/8/9 H.Q. & file.

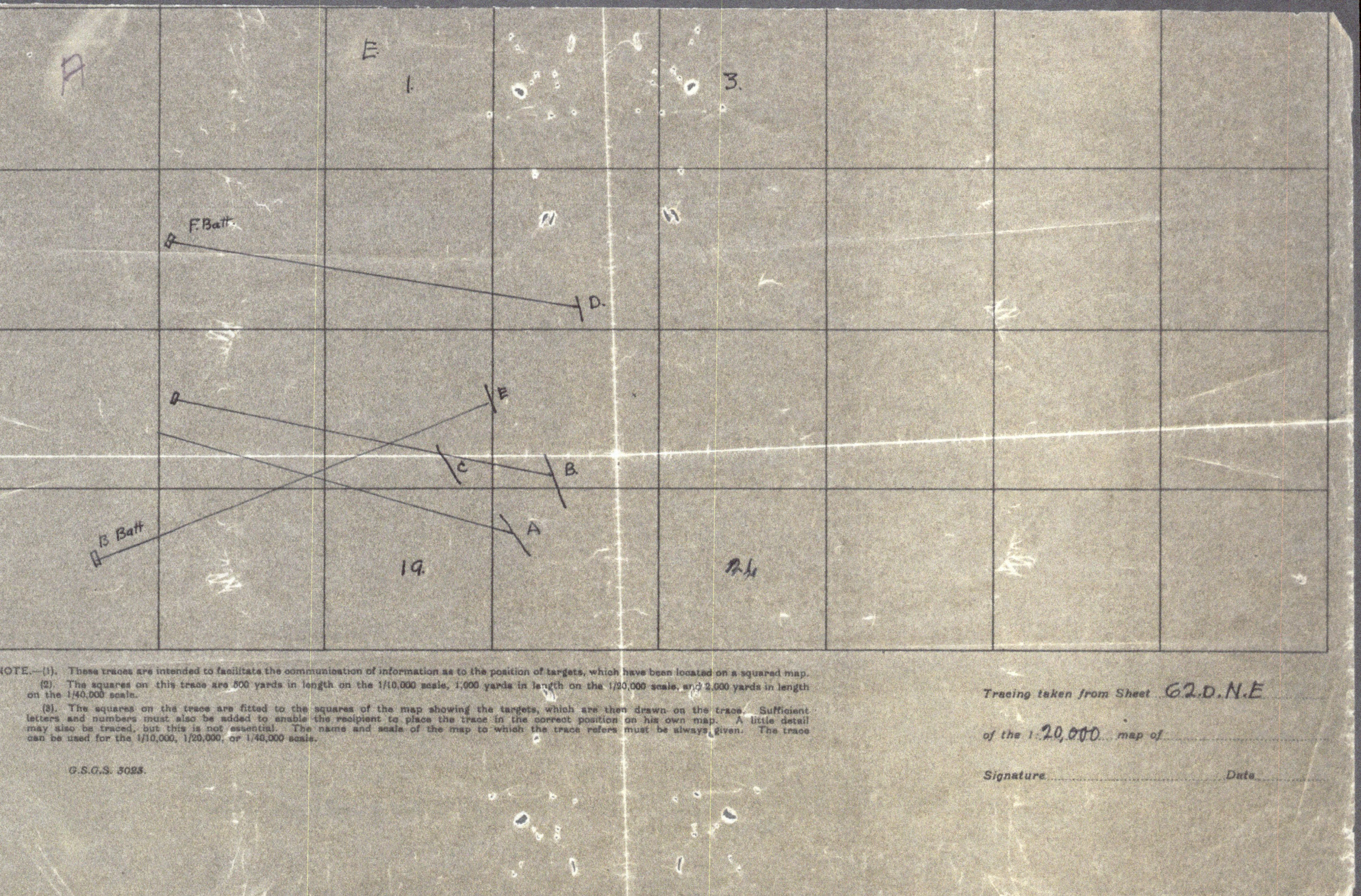

NOTE.—(1). These traces are intended to facilitate the communication of information as to the position of targets, which have been located on a squared map.

(2). The squares on this trace are 500 yards in length on the 1/10,000 scale, 1,000 yards in length on the 1/20,000 scale, and 2,000 yards in length on the 1/40,000 scale.

(3). The squares on the trace are fitted to the squares of the map showing the targets, which are then drawn on the trace. Sufficient letters and numbers must also be added to enable the recipient to place the trace in the correct position on his own map. A little detail may also be traced, but this is not essential. The name and scale of the map to which the trace refers must be always given. The trace can be used for the 1/10,000, 1/20,000, or 1/40,000 scale.

G.S.G.S. 3023.

Tracing taken from Sheet 62.D.N.E

of the 1:20,000 *map of* ....

Signature .... *Date* ....

S E C R E T.

APPENDIX 38

Copy No. 15

Reference Maps:- Sheets 57.d. and 62.d. 1/40,000.

22nd May 1918.

18TH BATTN. M. G. C. ORDER NO. 29.

1. The 47th Battn. M.G.Corps will relieve the 18th Battn. M.G.C. in the Right Sector of the III Corps front on nights 24th/25th and 25th/26th May 1918.

2. Reliefs of Companies will take place in accordance with attached table, which also shows dispositions to be occupied by Companies after relief.

3. All details of reliefs (guides etc) will be arranged direct between Company Commanders concerned.

4. The following will be handed over at Gun Positions:-
   All A.P. Ammunition.
   14 filled belt boxes per gun.
   All boxed S.A.A.
   Petrol tins - 2 per gun.
   T. Bases, emplaced.
   All Battery Charts, fire orders, air photos.
   Receipts will be obtained and forwarded to Battn. H.Q. by noon 26th inst.

5. Reliefs of Signal personnel and handing over of Signal communication will be arranged between respective Signal Officers

6. Completion of Reliefs will be wired to Battn. H.Q. using serial number of relief and hour.

7. Command of Machine Gun Dispositions in Divisional Sector to include 8 guns of 34th Bn. M.G.Corps in LAVIEVILLE LINE will pass to O.C. 47th Battn. M.G.C. at 10 a.m. 25th inst.

8. Rear Bn. H.Q. will be relieved by H.Q. 47th Bn. M.G.C. and will move back to MOLLIENS AU BOIS on morning of 25th May 1918.
   Advanced Battn. H.Q. will remain in BAIZIEUX until completion of reliefs.

9. A C K N O W L E D G E.

....................Capt & Adjt.,
18th Battn. Machine Gun Corps.

Issued at .... p.m. by D.R.L.S. Copies to:-

No.1.Copy C.O.
" 2 " 2nd-in-Command.
" 3 " Adjutant.
" 4 " Signal Officer.
" 5 " Transport Officer.
" 6 " Quartermaster.
" 7 " "A" Company
" 8 " "B" Company.
" 9 " "C" Company.
" 10 " "D" Company.
" 11 " 18th Division. "G"
" 12. " 34th Battn. M.G.C.
" 13. " 47th Battn. M.G.C.
" 14. " 58th Battn. M.G.C.
" 15/16" War Diary.
" 17 " File.

18TH BATTALION MACHINE GUN CORPS.

T A B L E   O F   R E L I E F S.
(To accompany O. Order No. 29.)

Serial No.	Date.	Unit of 18th Bn.	Relieved by Unit 47th Bn.	From.	After relief to.
1.	Night. 24/25th May.	"A" Coy. (less 4 guns at Bde.H.Q)	12 guns of "B" Coy.	C.20.b.3.6.	Woods C.8.a.7.1.
2.	do.	4 Guns "A" Coy. at Bde H.Q.	4 Guns "D" Company.	C.20.b.3.6.	Woods. C.8.a.7.1.
3.	do.,	4 Guns "D" Coy. at D.12.a.0.1.	4 Guns of "B" Coy.	C.20.b.3.6.	EBART FARM.
4.	25th May.	"C" Coy. EBART FARM.	12 Guns "D" Coy.	MOLLIENS-AU-BOIS.	MOLLIENS-AU-BOIS.
5.	Night. 25th/26th May.	"B" Coy. (less 4 guns at Bde H.Q)	12 Guns "C" Coy.	C.20.b.3.6.	C.20.b.3.6.
6.	do.,	4 Guns "B" Coy.at Bde H.Q.	4 Guns "D" Company.	EBART FARM.	C.20.b.3.6.
7.	do.,	6 Guns "D" Coy. in D.23.	6 Guns "D" Company.	EBART FARM.	EBART FARM.
8.	do.,	2 Guns "D" Company BAIZIEUX.	2 Guns "D" Company.	EBART FARM.	EBART FARM.
9.	do.,	4 Guns "D" Company. D.18.a.3.0.	4 Guns "C" Company.	C.20.b.3.6.	EBART FARM.

REMARKS.

Serial Number 1. Bivouacs in wood at C.8.a.7.1. are at present occupied by "C" Coy 47th Bn. M.G.C. This Coy. will move to bivouacs at C.20.b.3.6. on afternoon of 24th May.

Serial Number 3. On 25th will march with "C" Company to MOLLIENS-AU-BOIS.

Serial Nos. 7, 8, and 9. On 26th will proceed by route March to MOLLIENS-AU-BOIS.

-----------oOo---------

SECRET. 18th Battn. M.G.C. No.S.48.

18TH BATTALION MACHINE GUN CORPS.

Reference Maps:- SENLIS. 1/20,000. 29th May 1918.

APPENDIX 39.

ACTION OF MACHINE GUNS IN EVENT OF COUNTER ATTACK BY 18TH DIVN.

1. Should ~~either~~ any of the following situations arise;-
(a) Enemy capture HENENCOURT and British hold LAVIEVILLE.
(b) Enemy capture LAVIEVILLE and British hold HENENCOURT.
(c) Enemy capture both HENENCOURT and LAVIEVILLE.
the action of Machine Guns will be as follows:-

2. In all three situations 8 Guns of "A", "B" and "C" Coys. will report immediately to their respective Brigades and be Commanded by Company Commanders under orders of G.O.C. Brigades.
The remaining 16 guns of "B" and "D" Coys. will be in Divisional Reserve under orders of O.C. 18th Machine Gun Battalion.

3. Action of remaining guns.
In the event of Situation:-
(a) 8 Guns of "A" Company will take up Barrage positions in V.25.a.80.30.(approximately) and barrage along V.27.a.0.1. to V.27.d.3.3. and then lift on trench line in V.28.d.0.5.
16 Guns of "D" Coy. in V.25.d.4.6. will barrage along western edge of the Village from D.3.b.25.4. to V.27.c.9.3. (Approximately) and then lift to trench line in V.28.c. and d.
The company of [illegible] Battn. M.G.C. in reserve at BOIS [illegible] will take up positions under the brow in D.15.b.70.60. and will barrage the valley in V.29.a. and c.
(b) 8 Guns of "A" Company will take up position at D.2.d. 60.40. and barrage the valley in D.8.a. and c.
16 Guns of "D" Company will take up position in D.2.c.85.80. (CAVALRY TRENCH) and barrage along Western Edge of LAVIEVILLE from D.10.b.0.8. to D.10.d.0.5 and then lift to [illegible] AVENUE in D.11.c.
16 Guns of [illegible] Bn. M.G.C. in D.14.c.10.30. will barrage valley on the approximate line D.16.d.5.8 to D.17.c.7.3.
(c) 8 Guns of "A" Company in positions as for (a) will barrage on lines as for (a).
16 Guns of "D" Company in positions as for (b) will barrage on lines as for (b).
16 Guns of [illegible] Bn. M.G.C. in positions as for (b) will barrage on lines as for (b).

4. Artillery Tracings showing barrage lines are attached.
A separate tracing shows the action of guns of [illegible] Bn. M.G.C. at present in BAIZIEUX system.

5. Officers concerned will immediately reconnoitre positions and alternative routes for ammunition supply etc.,

6. A C K N O W L E D G E.

[signature]
.... Capt & Adjt.,
18th Battn. Machine Gun Corps.

Issued at ...... p.m. Copies to:-

No.1.Copy "A" Coy.
" 2 " "B" Coy.
" 3 " "C" Coy.
" 4 " "D" Coy.
" 5 " [illegible] Bn.M.G.C.
No.6.Copy 18th Division.
No.7.Copy. 53rd Inf. Bde.
" 8 copy. 54th Inf. Bde.
" 9 Copy. 55th Inf. Bde.
" 10 Copy. War Diary.
" 11 " File.

(A+C Situation)
A Coy. 8 Guns.

D. Coy.

25

V.

D.

D. Coy
16. Guns.

(A+C Situation)
A. Coy.

D. Coy.

28.

(A+C Situation)
A. Coy.

34. M.G.Bn

34. M.G.Bn
16. Guns.

13.

LEGEND

Situation A ....
" " B ....
" " C (Compiled from. A.B)

Sheet SENLIS.
1/20,000

NOTE.—(1). These traces are intended to facilitate the communication of information as to the position of targets, which have been located on a squared map.

(2). The squares on this trace are 500 yards in length on the 1/10,000 scale, 1,000 yards in length on the 1/20,000 scale, and 2,000 yards in length on the 1/40,000 scale.

(3). The squares on the trace are fitted to the squares of the map showing the targets, which are then drawn on the trace. Sufficient letters and numbers must also be added to enable the recipient to place the trace in the correct position on his own map. A little detail may also be traced, but this is not essential. The name and scale of the map to which the trace refers must be always given. The trace can be used for the 1/10,000, 1/20,000, or 1/40,000 scale.

G.S.G.S. 3023.

Tracing taken from Sheet ....

of the 1: .... map of ....

Signature .... Date ....

18th Bn. M.G.C. No. S. 43. Copy No. 7.

APPENDIX 40

18TH BATTALION MACHINE GUN CORPS.
W A R N I N G   O R D E R.

30th May 1918.

1. The sector now held by the 58th Division will be taken over by the 18th Division in the course of the next few days.

2. The 58th Battalion Machine Gun Corps will be relieved by the 18th Battalion Machine Gun Corps as given below:-

"C" Company on the night 1st/2nd June.

"A" Company on the night 2nd/3rd June.

"B" Company will be in reserve.

"D" Company: Orders re relief will be issued later.

3. A C K N O W L E D G E.

Capt & Adjt.,
18th Battn. Machine Gun Corps.

Copies to:-

No.1.Copy "A" Coy.
" 2 " "B" Coy.
" 3 " "C" Coy.
" 4 " "D" Coy.
" 5 " Transport Officer.
" 6 " Signal Officer.
" 7 " War Diary.
" 8 " War Diary.
" 9 " File.

SECRET. Copy No. 16...

Reference Maps-
Sheets 57d. and 62 d. 1/40,000.

APPENDIX 41

18th Battalion M.G.C. ORDER No. 30.

1. The 18th Bttn. M.G.C. will relieve the 58th Bttn. M.G.C. in the left sector of the III Corps Front on nights 1st/2nd and 2nd/3rd June 1918.

2. The relief of Companies will take place in accordance with the attached table.
Artillery tracings showing dispositions of Coys on relief is attached.

3. All details of relief (guides etc.) will be arranged between Company Commanders concerned.

4. The following will be taken over at all gun positions.:-

12 belt boxes S.A.A. (6 of these belts contain Armour piercing ammunition)
"T" Pieces and aiming marks.
Reserve rations and water.
Petrol tins.
S.A.A.
Battery and range charts. Fire Orders. etc. Receipts will be given and forwarded to Battalion Headquarters by noon 3rd June.

5. Signal Communication.
The handing over of Signal Communication will be arranged between respective Signal Officers.

6. The Company of the 34th Battalion M.G.C. in the area will come under the Command of the 18th Division on completion of relief.

7. "B" Coy. will hand over the work at present being done for the 158th Tunnelling Coy. R.E. to "B" Coy. 58th Battalion M.G.C.

8. "C" Coy. 18th Bn. M.G.C. will provide working parties to relieve working ~~xxxxxxx~~ party of "D" Coy. 58th Bn. M.G.C. on night 1st /2nd June.
"A" and "D" Coys. 18th Bn. M.G.C. will take over work at V 24 d. 8.8. from "A" and "C" Coys 58th Bn. M.G.C. on Night 2nd /3rd June.
Working party tables for Coys ~~xxxxxxxx~~ in the line are attached.

9. Completion of reliefs will be wired to Bttn. H.Qrs giving serial number of relief and hour.

[signature]
Capt. and Adjt.
18th Bttn. Machine Gun Corps.

Issued at..4.30...p.m.
Copies to:-.

1. C.O.	10. Quartermaster.
2. Second-in-Command.	11. 18th Division.
3. Adjutant.	12. 58th Bn. M.G.C.
4. "A" Coy.	13. 34th Bn. M.G.C.
5 "B" Coy.	14. 47th Bn. M.G.C.
6. "C" Coy.	15. War Diary.
7. "D" Coy.	16. War Diary.
8. Signal Officer.	17. File.
9. Transport Officer.	

(To accompany Order No. 30)

18th [illegible]

RELIEF TABLE

Serial No.	Date	Relieving Unit	From	Via	Route	Through?	Unit to be relieved
1	[illegible] 1st/2nd June	"B" Coy. 18th Battn	C.20.b.		WARLOY ~~CONTAY~~		D Coy 58th Battn.
2.	do.	"D" Coy. 18th Battn	CONTAY	V27b Central	V16.c. 7.5.	V16c 7.5.	C Coy 58th Battn.
3.	do.	"C" Coy 18th Battn	WARLOY/2	V27b 30.30.	CONTAY	V16c 7.5.	"D" Coy 58th Battn.
4.	2nd June.	HQ 18th Bn.	[illegible]		CONTAY		HQ 58th Battn.
5.	Night 2nd/3rd	A Coy 18th Battn	WARLOY	V27b Central	CONTAY	V16c 7.5.	"C" Coy 58th Bn.

NOTES. Probably on a date to be notified later [illegible] B Coy in WARLOY and B Coy will take over billets of [illegible] in WARLOY.

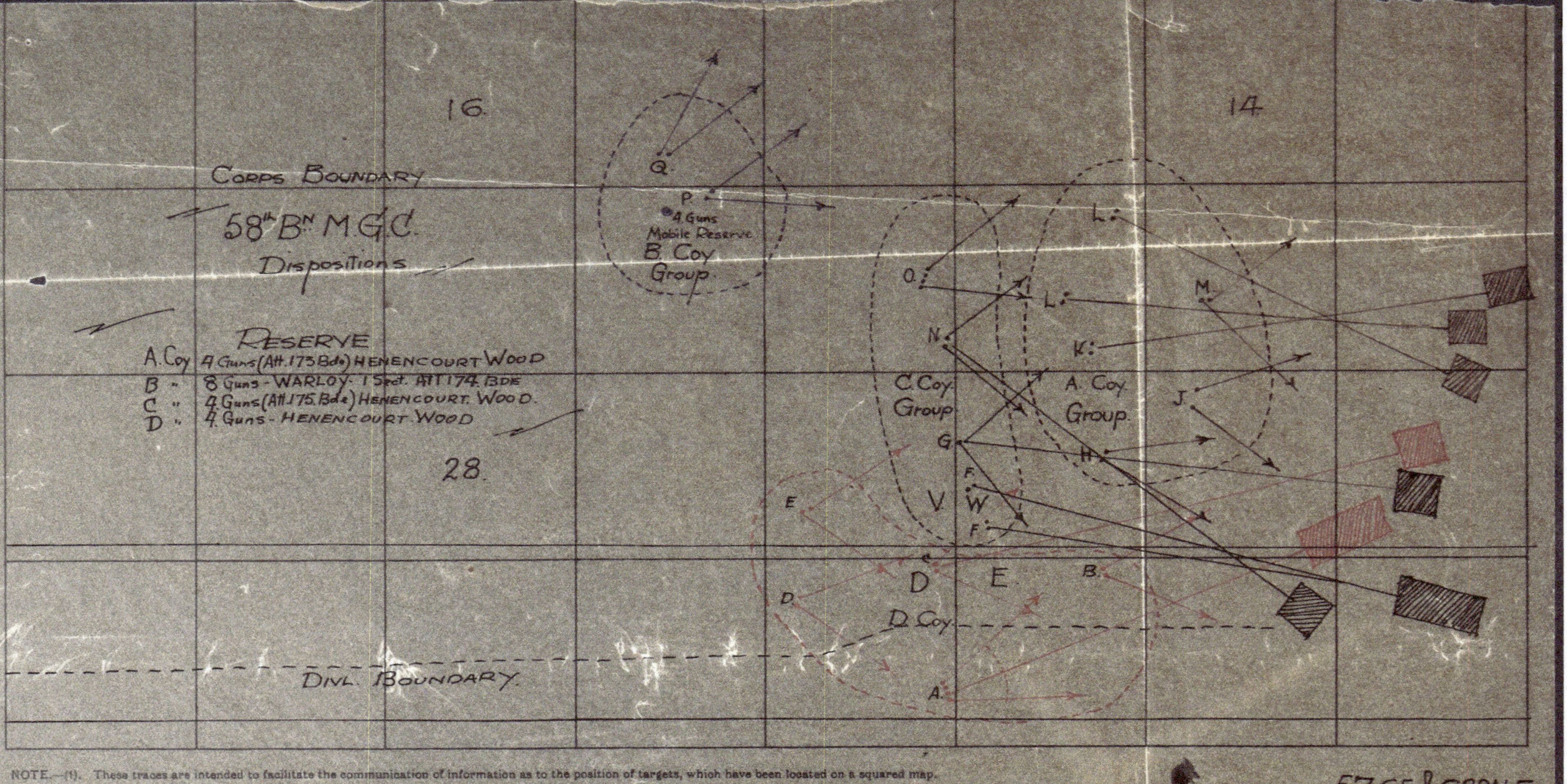

NOTE.—(1). These traces are intended to facilitate the communication of information as to the position of targets, which have been located on a squared map.

(2). The squares on this trace are 500 yards in length on the 1/10,000 scale, 1,000 yards in length on the 1/20,000 scale, and 2,000 yards in length on the 1/40,000 scale.

(3). The squares on the trace are fitted to the squares of the map showing the targets, which are then drawn on the trace. Sufficient letters and numbers must also be added to enable the recipient to place the trace in the correct position on his own map. A little detail may also be traced, but this is not essential. The name and scale of the map to which the trace refers must be always given. The trace can be used for the 1/10,000, 1/20,000, or 1/40,000 scale.

G.S.G.S. 3023.

Tracing taken from Sheet 57D SE & 62D N.E

of the 1:20,000 map of FRANCE

Signature .... Date 31.5.18.

APPENDIX 42.

CASUALTIES INCURRED BY THE BATTALION DURING THE MONTH OF MAY 1918.

Date.	Killed.	Wounded.	TOTAL.
16th.	-	1	1
17th.	1	3	4
19th.	-	4	4
20th.	-	% 1	1
26th.	1	-	1
31st.	-	2	2
	2	11	13

% Wounded but remained at Duty.

-----oOo----

APPENDIX 43.

CHANGES IN ESTABLISHMENT AND STRENGTH
CHANGES IN OFFICERS, DRAFTS ETC. RECEIVED
BY THE BATTALION DURING THE MONTH OF MAY.

PAPER STRENGTH of Battalion (excluding attached):-

1st May 1918.	48 Officers.	731 Other Ranks.
31st May 1918.	44 Officers.	862 Other Ranks.

The following are attached to Battn. and not included in above figures:-

Medical Officer.
Chaplain.
R.E.Signal Officer.
20 R.E's (Signal Section.)

REINFORCEMENTS.

2nd Lieut. G. Young. Rejoined Battn. from Hospital and taken on strength, 25.5.18.

Draft of 80 O.Rs. joined Battn. from M.G.C. Base Depot and taken on strength, 16.5.18.

Draft of 50 O.Rs. joined Battn. from M.G.C. Base Depot and taken on strength, 23.5.18.

OFFICERS - DECREASES.

Lieut. H. Carey. Evacuated Sick out of Corps Area and struck off strength 1.5.18.

Lieut. C. M. Coates.)
Lieut. J. H. Caesar, M.C.) Transferred to 58th M.G.C. Battn.
2nd Lieut. C. P. Watts.) and struck off strength,10.5.18.
2nd Lieut. C. Richardson) (Authy:- A/1/1081)

------oOo------

CONFIDENTIAL

Vol 5

War Diary

~of~

18th Battn MACHINE GUN CORPS.

From:- 1st JUNE 1918

To:- 30th JUNE 1918

APPENDICES ~

~ 44 to 53 ~

~ ATTACHED ~

(VOLUME. V)

Instructions regarding War Diaries and Intelligence Summaries are contained in F. S. Regs., Part II. and the Staff Manual respectively. Title pages will be prepared in manuscript.

18th Bn. M Gun Corps

WAR DIARY
or
~~INTELLIGENCE SUMMARY.~~
(Erase heading not required.)

June 1918

Army Form C. 2118.

Place	Date	Hour	Summary of Events and Information	Remarks and references to Appendices
MOLLIENS-AU-BOIS	1st		Dispositions Bn. HQ MOLLIENS-AU-BOIS	
			A Coy WARLOY	
			B " [illegible]	
			C " WARLOY	
			D " CONTAY	
			During night 1/2 June the following [illegible] took place to relieve 58th Bn MGC	
			B Coy from [illegible] to WARLOY	
			D Coy from CONTAY to V 27 b central	
			C Coy from WARLOY to line ~~Rt~~ Left Brigade Sector NO V27 b 3 3	[illegible]
	2	[illegible]	Bn H Q moved from MOLLIENS-AU-BOIS to CONTAY & relieved Bn HQ	
			58th Bn MGC at 12 noon	
			Night 2/3 June A Coy moved from WARLOY to take over	
			Left Brigade Sector [illegible] complete 12 midnight	[illegible]
CONTAY	3		Adv Batt H.Q established at ~~CONTA~~ WARLOY at 12 noon	Administrative Instructions Order No 30 issued [illegible]
			Capt & Adj. W. R. [illegible] proceeded on Leave to U.K.	APPENDIX A 3
	4		A. C & D Coys in line 12 guns each. B Coy 4 guns in line 12 guns reserve 4 guns A C D in reserve. Operation order no 31 issued	APPENDIX A 5. [illegible]

D. D. & L., London, E.C. (A7853) Wt. W593/M1672 350,000 4/17 Sch. 52a Forms/C2118/14

Army Form C. 2118.

Instructions regarding War Diaries and Intelligence Summaries are contained in F. S. Regs., Part II. and the Staff Manual respectively. Title pages will be prepared in manuscript.

WAR DIARY
or
INTELLIGENCE SUMMARY.
(Erase heading not required.)

Place	Date	Hour	Summary of Events and Information	Remarks and references to Appendices
	JUNE			
CONTAY	5		A Coy relieved by B Coy without incident night 5/6. Relief complete 11.45 pm	RM
	6		Locations. Batt HQ (Adv) WARLOY. B C & D Coys - line.	
			" (Rear) CONTAY. A Coy WARLOY	RM
CONTAY	7		B Coy, C Coy & D Coy in line. Harassing fire programme carried out	RM
	8		Operation order 32 issued - inter relief of Companies A to relieve C	RM App. 46
	9		Operation order 32 cancelled. Operation order 33 issued	RM App 47
	10		Positions prepared for 16 guns A Coy 34 M G Batt 16 Guns A Coy 18 Batt 6 Guns B Coy	
			18 Batt. 4 Guns D Coy 18 Batt. 4 Guns C Coy 18 Batt at following positions	
			W20 a 1.9. W19 b 8.8. (W25 b 8.3 & W26 a 3.4). W25 b. E1 b 8.8. Addendum to OO 33 issued.	Appendix 48
			All arrangements made & guns moved into position during night 10/11.	RM
CONTAY	11.		Operations for 11/12 postponed 24 hours. Harassing fire carried out	RM
	12		Operation order No 33 cancelled. Night 12/13 A Coy provided a	
			protective barrage for an operation by Right Brigade 6000 rds fired	
			night 12/13 Special programme of harassing fire carried out	
			25000 rds fired. A Coy 34 Batt M G C withdrawn to normal positions	RM
	13		Situation normal. Usual harassing programme carried out	RM

D. D. & L., London, E.C. (A7893) Wt. W2093/M1672 350,000 4/17 Sch. 52a Forms/C/2118/14

Instructions regarding War Diaries and Intelligence Summaries are contained in F. S. Regs., Part II. and the Staff Manual respectively. Title pages will be prepared in manuscript.

18th Bn Machine Gun Corps

WAR DIARY
or
~~INTELLIGENCE SUMMARY.~~
(Erase heading not required.)

June 1918

Army Form C. 2118.

Place	Date	Hour	Summary of Events and Information	Remarks and references to Appendices
CONTAY	June 14	–	Situation normal. Operation order 34 issued	Appendix [illegible] A9.
	15		On night 15/16 regrouping of guns of Battalion carried out.	
			Each company occupied a definite area in which it remains. Guns	
			disposed in depth. ½ Companies in reserve for relief purposes	
			Dispositions. A Coy 8 guns in line 4 Guns Brigade Reserve 4 Reserve	
			B Coy 10 guns – – 6 Guns Brigade Reserve	
			C Coy 8 guns in line 4 Brigade Reserve 4 Reserve	
			D 8 guns – – 4 Guns (Army Reserve) 4 Reserve	[illegible]
	16		Situation Normal –	[illegible]
	17		Situation Normal.	[illegible]
	18		Situation Normal.	
	19		Inter Corps relief according to Operation order No 34	[illegible]
	20		As per Operation order 34	[illegible]
	21		As per operation order 34.	[illegible]
	22		Captain J.W.K. Wenham returned from leave. Situation Normal	[illegible]
	23		Situation Normal	[illegible]

D. D. & L., London, E.C. (A7853) Wt. W2093/M1672 350,000 4/17 Sch. 52a Forms/C/2118/14

Instructions regarding War Diaries and Intelligence Summaries are contained in F. S. Regs., Part II. and the Staff Manual respectively. Title pages will be prepared in manuscript.

18th Bn Machine Gun Corps

WAR DIARY
or
~~INTELLIGENCE SUMMARY.~~
(Erase heading not required.)

June (cont)

Army Form C. 2118.

Place	Date	Hour	Summary of Events and Information	Remarks and references to Appendices
CONTAY	24		Lieut-Colonel E.T. Minet DSO MC proceeded on leave – Major Hebbert DSO assumed	
			Command – Lieut O.R.F. Batchelor proceeded to GHQ Small Arms School	
			MG Branch on Instructional Staff.	
			Situation in line normal	JW
	25		do	JW
	26		do Order No. 35 issued	JW APP 50
	27		do Addenda to O. No. 35 issued	JW APP 50.
	28		do Gun positions for operations prepared. Addenda to OO 35 issued	JW APP. 51
	29		do All gun teams & guns moved into position during night	JW
	30		Quiet in line during day – Our barrage opened at 9.35 pm	
			and continued until infantry had captured & consolidated	
			their objective which was complete by 12.30 am	
			Report on operation will be issued with next months diary	
			List of Casualties incurred during month attached	APP 52
			Statement showing changes in Establishment & Strength attached	APP 53.

[illegible signature]
Capt. Adjt
18th Bn M.G.C.

D. D. & L., London, E.C. (A7885) Wt. W593/M1672 350,000 4/17 Sch. 52a Forms/C/2118/14

SECRET. 18th Bn.M.G.C. No. S.48.

APPENDIX 44

JUN 3 1918

ADMINISTRATIVE INSTRUCTIONS IN CONNECTION WITH 18TH BN.M.G.C. ORDER NO. 30.

1. Baths allotted to 18th Division in this area are as below:-

Two 12 Spray Baths (including one for gassed cases at WARLOY)
One bath (tubs) at HENENCOURT.

2. TRAFFIC.
(a) Wheeled traffic by day will not proceed E. of Cross Roads in C.12.b. or E., N.E. or S. of HENENCOURT CHATEAU STABLES.
(b) Headlights will not be used on cars or lorries in the Corps Area East of DOULLENS - AMIENS Road.
Motor Cycles may use headlights but will cover them when halted.
Cars or lorries when halted will cover or extinguish sidelights, except on so far as it is necessary to mark convoys.
(c) All lights in billets and camps must be carefully screened from one hour after sunset till dawn.

3. BURIAL ARRANGEMENTS.
All burials will take place in one of the following cemeteries:-
WARLOY COMMUNAL CEMETERY EXTENSION...........U.24.b.9.5.
CONTAY BRITISH CEMETERY.....................U.27.c.5.4.
HENENCOURT WOOD BRITISH CEMETERY............V.26.b.1.5.
FRANVILLERS COMMUNAL CEMETERY EXTENSION.......C.29.b.1.1.
BAVELINCOURT..................................C.7.
MONTIGNY (BRITISH PLOT)......................B.17.d.5.6.
Isolated burials will be avoided as far as possible and no fresh cemeteries will be opened without reference to Divisional Headquarters.
Location of G.R.U. No.1. is at VIGNACOURT.

4. Horse Burials.
Brigades will be responsible for Divisional Area E. of the BRESLE - HENENCOURT - SENLIS Road within their Brigade area.
58th Div. Artillery will be responsible for area W. of above road and E. of BAIZIEUX - WARLOY - VARENNES Road.
West of this line the nearest Unit will be responsible.
Units are responsible for all burials in their own wagon lines.
A.P.M. will notify Units direct locations of unburied horses.

9. Waterpoints. Locations of Waterpoints in the Div. area are shown on attached table "A".
Bns. in line are supplied by petrol tins filled at WARLOY.
A reserve of 3 days supply at two pints per man per day is maintained in the front line system.

10. SALVAGE. H.Qrs Salvage Coy - WARLOY.
Dumps. WARLOY ...... No.14 Main Street.
HENENCOURT ...... No.25 Rue de Majistor.
CONTAY ...... No.121 Albion Street.
All Salvage is brought by limbers from HENENCOURT to WARLOY, from whence it is cleared by Train Wagons and taken to Supply Refilling Point the following morning for despatch by empty supply lorries.

12. RECOVERY OF SOLDER. Empty tins to be sent to Div.Solder Kiln. at C.1.d.4.8. (153 Coy. A.S.C)

13. R.E.DUMPS. III Corps.........EBART FARM.
Div. R.E.Dump.....Eastern drive of BAIZIEUX Chat.
HENENCOURT Dump...V.27.d.4.7.

14. S.A.A.DUMP. will be at C.3.d.central.

Capt. and Adjt.
18th Bn. Machine Gun Corps.

Secret

Copy No 5

A5

18th Bn M.G.C. Order No 31

1/ On night 5/6th June B Coy will relieve A Coy in the line. Details of relief will be arranged between Coy Commanders concerned

2/ BILLETS

A Coy will take over all billets at present occupied by B Coy and B Coy will take over billets of A Coy.

3/ BATTLE Surplus

Coys will arrange to accomodate battle surplus at their own Rear HQ until further notice

4/ Work in line will be handed over to relieving Coy.

5/ Bivouac Sheets and tents will be handed over and copies of receipts sent to Bn HQ

6/ Completion of relief will be wired to Bn HQ using as code word "BATCHELOR" & giving hour

7/ Acknowledge

Copies To

1/ A Coy

2/ B Coy

3/ 54th Inf Bde (for info)

4/ War Diary

5/6 File

C.H. Allen Major
18th Bn M G Corps

SECRET. 18th Bn M.G.C. Order
No 37.

Copy No 4

Appendix 46

1. A Coy 18th Bn M.G.C. will relieve "C" Coy 18th Bn M.G.C. in the line on the night 9/10th.
Details of relief will be arranged between Coy Commanders concerned.

2. Billeting will be done under Coy arrangements.

3. Work in the line will be handed over to relieving Coy.

4. Completion of relief will be wired to Bn HQ giving hour of relief and using as code word "NUT".

5. Acknowledge.

June 8/1918
Copies to –
1 A Coy
2 C Coy
3 53 Inf Bde
4/5/6 War Diary
7 File.

C. H. [illegible] Major
18th Bn M.G.C.

W A T E R   P O I N T S.

Location.	Drinking.	Horse.
FORWARD AREA. Henencourt and Millencourt	* V. 29.c.2.2. V.29.c.5.3. D.5.a.7.6. D.5.a.7.4. V.27.b.5.4. V.27.d.9.4. V.27.d.6.5. V.27.d.6.0.	
WARLOY AREA.	Pumping Station (U.24.d.9.2.) U.24.b.8.0. U.30.b.5.5. U.30.b.6.8. U.30.b.4.4. U.24.d.4.3. U.24.d.6.1. U.30.a.9.0.	U.30.a.1.9. V.19.c.1.1. V.19.c. Central. V.19.d.1.8. U.24.c.9.5.
CONTAY AREA.	U.21.c.8.3. CONTAY. Billet No. 1 (Pump) " " 9 " " " 17 " " " 21 " " " 25 (Well) " " 33 (Pump) " " 38 (Well) " " 40 (Pump) " " 86 " " " 90 " " " 98 " " " 103 " " " 106 " " " 107 " " " 119 " " " 129 " " " 134 "	U.26.c.4.3. U.27.c. U.27.a.6.1.

Chlorination required one measure per 100 Gallons.

SECRET.

Copy No. 11......

Appendix 47

[illegible]

9th June 1918.

19th Battn. M. G. C. ORDER No. 60.

1. On the night 11th/12th June 1918 an operation will be carried out in conjunction with the [illegible] Division on our left.

2. The 56th Infantry Brigade will attack, capture and hold the enemy trench [illegible] to [illegible].

3. Action of Machine Guns.
A Company [illegible] Battn. M. G. C.
"A" Company [illegible] Battn. M.G.C.
16 Guns 19th Battn. M. G. C. under O.C. "B" Coy.
will co-operate and provide a standing barrage on a line shown on attached tracing.
Company Commanders concerned will at once reconnoitre the positions, emplacements dug and all necessary arrangements made.
O.C. "C" Coy. will place 4 guns at [illegible] (approx) and lay on lines as per attached tracing for direct fire.

4. All work to be completed by dawn 11th inst.

5. Rates and time of fire as per attached appendix "A".

6. ZERO HOUR. Will be notified later.

7. Batteries will remain in their positions for 24 hours after zero, after which they will occupy their normal positions.

8. Copies of battery charts will be submitted to Battn. H.Q. for checking by 12 noon 11th inst.

9. Ammunition and water supply will be made under Company arrangements, care being taken to have a sufficient supply of S.A.A. [illegible] during the 24 hours after zero.

10. ACKNOWLEDGE.

Lieut & A/Adjt.,
19th Battalion Machine Gun Corps.

Issued at 7 a.m. Copies to:-
1. C.O.
2. Second-in-Command.
3. Adjutant.
4. 19th Division "G".
5. 56th Inf. Bde.
6. [illegible]
7. [illegible]
8. O.C. "A" Company.
9. O.C. "B" Company.
10. O.C. "C" Company.
11. War Diary.
12. War Diary.
13. File.

Appendix "D".

TIMES AND RATES OF FIRE.

Zero to Zero plus 10 ... ... Rapid.

Zero plus 10 to Zero plus 30 ... ... Medium.

Zero plus 30 to Zero plus 60 ... ... Slow.

During the remainder of the night alternating bursts of fire in conjunction with artillery.

Identification Trace for use with Artillery Maps.

V W

LEGEND

Barrage lines of 12th Bn. M.G.C. ... ...

S.O.S. do — do — ... ...

Barrage lines of 18th Bn. M.G.C. ... ...

do — do 38 Bn. M.G.C. ... ...

Ref Sheets 57.D S.E. 62 D. NE.
1/20,000.

V W

D E

NOTE.—(1). These traces are intended to facilitate the communication of information as to the position of targets, which have been located on a squared map.

(2). The squares on this trace are 500 yards in length on the 1/10,000 scale, 1,000 yards in length on the 1/20,000 scale, and 2,000 yards in length on the 1/40,000 scale.

(3). The squares on the trace are fitted to the squares of the map showing the targets, which are then drawn on the trace. Sufficient letters and numbers must also be added to enable the recipient to place the trace in the correct position on his own map. A little detail may also be traced, but this is not essential. The name and scale of the map to which the trace refers must be always given. The trace can be used for the 1/10,000, 1/20,000, or 1/40,000 scale.

G.S.G.S. 3023.

Tracing taken from Sheet 57 D. S.E. & 62 D. NE

of the 1: 20,000 *map of* ....

Signature .... *Date* ....

SECRET.   18th Bn. M.G.C. No.S. 49.
Copy No....12

ADDENDA to 18th Bn.M.G.C.ORDER No.33.

Reference Map:-
[illegible] 1/40,000.

appendix 48

10th June 1918.

Reference 18th Bn. M.G.C. Order No. 33 dated 9th inst.

1. Machine guns will not withdraw from their Battery positions until night 12th/13th June. The Company of 34th Bn. M.G.C. taking part in the Barrage, will, the tactical situation permitting, be withdrawn from the line on the morning of June 13th 1918. and revert to Corps Reserve.

2. S.O.S.
The S.O.S. signal to be employed by the troops of the 18th Division carrying out this operation will be the S.O.S. signal of the Corps on our left, viz.,
"A Rifle grenade bursting into 3 stars GREEN over RED over GREEN".
This S.O.S. signal will be in force from zero hour until 3.30 a.m. 13th June when the present S.O.S. signal will come into force again. 54th Infantry Brigade will arrange to collect and return any unexpended V.Corps S.O.S. Rifle Grenades.

3. Medical Arrangements.
(a) The Advanced Dressing station is at HENENCOURT.
(b) All Walking wounded will proceed to Aid Post V.24.b.3.8 thence to WARLOY by road running along North edge of HENENCOURT Wood.

4. Synchronisation of Watches.
1 Officer to be detailed by O.C. "A" Company will synchronise watch at Div. H.Qrs. at 3.30 p.m. 11th inst.
1 Officer "B" Company will synchronise watch at 54th Bde. H.Q. at 4 p.m. 12th.

5. Contact Aeroplane.
A Contact Aeroplane will fly over the objective at 5 a.m. on 13th June or as soon as light permits. Troops in the front line will indicate their position to the aeroplane when it sounds its Klaxon horn, by waving their helmets and placing their rifles in groups of three on the parapet of the trench, two feet between rifles and 10 yds. between each group of 3 rifles.

6. ACKNOWLEDGE.

R H Batchelor
......................Lieut & A/Adjt.,
18th Battn. Machine Gun Corps.

Issued at .... a.m.
Copies to recipients of Order No.33, and:-

14. O.C. "A" Company, 34th Bn. M.G.C.

SECRET. Copy No..12...

Reference Map:-
SENLIS 1/20,000. appendix 49 14th June 1918.

18TH BATTN. M.G.C. ORDER No. 34.

1. In order that Company Commanders may have better fighting control over their guns, and Officers, N.C.Os. and men a thorough knowledge of the ground opposite their front, each of the 4 Companies will be disposed in depth and will remain in the area allotted to it.

2. In order to conform with the above, on the night 15th/16th a re-grouping of the Machine Guns on the Divisional Front will take place as follows.

3. "A" Company from Reserve, will take over positions B.33. B.5. B.13. from "C" Company, and B.6. from "D" Company.
"D" Company, in the line, will take over B.3.a. from "B" Company.

4. The positions then held by Companies will be as shown on attached tracing.

5. "A", "B" and "C" Coys. will detail 4 guns to 53rd, 54th, and 55th Infantry Brigades respectively when those Brigades are holding the line.

6. When Brigades are in Divisional Reserve, Companies will detail 8 guns to their respective Brigades.

7. Inter-Company reliefs will take place as follows:-
"D" Company ... ... on night 19th/20th.
"C" Company ... ... on night 20th/21st.
"B" Company ... ... on night 21st/22nd
"A" Company ... ... on night 22nd/23rd.

8. Subsequent Inter-Company reliefs will be carried out every 6 days from above dates.

9. This system will ensure regular Company reliefs throughout the Battalion and enable training to be carried out.

10. Company Commanders will draw up Training Programmes for their gun teams out of the line and submit them to Battalion Headquarters two days before relief.

[signature]

Lieut & A/Adjt.,
18th Battalion Machine Gun Corps.

Issued at 12 midnight. Copies to:-
No.1.Copy C.O.
" 2 " 2nd-in-Command.
" 3 " Adjutant.
" 4 " "A" Company.
" 5 " "B" Company.
" 6 " "C" Company.
" 7 " "D" Company.
" 8 " 18th Division 'G'.
" 9 " 53rd Infantry Brigade.
" 10 " 54th Infantry Brigade.
" 11 " 55th Infantry Brigade.
" 12/13" War Diary.
" 14 " File.

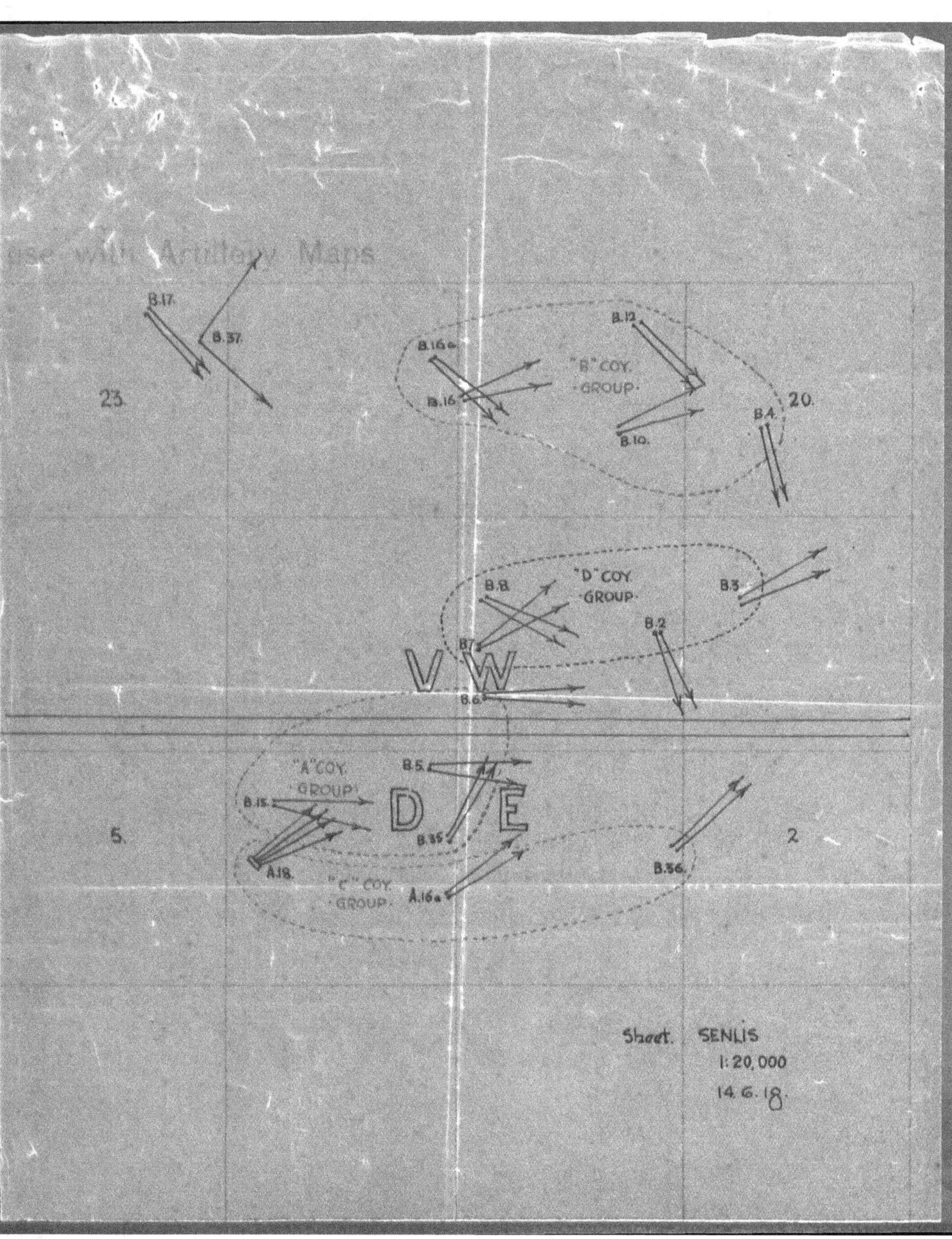

use with Artillery Maps
B.17.
B.37.
23.
B.16a
B.16.
"B" COY.
GROUP.
B.12.
B.10.
B.4.
20.
B.8.
"D" COY.
GROUP.
B.3.
B.7.
B.2.
V
W
B.6.
B.5.
"A" COY.
GROUP.
B.15.
D
E
B.35.
5.
A.18.
"C" COY.
GROUP.
A.16a
B.36.
2
Sheet. SENLIS
1:20,000
14.6.18.

SECRET. Copy No.....

Reference Map:- [illegible]
1/20,000 26th June 1918.

Appendix 50a

18TH BATTN.M.G.C. ORDER NO. 36.

1. On the night of June 30th/July 1st. an operation will be carried out in conjunction with the 12th Division on our left.

2. The 54th Infantry Brigade will capture and hold the German front line system from W.21.d.1.7 to W.16.d.9.10. The 12th Division will simultaneously capture and hold the line of the road from W.16.d.9.0 to W.16.a.8.4 (approximately).

3. Action of Machine Guns.

Batteries will be found as under;-

"A" Coy. 4 guns from Bde.Reserve V.21.c.4.6. under Command of O.C. "A"Coy.
"D" Coy. 2 guns from B.5.position do., do.,
"D" Coy. 2 guns from B.6.position, do., do.,

"C" Coy. 8 guns from Bde.Res.WARLOY, under command of O.C. "C" Coy.

"B" Coy. 4 guns from Bde.Res. V.29.b.5.2. under Command of O.C."B" Coy.
"B" Coy. 2 guns from Div.Res. WARLOY, do., do.,

and will co-operate and provide a standing barrage on lines shown on attached tracing.

In addition the following batteries will assist on targets shown on tracing:-

B.10........2 Guns	B.11......2 guns.
B. 7........2 Guns.	B. 6......2 Guns.
B. 3........2 Guns.	B.40......2 Guns.
A.16........2 Guns.	B.42......2 Guns.

4. Battery positions to be completed and firing line marks laid out and checked by dawn 29th June.

5. Battery positions will be manned on night of June 29th and teams will remain in position after the operation until ordered to withdraw.

6. Rate and time of fire as per attached Appendix "A".

7. Copies of Battery charts will be submitted to Battalion H.Q. by noon 29th June.

8. Ammunition and water supply will be made under Coy.arrangements, care being taken to keep an ample supply of S.A.A. for M.G.C. during the 48 hours after zero.

9. ZERO hour will be notified later.

10. The 54th Bde. Battle Posts will be:-
2nd Bedfordshire Regiment ... ... The Left Battn. H.Qrs.
6th Northamptonshire Regiment ... The Right Battn. H. Qs.
The Brigade Battle Post ... ... V.22.c.9.6.

11. Watches will be synchronised at 54th Brigade Headquarters at 5 p.m. June 30th. Company Commanders concerned will each send a representative.

12. Signal communications as per attached Appendix "B".

13. The ordinary light signals will be used in addition to the S.O.S. and will be repeated by all light signal stations and confirmed, and direction in which seen at once reported by signal.

14.(a) 1st objective gained)
       2nd objective gained) Succession of White Very Lights.
       3rd objective gained)

(b) Arty. & M.G. support required:- Succession of Green Very Lights.

(c) Lengthen Barrage:- Succession of Red Very Lights.

(d) Arty. and M.G.'s cease fire:- Succession of White Very Lights.

(e) Consolidation completed and all covering parties withdrawn) Pairs of Red and Green Very lights sent up in succession.

15. Special care should be taken to avoid making tracks round battery positions and movement in trenches or vicinity by day.

16. Rations.
Probably rations for 30th June and 1st July will be issued on 29th June.

17. A C K N O W L E D G E.

Major,
Commanding 18th Battalion Machine Gun Corps.

Issued at .... p.m. Copies to:-

No.1.Copy C.O.
" 2 " 2nd-in-command.
" 3 " Adjutant,
" 4 " O.C. "A" Company.
" 5 " O.C. "B" Company.
" 6 " O.C. "C" Company.
" 7 " O.C. "D" Company.
" 8 " Signal Officer.
" 9 " C.M.G.Officer.
" 10 " 18th Division 'G'.
" 11 " 53rd Infantry Brigade.
" 12 " 54th Infantry Brigade.
" 13 " 55th Infantry Brigade.
" 14 " 12th Battn. M.G.C.
" 15 " 58th Battn.M.G.C.
" 16 " War Diary.
" 17 " War Diary.
" 18 " File.

APPENDIX "[illegible]".

TIMES AND RATE OF FIRE.

Zero to Zero plus 10 ... ... Rapid.

Should the S.O.S. go up all guns will open fire with;-
10 minutes, Rapid.
10 minutes, Medium.
and slow off with Artillery, unless orders are received to the contrary.

---------000---------

APPENDIX "[illegible]".

M.G. SIGNAL COMMUNICATIONS.

Telephones ◯ and lamps ⚒ will be manned as shown on attached tracing. issued to all concerned

There is also a Brigade wireless station at the Brigade Battle Post connected with;-

Left Battn. Right Brigade.

Report Centre. W.19.d.8.1.

Left Battn. Right Brigade, W.19.b.6.6.

-----------000-----------

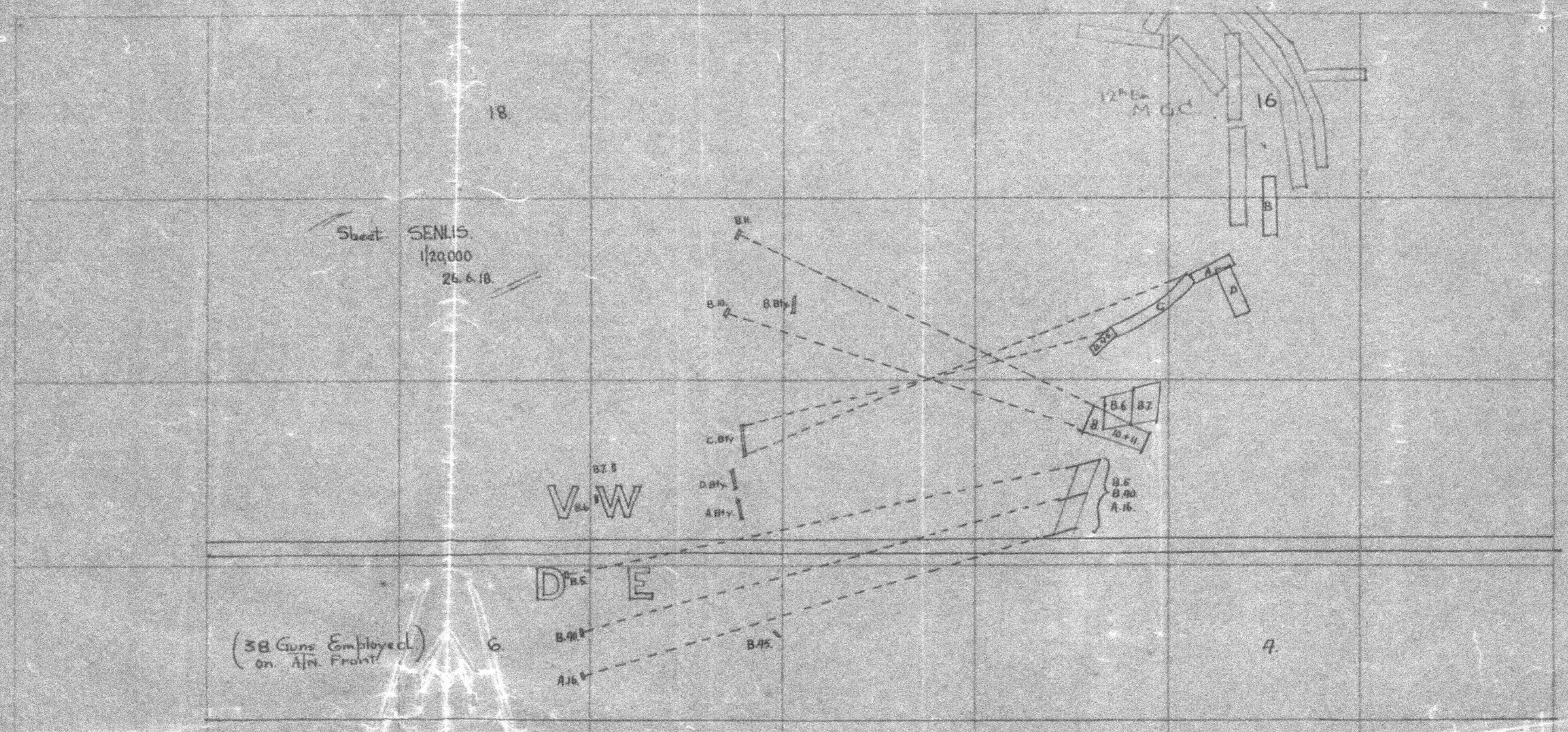

18

16

12th Bn. M.G.C.

Sheet SENLIS.
1/20,000
26.6.18.

B.11.

B.10. B.Bty.

C.Bty.

D.Bty.

A.Bty.

B.6 B.7

B. 10 + 11.

A. D. C. B. B.

B.5.
B.10.
A.16.

V B.6 W
B.7. B

D B.5. E

B.10.

A.16.

B.45.

(38 Guns Employed on A/N. Front)

6.

4.

Refce map. SENLIS 1/20000 { A B C & D Coys | SECRET
War Diary | Appendix -51-

18th Batt M G C

Addenda to O.O No. 35.

1. Slow fire will be maintained from Z + 10 until the signal "Consolidation completed & all covering parties withdrawn" is received.

2. The S.O.S. RED over RED over RED will be used after signal is given "Consolidation completed & all covering parties withdrawn".

3. Ten more Guns as under are being employed in the operation.

B.35	– 2	Guns
B.37	2	"
B.38	2	"
B.39	2	"
B.17	2	"

Positions & Targets have been given separately to those concerned.

(Sgd.) B B Hibbert
Major
29/6/18 Commdg 18th Bn MGC

APPENDIX 52.

CASUALTIES INCURRED BY THE BATTALION
- DURING THE MONTH OF -
- JUNE 1918 -

.....

OFFICER.

Lieut. P. G. MACMASTER. Killed in Action 20.6.1918.

OTHER RANKS.

Date.	Killed.	Wounded.	Wounded (Gas)	TOTAL.
2nd.	-	-	1	1
9th.	-	1	-	1
16th.	-	1	-	1
17th.	1	2	-	3
18th.	-	-	1	1
20th.	-	1 ø	-	1
30th.	-	1	-	1
TOTALS:-	1	6	2	9

ø Wounded at Duty.

APPENDIX 53.

CHANGES IN ESTABLISHMENT AND STRENGTH, INCREASES & DECREASES OFFICERS, DRAFTS RECEIVED ETC., BY THE BN. DURING JUNE.

PAPER STRENGTH of Battalion (excluding attached):-

1st June 1918:-	45 Officers,	862 Other Ranks.
30th June 1918:-	44 Officers,	906 Other Ranks.

INCREASES.

2nd Lieut. A. F. Woodrow (M.M) Joined Battalion as reinforcement and taken on strength, 12.6.18.

Draft of 26 Other Ranks joined Battn. from M.G.C. Base 9.6.18.
Draft of 50 Other Ranks joined Battn. from M.G.C. Base, 15.6.18.
Draft of 1 Other Rank, joined Battn. from M.G.C. Base, 16.6.18.
Draft of 1 Other Rank, joined Battn. from 7th Bedfords, 15.6.18.
Draft of 1 Other Rank, joined Battn. from M.G.C. Base, 21.6.18.
Draft of 4 Other Ranks joined Battn. from M.G.C. Base, 27.6.18.

DECREASES.

Lieut. P. G. MACMASTER. Killed in Action, 20.6.18.

Lieut. O. R. F. BATCHELOR. To G.H.Q. Machine Gun School as Instructor and struck off strength, 23.6.18.

Other Ranks.

To Base, Medically Unfit	1
Transferred to 47th Bn. M.G.C.	1
To England as Candidates for Commissions,	3
Transferred to 7th Bedford Regt... ...	1
To C.C.S. and struck off strength ...	25
Casualties in action	8
TOTAL:-	39

Strength 1st June 1918:-	45 Officers	862 O.Rs.
Add Reinforcements:-	1 "	83 O.Rs.
	46 "	945 "
Deduct decreases shown above:-	2 "	39 "
TOTAL:-	44 Officers.	906 O.Rs.

OFFICERS TO HOSPITAL DURING MONTH.

Lieut D. C. IMRIE. Admitted 6.7.1918.

----------ooo----------

CONFIDENTIAL

Vol 6

War Diary.

~ of ~

18th Battn MACHINE GUN CORPS

From:- 1st July 1918.

To:- 31st July 1918.

APPENDICES ~

Nos 54 to 67

~ ATTACHED.

(VOLUME VI)

Instructions regarding War Diaries and Intelligence Summaries are contained in F. S. Regs., Part II. and the Staff Manual respectively. Title pages will be prepared in manuscript.

18th Bn Machine Gun Corps

WAR DIARY or ~~INTELLIGENCE SUMMARY.~~

(Erase heading not required.)

July 1918

Army Form C. 2118.

Place	Date	Hour	Summary of Events and Information	Remarks and references to Appendices
CONTAY	1st		Operation on night 30th June - July 1st (cont)	
			Barrage ~~fire~~ & harassing fire continued until infantry had consolidated their objective 12.30 am	
		1.45am	S.O.S. call was replied to with 10 mins rapid fire	
			Quiet in line during the day but hostile artillery very active during the night	
		9pm - 10.15pm	Batteries in W.25.d spotted by E.A. & shelled with 5.9 - 4.2s. The whole of the right group received considerable attention.	
		8.58pm	S.O.S calls answered } Hostile counter attacks suspected but did	[initials]
do	2nd	2.30am	do } not develop.	[initials]
			Fairly quiet during the day. Order No MG 152F issued	App 54
		9.30pm	Enemy put down fairly heavy barrage and on the SOS being sent up, all batteries opened fire on SOS lines and continued throughout the night - No hostile counter attack developed on our front but troops were forced to evacuate our gains of the night June 30 - July 1 owing to severity of [illegible] shell & TM fire	[initials]
			Report of action see appendix 54A	App 54a

D. D. & L., London, E.C. (A7883) Wt W809/M1672 350,000 4/17 Sch. 52a Forms/C/2118/14

18th Bn Machine Gun Corps

WAR DIARY
or
~~INTELLIGENCE~~ SUMMARY.
(Erase heading not required.)

July 1918 (cont)

Army Form C. 2118.

Instructions regarding War Diaries and Intelligence Summaries are contained in F. S. Regs., Part II. and the Staff Manual respectively. Title pages will be prepared in manuscript.

Place	Date	Hour	Summary of Events and Information	Remarks and references to Appendices
CONTAY	3rd		Quiet in line – Order under MG 160F issued see Appendix 54	JWS App 55
"	4th		do. (PUO (Spanish Fever) very prevalent in Battalion during	JWS
"	5th		do. } this period	JWS
"	6th		do	JWS
"	7th		do	JWS
"	8th		do Lieut-Colonel E.C.T. Minet rejoined from leave	JWS
"	9th		do	JWS
"	10th		do Orders for relief issued (Order No 36) see Appendix 55	JWS App 56
"	11		do Reliefs and moves carried out in accordance with Order 36	JWS
"	12th		do Amendment to Order 36 issued. Reliefs and moves carried out in accordance with Order 36 & amendment	App 57 JWS
"	13		Remainder of Battalion + Bn HQ relieved in line by 47th Bn Machine Gun Corps – Relief complete 1.30 am – embussed 4.30 am and clear of forward area by 5.30 am – arrived Fourdrinoy 9.30 am. Billets not very good and extremely dirty – Remainder of day resting. Map showing position of Guns handed over attached Marked "H"	JWS App 58

D. D. & L., London, E.C. (A7883) Wt. W809/M1672 350,000 4/17 Sch. 52a Forms/C/2118/14

Army Form C. 2118.

Instructions regarding War Diaries and Intelligence Summaries are contained in F. S. Regs., Part II. and the Staff Manual respectively. Title pages will be prepared in manuscript.

18th Battn Machine Gun Corps

WAR DIARY
or
INTELLIGENCE SUMMARY.
(Erase heading not required.)

July 1918 (cont)

Place	Date	Hour	Summary of Events and Information	Remarks and references to Appendices
FOURDRINOY	14th		Resting – Church Parade 11 am 12 days Training Programme issued	JWS App 59
"	15th		Cleaning up refitting and repacking limbers etc	JWS
"	16		do do	JWS
"	17		Recruit Training on Battalion Parade Ground – Warning Order (Bn in GHQ Reserve and ready to move at 9 hrs notice) issued	App 60 JWS
"	18		Recruit Training on Battalion Parade Ground – Dr Devine addressed Bn on "America & the War"	JWS
"	19		Recruit Training on Battalion Parade Ground	JWS
	20		Battalion Sports – No parades – Commenced 9 am finished 6 pm Band of 10th Essex Regt assisted – "Zeros" 53rd Bde Concert Party performed in evening – very successful day. Tactical & Technical Lessons learnt sent to Bns	JWS App 61
"	21		Battalion Resting – Church Parade 11.30 am Parade Strength 561	JWS
"	22		Training (P.T. – Gun Drill – Close Order Drill & Immediate Action) on Bn Parade Ground	JWS
	23		Very Wet – Training in Billets	JWS
"	24		Training in Vicinity of Billets	JWS
"	25-26		do	JWS

D. D. & L., London, E.C.
(A7883) Wt. W809/M1672 350,000 4/17 Sch. 52a Forms/C/2118/14

Ref Maps:- 57d NE & NW. 1/20.000.
AMIENS. 1/100.000.
Sheet 62d NW. & NE. 1/20.000.

18th Battalion Machine Gun Corps

Instructions regarding War Diaries and Intelligence Summaries are contained in F. S. Regs., Part II, and the Staff Manual respectively. Title pages will be prepared in manuscript.

WAR DIARY
or
~~INTELLIGENCE SUMMARY.~~

(*Erase heading not required.*)

July 1918

Army Form C. 2118.

Place	Date	Hour	Summary of Events and Information	Remarks and references to Appendices
FOURDRINOY	27		Resting – no training – Church Parade 11.30 am.	JW
"	28		Orders for move to Forward Area issued – Repacking limbers etc.	JW see app 62
"	29		Officers A B & C Coys moved forward 8 am to reconnoitre forward area – B & C Coys moved as per Order 37 to FRANVILLERS arriving 4 pm.	JW
"	30		A Coy & Bn H.Q. proceeded as per Order 37 – A Coy to FRANVILLERS arriving 6 pm. – Bn H.Q. to LA HOUSSOYE arriving 5.45 pm. 14 guns C Coy moved during night from FRANVILLERS to line left subsector Divisional Front as per attached map "B"	JW
La HOUSSOYE	31		"D" Coy moved as per Order 37 arriving FRANVILLERS 6.30 pm. During night 8 guns D Coy relieved 8 guns of 5th Austn M.G. Bn in BONNAY Sector also B Coy relieved in line 16 guns of 5th Austn M.G. Bn in right subsector of 5th Austn Div Front & A Coy relieved 12 guns of 3rd Austn M.G. Bn in right subsector of 18th Divn Front – this being the left subsector of the Division on right of 5th Austn Division – reliefs complete 2 am. Dispositions as per Map "B" attached	Orders for move of D Coy app 63 Orders for "D" app 64 Map "B" App 65 [illegible] Capt for Lt Col [illegible] 18th Bn MGC

D. D. & L., London, E.C. (A7883) Wt W809/M1672 350,000 4/17 Sch. 52a Forms/C/2118/14

SECRET. 18th Bn. M.G.C. M.G.152 F.

To: A B C & D Coys.
18th Division

APPENDIX
54

1. A series of Chinese attacks on the Division Front to be known & referred to as "Scheme A" will be undertaken at not more than 48 hours notice. All Arms are to co operate. A M.G. Barrage Scheme is being submitted to Division today for approval.

2. The following Guns will be used –

A. Coy.	B.40	2 Guns	From Battle Positions.
	B.5	2 "	
	B.6	2 "	

2 Guns from B.35 position to Battery positions in W.25.b. behind VALLEY NORTH TRENCH

B. Coy.	B.10	2 Guns	From Battle positions
	B.11	2 "	

6 Gun Battery as at present occupied in W.20.c.

C. Coy.	B.45	2 Guns	From Battle positions
	A.16	2 "	

Four Guns from Battery position in W.25.b behind VALLEY NORTH TRENCH

D. Coy B.2 2 Guns } From harassing
B.36 2 " } fire positions
B.7 2 " from Battle positns
4 Guns Battery position in W.20.d.

3. The following moves will, therefore, take place tonight:-

A Coy.
Four Gun Battery in W.25.d to be withdrawn
B.35. 2 Guns to Battery position in W.25.b
Otherwise all normal Battle positions to be occupied

B. Coy
No change, except that the 4 Guns now forming a Battery in Trench at W.19.b.8.5. may, with the consent of the Brigdr. Genl. Commdg. 54 Brigade withdraw to their normal battle positions

C. Coy
Four Guns in Battery position at

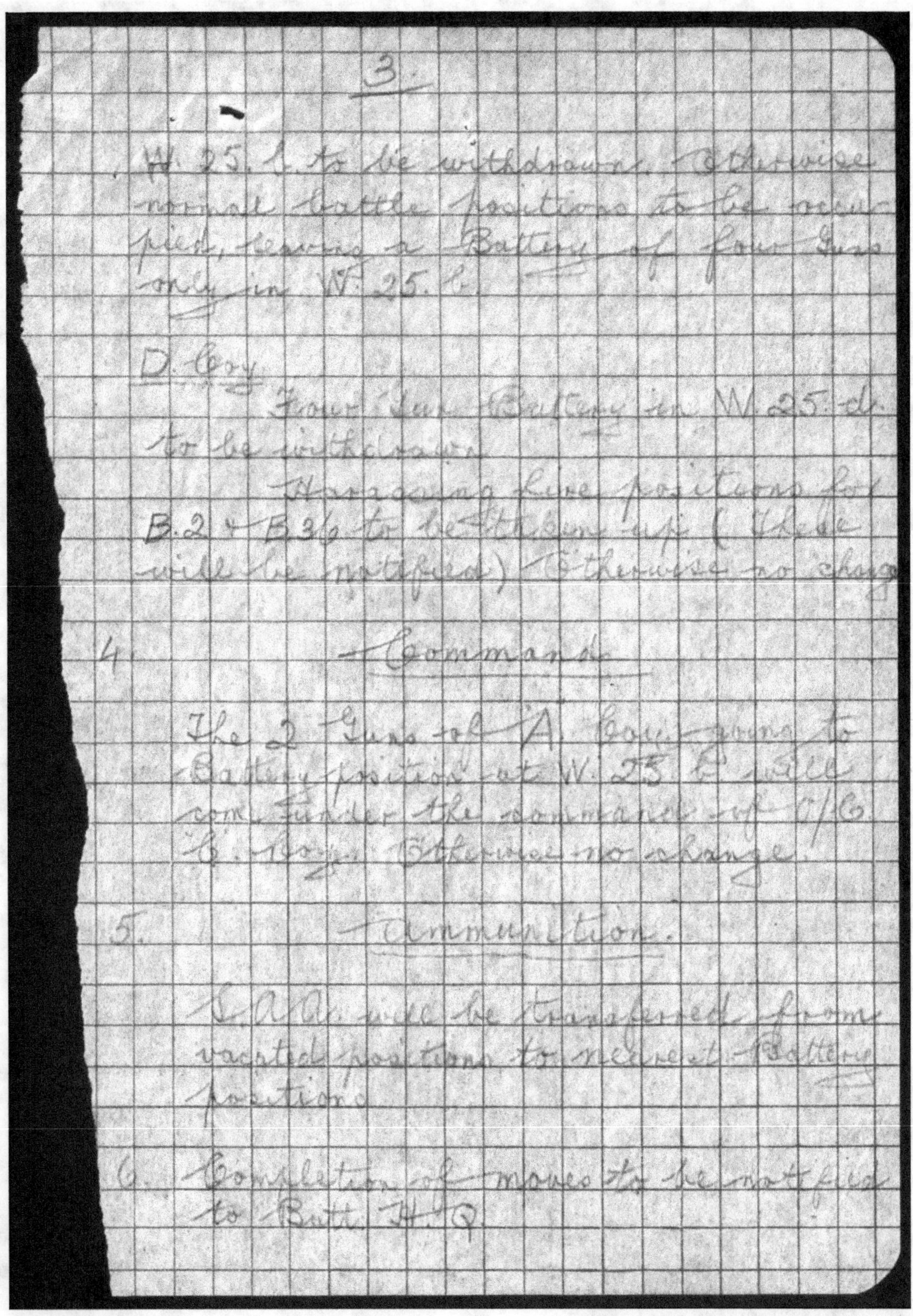

3.

W. 25. b. to be withdrawn. Otherwise normal battle positions to be occupied, leaving a Battery of four Guns only in W. 25. b.

D. Coy

Four Gun Battery in W. 25. d. to be withdrawn.

Harassing fire positions for B.2 & B.3b to be taken up (These will be notified) Otherwise no change

4. Command

The 2 Guns of A. Coy going to Battery position at W. 25 b will come under the command of O/C C. Coy. Otherwise no change.

5. Ammunition.

S.A.A. will be transferred from vacated positions to nearest Battery positions.

6. Completion of moves to be notified to Batt. H.Q.

4

7. — Drawings & fire instructions for "Scheme A" will be submitted as soon as possible.

8. <u>Fire Orders for night 2/3rd July.</u>

All Batteries & pairs of guns will remain laid on present Battery S.O.S. Lines for protection of newly captured ground.

Where guns have been removed to normal battle positions Coy. Commanders will arrange to lay out fresh lines tonight in accordance with the general S.O.S. Scheme of Defence.

9. ACKNOWLEDGE.

(Sgd) C. B. [illegible] Major
Commdg 8th Bn. M.G.C.

Appendix 54A

REPORT ON ACTION OF 18TH BATTALION M.G.CORPS.
IN MINOR OPERATION CARRIED OUT BY THE 54th
INFANTRY BRIGADE on 30th JUNE - 3rd JULY 1918.

1. Infantry Trench-to-trench attack was carried out by two Battalions.

MACHINE GUNS.

Organisation.

To cover the attack 32 guns organised in 3 groups and disposed in batteries were detailed to put down a protective barrage covering the whole front of attack (with average frontage of 40 yards per gun) in close co-operation with Machine Guns of left flank Division, while 16 guns firing from Battle positions swept selected areas.

Communication.

Direct communication by Lucas lamp and telephone was arranged from Brigade Battle Post to each Group H.Qrs.

Action of Machine Guns.

Night of 30th June/1st July.

At 9.35 p.m. artillery, trench mortar and machine gun barrage was put down simultaneously with Infantry Advance; Machine Guns firing 250 rounds per minute for 1st 10 minutes, 50 rounds per minute until final objective was reached, 10.15 p.m. and continuing at slow rate until consolidation was completed 12.30 a.m.

At 1.45 a.m. an S.O.S. call was answered with 10 minutes rapid fire, slowing down with artillery.

301,500 Rounds were fired during night.

Night of 1st/2nd July.

New front line having been accurately plotted, the protective barrage was drawn as close as possible, and 2 more guns brought in to thicken the barrage.

S.O.S. calls were answered at 9 p.m. and 2.30 a.m. and 225,000 rounds fired.

At 9 p.m. right group was spotted by enemy aeroplane which signalled to artillery. Area was searched with 4.2's and 5.9's at 9.15 p.m. and a few casualties caused in trenches near Battery positions. No casualties in Battery positions themselves.

Night of 2nd/3rd July.

Right group shifted Battery positions after dark and no more casualties were sustained in this group.

S.O.S. call was answered at 9.30 p.m. and fire continued throughout the night.

191,500 rounds were fired.

General.

It was found that battery positions dug well clear of trenches, with deep slits camouflaged during the day, afforded excellent protection, and casualties in proportion to the weight of enemy barrage were very slight in specially prepared positions and relatively heavy in trenches.

S.O.S. calls were in every case answered very promptly. The Machine Gun barrage coming down several minutes before the artillery.

Communication was maintained throughout the operation, with one exception, when a group signal station was damaged by a shell. Communication was resumed within 20 minutes.

Effect of M.G.Fire.

No evidence is available as to the effect of M.G. protective barrage in this operation. It appears however that no Infantry Counter-attack against the captured positions developed across the open ground covered by M.G.fire.

TOTAL AMMUNITION EXPENDED:- 718,000 rounds.

Casualties.

Killed:-	1	Officer,	1	O.R.
Wounded:-	-		7	O.R's.

No damage to guns.

..........C B Hilbert.........Major,
Commanding 18th Battalion M. G. Corps.

5th July 1918.

SECRET. 18th Bn. M.G.C. M.G. 160 F.

To O.C. B. & D. Coys. APPENDIX 55

The following order of moves cancels order M.G. 152 F. of 2/7/18 & will come into operation night of 3/4th inst.

A. Coy. 4 Gun Batty in W. 25. b. to withdraw. A. Coy. will then occupy its normal positions only.

B. Coy.

6 Gun Batty in W. 20 c. to withdraw. 4 Guns from B. 37 & 38 positions to remain in Battery position in W. 19. b. Other positions normal.

C. Coy.

8 Gun Batty in W. 25. b. to withdraw. 4 Gun Batty at A. 18 to move forward & take nos 1 & 4 positions in W. 25. b. vacated by other 2 sections. Other positions normal.

D. Coy.

Battery in W. 20. a. to remain also Battery made up of B. 2 & B. 36 in positions just moved at W. 25. b. 95. 55. Other positions normal.

S.O.S.

Targets for Batteries & pairs of guns attached.

2.

Should Scheme "A" be ordered Guns will fire on same S.O.S targets.

ACKNOWLEDGE.

(Sgd) C.B. Hubbert Major
Commdg 18th Bn M.G.C.

3rd July 1918

3

Battery Lines

On & after night of July 3rd/4th following Battery positions will be occupied & targets engaged as under –

Battery	Coy.	Position	Targets
B. 5.	A.	Normal	W.27.b.15.15 to
B. 40			W.27.c.95.40
A. 16	C	Normal	
B. 37	B.	W.19.b.90.75	No change
B. 38		W.19.b.90.60	Tasks as W.22 [illegible]
B. 10	B		W.22.b.05.05 to
B. 11		Normal	W.22.b.02.63
A. 18	C	W.25.b.60.50	W.22.c.70.70 to
(4 Guns)		or W.25.b.45.60	W.22.a.70.35
B. 45	C	Normal	W.22.c.00.00. to
			W.22.c.30.23
B. 6	A	Normal	W.27.b.42.90
B. 7	D	Normal	W.27.b.65.95
B. 2	D	W.25.b.95.25	W.22.a.15.20 to
B. 36			W.22.a.90.40
B. 17	D	W.20.a.15.15	W.22.b.02.63 to
B. 39			W.16.d.00.22

SECRET. Copy No. 19....

APPENDIX. 56.

Reference Maps:- SHEET [illegible]
1/40,000 [illegible] 1/100,000.

10th July 1918.

18th BATTN. M.G.C. ORDER No. 36.

1. (a) The 18th Bn. M.G.C. will be relieved by the 47th Battn M.G.C. during the period 11th to 14th July (both dates inclusive).
(b) On relief the 18th Bn. M.G.C. will move to FOURDRINOY.

2. Reliefs and subsequent moves of Coys. will take place in accordance with the attached table.

3. All details of reliefs, guides, etc., will be arranged direct between Company Commanders concerned.

4. (a) The following will be handed over to the relieving Unit and will be left in the forward area :-
All Fortress Rations.
16 Filled Belt Boxes per gun.
2 Full water tins per Gun.
(1,024 Belt Boxes - 16 per gun - and 128 water tins - 2 per gun - are being left behind in a Battn. Dump at FOURDRINOY by the 47th Battn. and will be drawn by Coys on their arrival.)
(b) In addition the following will be handed over at Gun positions :-

All boxed S.A.A.	All Armour Piercing S.A.A.
"T" Bases.	Battery Charts.
Fire Orders.	Air Photographs, etc.,

Receipts will be obtained and forwarded to Battn. H.Q. by 12 noon 15th inst.

5. Advance Party. The C.Q.M.S. (or representative) from each Coy. will proceed to MOLLIENS AU BOIS and report to the R.Q.M. at the Town Major's Office by 7.45 a.m. to-morrow 11th inst. Lorries leave MOLLIENS AU BOIS 8 a.m.

6. (a) All tents and shelters in present area will be handed over to incoming Units. Receipts will be taken and forwarded to Orderly Room with Trench Store Receipts.
(b) Tents and shelters in new area will be taken over from the 47th Battn. M.G.C. Duplicates of receipts given, to be forwarded to Orderly Room.

7. Communication. Relief of Signal personnel and handing over of Signal communication will be arranged between respective Signal Officers.

8. Battn. H.Qrs will close at WARLOY on the morning of the 14th July and re-open at FOURDRINOY on arrival.

9. ACKNOWLEDGE.

Capt & Adjt.
18th Battalion Machine Gun Corps.

Issued at .... p.m. Copies to:-

No.1.Copy	C.O.	No.10. Copy	Quartermaster.
" 2 "	Second-in-command.	" 11. "	R.S.M.
" 3 "	Adjutant.	" 12 "	18th Div. 'G'
" 4 "	"A" Coy.	" 13 "	53rd Inf. Bde.
" 5 "	"B" Coy.	" 14 "	54th Inf. Bde.
" 6 "	"C" Coy.	" 15 "	55th Inf. Bde.
" 7 "	"D" Coy.	" 16 "	47th Battn.M.G.C.
" 8 "	Signal Officer.	" 17/18"	War Diary.
" 9 "	Transport Officer.	" 19 "	File.

R E L I E F T A B L E.

(To accompany 18th Battn. M.G.C. Order No.36)

Serial No.	Date.	Guns 18th Battn.M.G.C. to be relieved.	Unit of 47th Bn. relieving.	18th Bn. M.G.C.On relief etc.move to.
1.	11th.	Transport of:- 4 Guns "A" Coy.HARLOY. 4 Guns "B" Coy.HARLOY. 4 Guns "C" Coy.HARLOY. 4 Guns "D" Coy.VARENCOURT.	-	Move by road to FOURDRINOY.
2.	Night 11/12th	10 Guns "B" Coy. in line.	"C" Coy.	4 Guns "B" Coy. billet HARLOY. 4 Guns "A" Coy. billet HARLOY. 2 Guns "C" Coy. billet HARLOY.
		2 Guns "B" Coy. HARLOY		2 Guns "C" Coy. billet HARLOY.
		4 Guns "D" Coy. HAMENCOURT.		VARENCOURT
3.	12th	Gun Teams of Serial No. 1.		Embus for FOURDRINOY.
4.	12th	Transport of Serial No. 2.		Move by road to FOURDRINOY.
5.	Night 12/13th	6 Guns "D" Coy. (B.48 B.8 and B.7) 6 Guns "A" Coy. (B.3 B.6 and B.40) 2 Guns "C" Coy. (A.16)	"B" Coy.	VARENCOURT HARLOY HARLOY
6.	13th	Personnel Serial No. 2		Embus for FOURDRINOY.
7.	Night 13/14th	2 Guns "A" Coy. (B.30) 6 Guns "C" Coy. (B.46 and A.18) 4 Guns "C" Coy. HAMEN-COURT. 4 Guns "A" Coy. HAMEN-COURT	"D" Coy.	Embus for FOURDRINOY
8.	Night 13/14th	Personnel Serial No. 5	"A" Coy.	Embus for FOURDRINOY
9.	14th.	Remainder of Coy. Transport and Bn. H.Q. Transport		Move by road to FOURDRINOY.
10.	14th	Battn. H.Q. and Personnel	Bn. H.Q.	Embus for FOURDRINOY.

NOTES. Completion of reliefs will be reported to Battn. H.Qrs using Serial number of relief.

Serial No.3. Debussing Point:- SOUES - PICQUIGNY Road facing West. Tail of Column at West end of PICQUIGNY.

Serial No.6. Embus 4 a.m. Debussing Point:- CAVILLON - BRIQUEMESNIL Road. Head of column facing South at North end of BRIQUEMESNIL.

Serial No.7. B.30 position will not be taken over by 47th Battn.M.G.C. but will withdraw as soon as possible on night of 13th. Corresponding guns of 47th Battn. will remain in HARLOY.

RELIEF TABLE (continued)

Serial No. [illegible]. Embus 4 a.m. 14th. Debussing point;- [illegible] [illegible] Road. Facing West. Tail of Column at East end of [illegible] facing West.

Serial Nos [illegible] and 10. Embussing Point;- [illegible] - [illegible] Road, Facing West. Tail of Column at West end of [illegible].

----------000----------

SECRET.

APPENDIX "B".
(To accompany 18th Batt. M.G.C.
Order No. 36)

E M B U S S I N G   T A B L E.

1. Embussing Strengths as rendered by Companies are as follows:-

To embus on:-	"A"	"B"	"C"	"D"	"H.Q".
12th	75	50	51	50	Nil
13th	Nil	140	Nil	55	Nil
14th	86	Nil	127	60	77

2.

Date.	Coy.	Number of Lorries allotted.	Lorry Nos. Front to rear of Lorry Column.	Embussing Point.	Debussing Point.
12th	"A"	4	126 - 129 (incl)	Embus 4 a.m. VADENCOURT - WARLOY Road facing West. Tail of Column at West end of WARLOY.	SOUES- PICQUIGNY Road facing West. Tail of Column at West end of PICQUIGNY.
	"B"	3	130 - 132 (incl)		
	"C"	3	133 - 135 (incl)		
	"D"	3	136 - 138 (incl)		
13th	"B"	8	161 - 168 (incl)	As above	Debussing Point CAVILLON - BRIQUEMESNIL Road. Head of Column facing S. at North end of BRIQUEMESNIL.
	"D"	4	169 - 172 (incl)		
14th	"A"	5	155 - 159 (incl)	As above	BRIQUEMESNIL - FERRIERES Road facing West. Tail of Column at E. end of FERRIERES.
	"C"	7	160 - 166 (incl)		
	"D"	4	167 - 170 (incl)		
	"H.Q".	5	171 - 175 (incl)		

3. Lorries will be marked showing number allotted to each Unit as per above Table.

4. Carrying capacity - each Lorry - 20 O.R's.

5. In addition to above, 1 Lorry has been detailed to report to Q.M. Stores CONTAY, at 9 a.m. on 14th inst. to convey surplus kit etc. to new area.

TO:- .......W.D.......

Capt. & Adjt.
18th Battn. M. G. C.

11th July 1918.

18th Battn. M.G.C. No. G.80.

APPENDIX 57

AMENDED EMBUSSING TABLE.

1. Estimated Embussing Strengths are as follows:-

Time.	Date.	"A"	"B"	"C"	"D"	H.Q.
4 a.m.	15th	80	76	82	80	Nil.
6 p.m.	15th.	86	115	Nil	88	80
4 a.m.	16th.	86	Nil.	127	60	80.

2.

Date.	Coy.	Number of busses or lorries allotted.	Lorry Numbers front to rear of Column.
4 a.m. 15th.	"A"	3 Busses.	7 - 9 (inclusive)
	"B"	4 Busses.	9 - 12 (inclusive)
	"C"	2 Busses.	13 - 14 (inclusive)
	"D"	2 Busses.	15 - 16 (inclusive)
6 p.m. 15th.	"A"	3 Lorries.	124 - 126 (inclusive)
	"B"	7 Lorries	126 - 132 (inclusive)
	"D"	4 Lorries.	133 - 136 (inclusive)
	H.Q.	4 Lorries.	137 - 140 (inclusive)
4 a.m. 16th.	"A"	5 Lorries.	144 - 148 (inclusive)
	"C"	7 Lorries.	149 - 155 (inclusive)
	"D"	4 Lorries.	156 - 159 (inclusive)
	H.Q.	3 Lorries.	160 - 162 (inclusive)

3. Bus capacity - 25. Lorry capacity 20.

4. Embussing Point:- 4 a.m. 15th and 4 a.m. 16th:-
VADENCOURT - CONTAY Road, facing West, Tail of column at West end of WARLOY.
6 p.m. 15th :-
CONTAY - HERISSART Road facing West, Tail of Column at CONTAY.

5. Debussing. Arrangements have been made to debus personnel as near as possible to FOURDRINOY.

6. Lorry for Surplus Kit will now report Quartermaster's Stores CONTAY, 9 a.m. 15th and not as previously stated.

[signature]
Capt & Adjt.,
18th Battalion Machine Gun Corps.

12th July 1918.

To:- ....

18th Battn. M.G.C. No. S.54.

AMENDMENT TO RELIEF TABLE ISSUED WITH ORDER NO. 36.

As the 18th Division has to be clear of this area by 10 a.m. 13th inst. it has been necessary to amend Relief and Embussing Tables issued with Order No. 36. accordingly.

Reference Relief Table. Serials 5, 6, 7, 8, 9, 10 are cancelled and the following substituted.

Serial No.	Date.	18th Battn. M.G.C. to be relieved.	Unit of 47th Battn. relieving.	18th Battn.M.G.C. on relief move to.
11.	12th.	Personnel serial No.2.	"A" Coy.	Embus 6 p.m. for FOURDRINOY.
12.	12th.	Battn. H.Qrs. (less 30 Signallers).	Bn.H.Qrs.	As above.
13.	Night. 12/13th.	8 Guns "D" Coy. (B.46. B.8. and B.7.) 6 Guns "A" Coy. (B.5. B.6. and B.40) 2 Guns "C" Coy (A.16)	"B" Coy.	WARLOY.
14.	Night. 12/13th.	2 Guns "A" Coy. (B.38) 6 Guns "C" Coy. (B.45 and A.18) 4 Guns "C" Coy. HENENCOURT. 4 Guns "A" Coy. HENENCOURT.	"D" Coy.	WARLOY.
15.	13th.	Personnel of serial Nos. 13 and 14. and 30 Bn.H.Q.Signallers.	-	Embus ~~2~~ 4 a.m. for FOURDRINOY.
16.	13th.	Remainder of Company Transport and Bn.H.Q. Transport.	-	By Road to FOURDRINOY.

[signature]

Capt & Adjt.,
18th Battalion Machine Gun Corps.

12th July 1918.

To:- Bn. H.Q. (File).

SECRET.

Appendix 64

Copy No....4......

Reference Map - 62 D.

31st July 1918.

18th BATTALION MACHINE GUN CORPS ORDER NO. 39.

1. 8 Guns of "D" Company, 18th Battalion M.G.C. will relieve 8 Guns 5th Australian M.G. Battalion, in BONNAY, on the night of 31st July/1st August 1918.

2. All details of relief will be arranged between Company Commanders concerned.

3. Company Headquarters 5th Australian M.G. Batt. are at C.21.C.central

4. Completion of relief will be reported to Battalion H.Q. by wire using code word " NARROC".

5. ACKNOWLEDGE.

H Corran Lt
..................Capt. & Adjt.
18th Battalion Machine Gun Corps.

Issued at..7 pm....p.m.

Copies to:-
No. 1 C.O.
2."D" Coy.
3. 5th Australian M.G.Batt.
4/5. War Diary.
6. File.

Appendix 63

SECRET. Copy No...4...

Reference Map:- Sheet 62.d. **30th July 1918.**

18TH BATTN.M.G.C. ORDER NO. 38.

1. "A" Company 18th Bn.M.G.C. will relieve 9th Company 3rd Australian M.G.Battn. in right sector of Divisional front on night 31st July/1st August 1918.

2. All details of relief will be arranged between Company Commanders concerned.

3. Rear Bn. H.Qrs. 3rd Aust. M. G. Bn. - BUSSY-LES-DAOURS.
Forward Bn.H.Q. -do- HAMLET. 0.6.b.75.55.
9th Company Headquarters - J.28.d.70.55.

4. Completion of relief will be reported to Battalion H.Q. by wire using code word "WERNHAM".

5. A C K N O W L E D G E.

J W K Woods(?)
....................Capt & Adjt.,
18th Battn. Machine Gun Corps.

Issued at ..10.45.. p.m.

Copies to:-
No.1. C.O.
" 2. "A" Coy. 18th Bn.M.G.C.
" 3. 3rd Australian M.G.Bn.
"4/5. War Diary.
" 6. File.

SECRET. 18th Battn. M.G.C. No.S. 64.

ADMINISTRATIVE INSTRUCTIONS
IN CONNECTION WITH ORDER 37.

1. CANVAS.

All tents and shelters in forward area will be taken over by relieving Units and receipts given.

Return of all tents and shelters taken over will be rendered to reach Orderly Room by 12 noon 1st August.

Orders with regard to tents in present area will be issued later.

Any tents in possession of "B" or "C" Coys. will be handed into Quartermaster's Stores by 9 a.m. 29th inst.

2. SUPPLIES.

Supplies for 29th.

Have already been issued.

Supplies for 30th.

"B" and "C" Coys. are being rationed by 54th Infantry Brigade. Instructions have already been issued by QrMr.

"A", "D" and H.Q. as at present.

Supplies for 31st.

"A", "B", "C" H.Q. will be rationed by 54th Inf. Bde.

"D" Company as at present.

Supplies for 1st.

Under Battalion arrangements in Forward Area. Quartermaster will ascertain that the necessary arrangements are made.

3. TRENCH AND AREA STORES.

All returns of Ammunition, grenades and fireworks, water tins and fortress rations taken over will be rendered in duplicate to Battalion Headquarters by noon 1st August.

4. S.A.A.

Demands for S.A.A. will continue to be made on Battn. H.Qrs. as required.

J.W.K. Wand ....Capt & Adjt.,
18th Battalion Machine Gun Corps.

Distribution as for Order No.37.

TABLE "B".

EMBUSSING TABLE.
(To accompany 18th Bn.M.G.C.Order 37)

Coy.	Embussing Point.	Date and Time.	Head of Column.	Busses for.
"B"	BRIQUEMESNIL - FERRIERES Road.	29th July. 12 noon.	Facing East at West end of FERRIERES.	200 O.Rs.
"C"	As above.	As above.	As above.	200 O.Rs.
"A"	CAVILLON - BRIQUEMESNIL Rd.	30th July. 12 noon.	Facing South at N. end of BRIQUEMESNIL.	200 O.Rs.
Bn. H.Q.	As for "A".	As for "A"	As for "A"	60 O.Rs.
"D"	PICQUIGNY & SOUES Road.	31st July. 12 noon.	Facing East at W. end of PICQUIGNY.	200 O.Rs.

DEBUSSING POINT FOR ALL COMPANIES.

QUERRIEUX ALBERT Road. Facing East.
Head of Columns I.8.a.5.8.

Busses and lorries will be numbered off accordingly to strengths of units. Companies will send on in advance 1 Officer to ascertain exact lorries allotted to their respective Companies, which in all cases will be those to the rear of the column.

Officers should report at embussing Point at least one hour before 12 noon on the day of departure with exact numbers of Officers and Other Ranks embussing.

---------ooo---------

TABLE "A".

MARCH TABLE.
(To accompany Order No. 37. dated 28.7.1918)

Serial No.	Date.	Coy.	Starting Point.	Time to Pass S.Point.	Route.	Destination.
1.	29th.	"B"	Junction of BREILLY - FOURDRINOY and SAISSEMONT - FOURDRINOY Rds.	10 a.m.	SAISSEMONT SAISSEVAL.	To Embus at 12 noon.
2.	29th.	"C"	As above.	10.5.a.m.	As above.	As above.
3.	29th.	Trans -port of "B"Co.	Junction of PICQUIGNY - FOURDRINOY and BREILLY - FOURDRINOY Road.	8.30 a.m.	BREILLY - AILLY-SUR-SOMME - AMIENS - QUERRIEU.	Reserve Brigade Area.
4.	29th.	"C" Trans -port.	As for Serial No.3.	8.40 a.m.	As for Serial No.3.	Reserve Bde.Area.
5.	30th.	"A"	Crucifix at Junction of Rd. S.W. entrance to FOURDRINOY.	11.30 a.m.	CAVILLON - FOURDRINOY Road.	To embus at 12 noon.
6.	30th.	Bn. H.Q.	As for Serial No.5.	11.35 a.m.	As for Serial No.5.	
7.	30th.	Trans -port of"A" Coy.	As for Serial No.3.	8.30 a.m.	As for Serial No.3.	Reserve Brigade Area vacated by "C" Company.
8.	30th.	Trans -port Bn.HQ.	As for Serial No.7. to move under Orders of Transport Officer "A" Company.			
9.	night 30/31st.	"A"	-	-	-	To relieve guns in line left Sub-Sector.
10.	31st.	"D"	Crucifix at Rd Junction N. entrance of FOURDRINOY.	11 a.m.	Rd.Junction J.8.d.5.8. PICQUIGNY.	To embus 12 noon.
11.	31st.	Trans -port "D"Co.	As for Serial No. 3.			Reserve Bde.Area vacated by "B" Coy.
12.	Night. 31. July/ 1stAug.	"B"	-	-	-	To relieve Right Sub-sector guns in line.

-------oOo-------

REMARKS. Coys. will make their own arrangements as to providing guides to meet incoming transport at QUERRIEU to guide it to Coy.Transport lines. Transport will probably take 6 - 7 hours on the journey and arrangements should be made accordingly.

Embussing Table attached.

--------oOo---------

18th Battn.M.G.C./No.G.891.

Appendix 59

18TH BATTALION MACHINE GUN CORPS.

P R O G R A M M E   O F   T R A I N I N G.

- FOR PERIOD 15th - 20th JULY 1918 -

Date.	Day.	Subject.
15th.	Monday.	Overhauling and cleaning all gun equipment, repacking limbers, kit inspection, etc.,
16th.	Tuesday.	As for 15th.
17th.	Wednesday.	Recruit Training. (To include, Saluting, Squad Drill, Arms Drill, P.T. etc.,
18th.	Thursday.	
19th.	Friday.	Officers.. Special Training under Company Commanders.
20th.	Saturday.	Company Route Marches.

Inspection of Box Respirators and Anti-Gas Training will be included in the above Training.

On every third day's training Box Respirators will be worn for 10 minutes during whatever training may be in progress.

J. C. K. Wenden

Capt & Adjt.,
18th Battalion Machine Gun Corps.

14th July 1918.

SECRET. 18th Battn.M.G.C.No.S.56.

Subject:- ENTRAINMENT OF DIV. AT 9 HOURS NOTICE. Copy No.10...

appendix 60

To:- "A", "B", "C", "D" Coys.
Signal Officer, Quartermaster,
Transport Officer.

---

1. The Division is at present held in G.H.Q. Reserve and all Units must be prepared to move at 9 hours notice.

2. The move may be ordered to be carried out in any of the following ways:-

(a) By a Strategical Move.
(b) By Bus.
(c) By Road.

3. Move by Train.
In the event of a move of the "complete Division in Strategical Trains" the 18th Division (less artillery) has been allotted 21 trains and the personnel divided into three groups:-

(a) 53rd Bde. Group and attached troops.
(b) 54th Bde. Group and attached troops.
(c) 55th Bde. Group and attached troops.

each group being allotted 7 trains and entraining at different stations.
Two stations have been allotted to each according as to whether the 18th Division is ordered to move North or South in which case different lines have to be used.
Entraining Table is attached marked "A".

4.(a) Each Company will detail an Officer as entraining Officer. This Officer will proceed to his Company's entraining stations to make a reconnaissance of approaches to the stations and entraining facilities. Stations for a move South will be reconnoitred first.
(b) These representatives will report to the R.T.O. from whom they will obtain information as to any special regulations in force at that particular station.

5. (a) Transport will arrive at entraining station three hours before time of departure of trains.
(b) Personnel will report one hour before time of departure of trains.

6. On arrival at the entraining station, Officers Commanding Companies will report to the R.T.O.
No troops will be permitted to enter the Station Yard until permission has been obtained from the R.T.O.

7. (a) Horses will be watered before entrainment.
(b) Units must provide head ropes for tying up horses in the trucks.
(c) Horses will not be unharnessed unless the scheduled time for the journey exceeds 15 hours; two men must travel in each truck

8. Supplies etc., will be notified later.

9. Water Carts will travel full

10. Blankets will be rolled into bundles of 10 and carried on trains of Units to whom they belong.

appendix 61

18th Battalion M.G.C. No. L.3/201.

Subject:- TACTICAL LESSONS LEARNT DURING THE PAST MONTH.

To/-
Headquarters,
18th Division.

From experience gained during active operations, it seems more and more advisable to keep Barrage Gun positions as far away as possible from any definite system of trenches. During operations on the 30th June 1918 and following days, the hostile shelling of our trenches was in many cases heavy. The gun emplacements were constructed well away from these trenches, and, with one exception, did not receive any attention from hostile artillery.

Special precautions, however, must be taken to camouflage all tracks to and from the gun position, and the gun position itself. Natural camouflage from material surrounding the gun position was found to be most satisfactory.

The exception referred to above, with reference to immunity from enemy shelling occurred as follows:-

At zero a low flying enemy plane flew over one of our Battery positions, and, on spotting it, signalled the position to its artillery by firing white Verey lights over the emplacements. A hostile bombardment was the result.

It is suggested that M.G. Battalions should be issued with 16 Lewis Guns (1 per section) to be manned by teams chosen from the present sections, no increase in personnel in a Battalion being recommended.

These Lewis Guns are intended for protection against low-flying hostile aeroplanes, and against enemy infantry in case of open warfare, when escorts provided for Machine Guns from our own infantry generally get detached, thus leaving the guns and teams to defend themselves instead of carrying out their allotted tasks.

(Sgd) E.C.T. Minet
Lieut. Colonel,
Commandg. 18th Batt. M.G.C.

22nd July 1918.

APPENDIX "A".

ENTRAINING TABLE.

Coy.	To Move with.	Entraining Station for move, North.	South.	Train No.	Time of Departure.
"A"	53rd Bde.Group.	PONT REMY.	SALEUX.	1	Zero.
"B"	54th Bde.Group.	HANGEST-SUR-SOMME.	PROUZEL.	2	Zero.
"C"	55th Bde.Group.	LONPRE-LES-CORPS-SAINTS.	BACOUEL.	3	Zero.
"D"	55th Bde.Group.	LONGPRE-LES-CORPS-SAINTS.	BACOUEL.	15	"Z" plus 12 hours.
Bn.H.Q.	ditto.,	ditto.,	ditto.,	3	Zero.

When Orders are received to move exact time of departure of trains will be notified.

--------ooo--------

APPENDIX "B".

EMBUSSING TABLE.

Coy.	Bde.Group.	Embussing Point.	Head of Column.	Lorry Numbers front to Rear.
"A"	53rd.	PICQUIGNY-SOUES Road.	Facing E. at W. end of PICQUIGNY.	177 - 186.
"D"	53rd.	ditto.,	ditto.,	187 - 197.
"B"	54th.	BRIQUEMESNIL) Rd. FERRIERES,)	Facing E. at W. end of FERRIERES.	122 - 132.
"C"	55th.	CAVILLON-BRIQUEMESNIL Rd.	Facing S. at N. end of BRIQUEMESNIL.	133 - 142.
Bn.H.Q.	55th.	ditto.,	ditto.,	143 - 146.

--------ooo----------

11. Each Company and Battalion Headquarters will detail 1 Officer and 2 O.Rs. as billeting party for the Company. Billeting Party of "D" Company will proceed in Train No.3. with "C" Coy. All billeting parties will report to Brigade Group Billeting representative immediately on arrival at detraining station.

12. Each Unit will detail 2 Cyclist Orderlies to report for duty to the Officer representing their Brigade Group, three hours prior to the time laid down on the attached time table for the departure of their train.

13. Move by Bus.
If the Division is ordered to move by bus, personnel will embus as per table "B" attached.
Transport will move by road.

14. Move by Road.
In the event of a move by road orders and march tables will be issued in accordance with the tactical situation.

15. Extra Transport.
It must be clearly understood that if the Division receives orders to move at 9 hours notice all units must be mobile.
A surplus kit store has been formed at Billet No.30, CAVILLON (On CAVILLON - OISSY Road). Companies will at once dump all surplus kit etc., neatly packed and clearly labelled at this store. In case of a hurried move, the dump will be cleared to new area by Divisional lorries.
In the event of the Division not being ordered to move under 9 hours notice, Companies will draw their kit and move it with them.

16. ACKNOWLEDGE.

Capt & Adjt.,
18th Battalion Machine Gun Corps.

Issued at .... a.m.
17th July 1918.

18th Bn.M.G.C.No.G.[illegible]

18TH BATTALION MACHINE GUN CORPS.

P R O G R A M M E   O F   T R A I N I N G.

- for PERIOD 21st - 26th JULY 1918 -

Date.	Day.	Subject.
21st.	Monday.	1 Hour ... ... Close Order Drill. 1 Hour ... ... Gun Drill. 1½ Hours ... ... Immediate Action and Mechanism. ½ Hour ... ... Physical Training.
22nd.	Tuesday.	Battalion Barrage Scheme.
23rd.	Wednesday.	As for Monday, 21st.
24th.	Thursday.	Company Tactical Schemes.
25th.	Friday.	Intensive digging of slits and construction
26th.	Saturday.	of Machine Gun Emplacements.

---------------000---------------

During the week special classes will be held as follows;-

4 men per Company ... ... Range and Visual Course under an officer to be detailed by Battn. H.Qrs.,

Backward Men ... ... On mechanism, stoppages, immediate action and task of elementary training under specially selected N.C.Os.

Junior N.C.Os. Class .. ... Daily under R.S.M.

Senior N.C.Os. Class .. ... Daily on Map Reading, Theory of fire etc. under Company Officers.

Signallers . ... Under Battalion Signal Officer.

Inspection of Box Respirators and Anti-Gas Training will be included in the above Training. On every third day's training Box Respirators will be worn for 10 minutes during whatever training may be in progress.

[illegible signature]

Capt & Adjt.,
18th Battalion Machine Gun Corps.

14th July 1918.

SECRET. Copy No. 10

appendix 62

Reference Maps:- AMIENS 1/100,000.
Sheets 62.d.N.E. & 62.d.N.W.1/20,000.

28th July 1918.

18TH BATTN. M.G.C. ORDER NO. 37.

1. (a) The 18th Battn.M.G.C. will relieve the 5th Australian M.G.C. in the line from the SOMME to K.1.d.6.3. Relief to be completed by dawn August 1st.,
   (b) The 18th Division is released from G.H.Q. Reserve for this purpose and on completion of relief will come under the orders of III Corps.

2. The Battn. will move from FOURDRINOY; personnel by bus, transport by road in accordance with attached table.

3. (a) All details of reliefs, guides, etc., will be arranged between Company Commanders concerned.
   (b) The M.Gs. in the left sub-sector will be relieved by "C" Company on the night of 30th/31st July, and those in the right sub-sector by "B" Company on the night 31st July/1st August 1918.

4. (a) Defence Schemes, Maps, Aeroplane Photographs and Documents relating to the sectors, also A.P. Ammunition, S.O.S. Grenades and Message carrying rockets will be taken over on relief.
   (b) Coys. will take over reserve rations and water in positions.

5. Administrative arrangements in connection with the relief will be issued separately.

6. Completion of all reliefs and moves will be reported to Bn. H.Q by wire giving serial number of relief.

7. ACKNOWLEDGE.

J O K Wem[illegible] ....Capt & Adjt.,
18th Battalion Machine Gun Corps.

Issued at 9.30 p.m. Copies to:-
No.1. C.O.
" 2 Second-in-Command.
" 3 Adjutant.
" 4 "A" Company.
" 5 "B" Company.
" 6 "C" Company.
" 7 "D" Company.
" 8 T.O. & QrMr.
" 9 R.S.M.
"10/11 War Diary.
" 12 File.

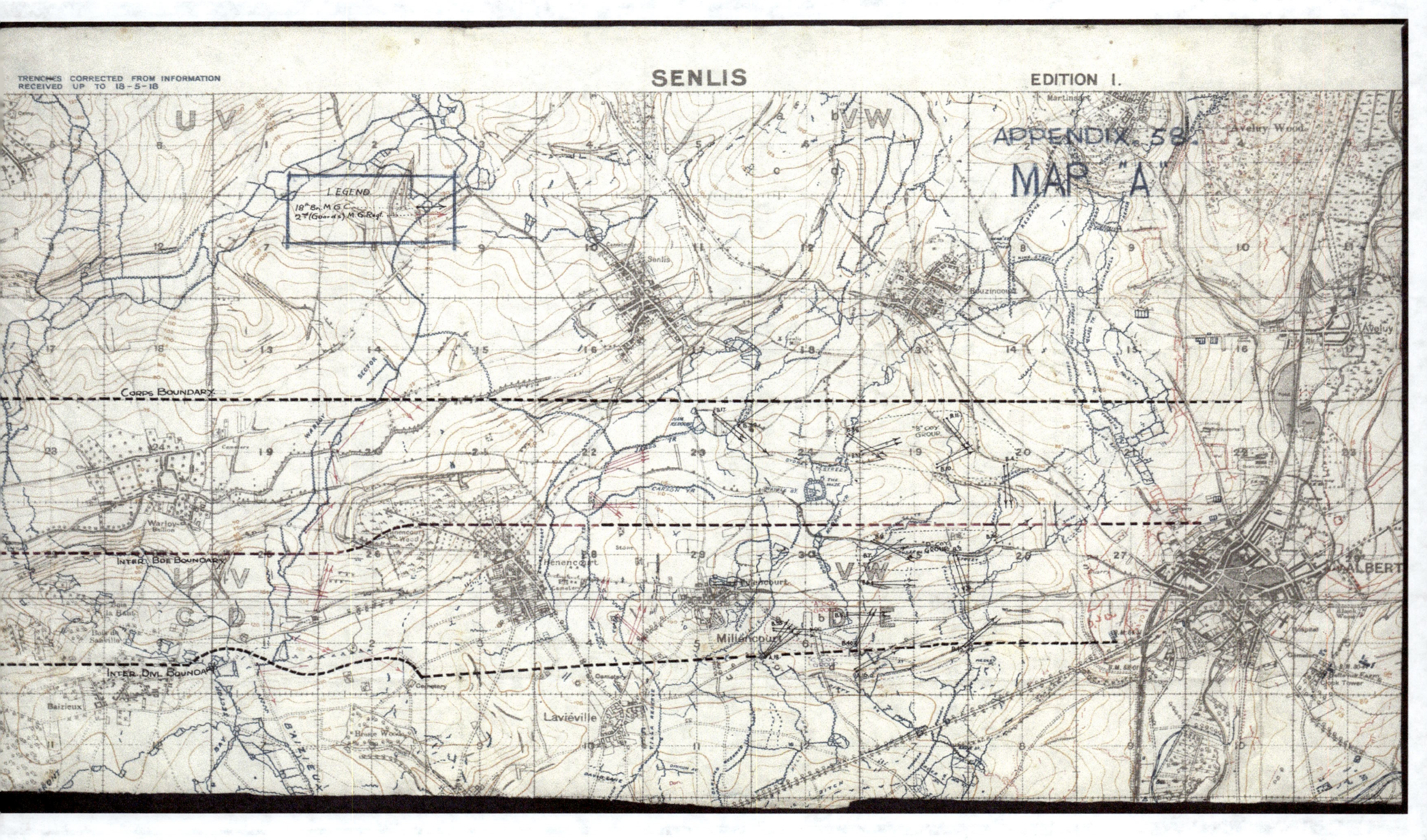

TRENCHES CORRECTED FROM INFORMATION RECEIVED UP TO 18-5-18
SENLIS
EDITION I.
APPENDIX 58.
MAP "A"
LEGEND
18th Bn. M.G.C.
2nd (Guards) M.G. Regt.
CORPS BOUNDARY
INTER. BDE BOUNDARY
INTER. DIVL BOUNDARY
Senlis
Bouzincourt
Martinsart
Aveluy Wood
Aveluy
ALBERT
Henencourt
Millencourt
Laviéville
Warloy-Baillon
Baizieux
BAIZIEUX

Dispositivo

APPENDIX 66.

CASUALTIES INCURRED BY THE BATTALION
DURING THE MONTH OF JULY 1918.

OFFICERS.

2nd Lieut. F. W. TAPPENDEN. Killed in Action 2.7.18.

OTHER RANKS.

Date.	Killed.	Wounded.	W at Duty.	Total.
1st.	-	1	-	1
2nd.	1	1	2	4
3rd.	-	1	-	1
7th.	-	1	-	1
13th.	1	1	-	2
TOTALS:-	2	5	2	9

------oOo------

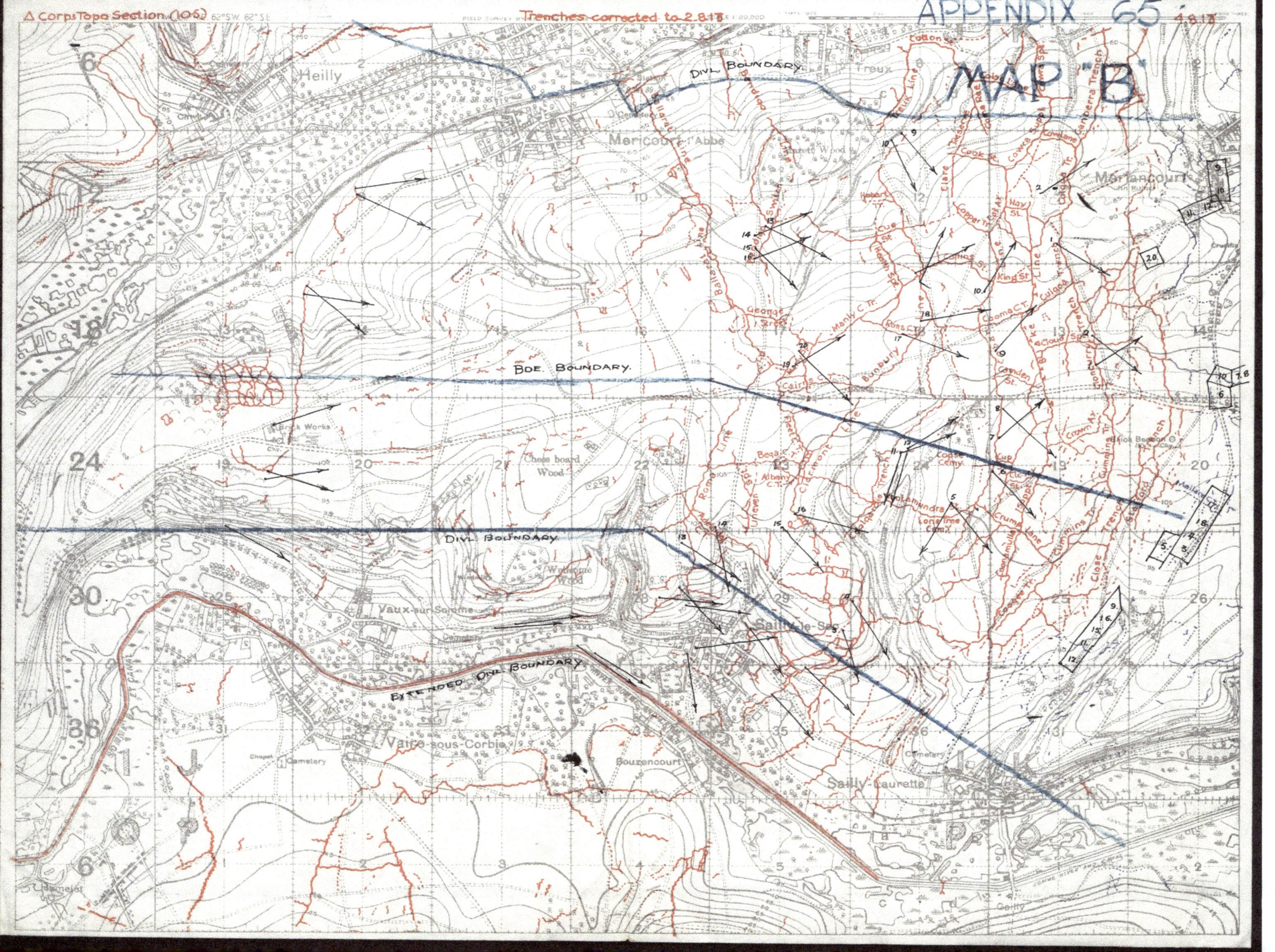

APPENDIX 65
4.8.18
MAP "B"
Δ Corps Topo Section (106)
Trenches corrected to 2.8.18
DIVL. BOUNDARY
BDE. BOUNDARY
DIVL. BOUNDARY
EXTENDED DIVL. BOUNDARY
Heilly
Treux
Mericourt l'Abbé
Morlancourt
Chess board Wood
Vaux-sur-Somme
Vaire-sous-Corbie
Bouzencourt
Sailly-le-Sec
Sailly-Laurette
Brick Works
Cemetery
Chapel
Ballarat Line
Cotton St.
Canberra Trench
Manly C.Tr.
George Street
Cairns
Bunbury
Roma Line
Cumming Trench
Close Trench
Crown Av.
Coongewarra Trench
Cook St.
Collins St.
King St.
Camden St.
Wooloomooloo Trench
Lone Tree Cemy.
Crump Lane

APPENDIX 67.

CHANGES IN ESTABLISHMENT & STRENGTH
CHANGES IN OFFICERS - DRAFTS RECEIVED
ETC. IN BATTN. DURING MONTH OF JULY 1918.

Paper Strength of Battalion (excluding attached):-

1st July 1918	... ...	44 Officers	906 Other Ranks
31st July 1918	... ...	47 Officers	922 Other Ranks.

INCREASES.

Lieut. H. J. Prout. Lieut. J. P. Godfrey. 2nd Lieut. H. P. G. Duplock. 2nd Lieut. A. W. Billbrough.	)	Joined Battalion as reinforcements from M.G.C. Base Depot and taken on strength, 13.7.18.
Lieut. D. J. Hutson. 2nd Lieut. W. P. Nash. 2nd Lieut. C. Pettitt.	)	Ditto., do., 18.7.18.
2nd Lieut. J. H. G. Clark.		Ditto., do., 19.7.18.

1 O.R.	joined Battn.	as reinforcement	from M.G. Base Depot	9.7.18.
3 O.Rs.	do.,	do.,	do.,	15.7.18.
20 O.Rs.	do.,	do.,	do.,	13.7.18.
35 O.Rs.	do.,	do.,	do.,	19.7.18.
1 O.R.	do.,	do.,	do.,	24.7.18.

DECREASES.

Officers.

2nd Lieut. F. W. TAPPENDEN,		Killed In Action, 2.7.18.
Lieut. D. C. Imrie. 2nd Lieut. A. F. Woodrow (M.M)	)	Evacuated out of Corps Area, Sick, and struck off strength, 4.7.18.
Lieut. G. H. Brownrigg-Jay Lieut. W. Mailer.	)	Ditto., do., 26.7.18.

Other Ranks.

Casualty Clearing Stations ...	27.
Casualties	7
Candidates for Commissions. ...	4
Struck off over 7 days in Hospital,	5
To Base for Further Training ...	1
	44

-------oOo---------

Strength 1st:-	44 Officers,	906 O.Rs.
Increases:-	8 "	60 O.Rs.
	52 "	966 "
Decreases:-	5 "	44 "
Strength 31st:-	47 "	922 "

18th Division

Divl. Troops.

18th BATTALION

MACHINE GUN CORPS,

AUGUST 1918.

Army Form C. 2118.

WAR DIARY
or
~~INTELLIGENCE SUMMARY.~~
(Erase heading not required.)

Instructions regarding War Diaries and Intelligence Summaries are contained in F. S. Regs., Part II. and the Staff Manual respectively. Title pages will be prepared in manuscript.

18th Battalion Machine Gun Corps — August 1918

Place	Date	Hour	Summary of Events and Information	Remarks and references to Appendices
LA HOUSSOYE	1st		Bn HQ unable to take over from Bn HQ 5th A M G Bn in C 21 c cent. owing to this Battalion being unable to vacate billets — Quiet in line — 2 pm. Conference for C.O. at Divisional H.Q.	[initials]
	2nd	6.30 am	Conference of Company Commanders at BONAY CHURCH	
		2 pm	Battalion H.Q. moved from LA HOUSSOYE and all Rear Coy H.Qrs in FRANVILLERS moved to Valley in C 21 c	
			8 guns of A. Co. relieved by D. Co Relief complete 9 45 pm.	
			8 guns of D. Co in BONNAY relieved by 8 guns of 50th Bn. M.G.C. Relief complete 9.30 pm.	
			4 guns of 'C' Co relieved by 58th Bn. M.G.C who took over portion of the front.	
			2 guns of 'C' Co & 4 guns of 'B' Co withdrawn from the line	[initials]

D. D. & L., London, E.C.
(A7883) Wt. W809/M1672 350,000 4/17 Sch. 52a Forms/C/2118/14

Army Form C. 2118.

WAR DIARY
or
~~INTELLIGENCE SUMMARY.~~
(Erase heading not required.)

Instructions regarding War Diaries and Intelligence Summaries are contained in F. S. Regs., Part II. and the Staff Manual respectively. Title pages will be prepared in manuscript.

18th Battalion Machine Gun Corps — August 1918.

Place	Date	Hour	Summary of Events and Information	Remarks and references to Appendices
LA HOUSSOYE	3	5.30pm	Commanding Officer attended conference at D. H. 2	
		9.30pm	16 guns "D" Co. 50th Bn. took up positions in BALLARAT – ROMA LINE in accordance with instructions from G. O. C.	
		"	8 guns D Co. 18th Bn. took over positions in BONNAY evacuated by "D" Co. 50th Bn.	H.C.
		7.30am	Capt + Adjt. J.W.K. Wernham M.C. left Camp to attend Course at Camiers + Lieut. H. Corrow appointed to act in his absence.	
	4	9am	Conference of Company Commanders	H.C.
	5	1.15am	Operation Order No. 40 issued See Appendix No 68	App 68
			All preparations for the attack ~~completed~~ being made by Companies.	H.C.

Army Form C. 2118.

Instructions regarding War Diaries and Intelligence Summaries are contained in F. S. Regs., Part II. and the Staff Manual respectively. Title pages will be prepared in manuscript.

WAR DIARY
or
~~INTELLIGENCE SUMMARY~~.
(*Erase heading not required.*)

Place	Date	Hour	Summary of Events and Information	Remarks and references to Appendices
Valley C 21 c	6th	4 am	Enemy attacked on right front astride Bray Corbie Road - all guns fired on S.O.S. lines - . Enemy penetrated front system & surrounded & captured 1 gun team - team afterwards escaped with exception of 1 man reported missing - no guns lost	
			During night 8 guns D Coy relieved by 58th Bn M.G.C. - Order No 41 issued (See Appendix 69.)	HC App 69
	7th	4.20 am	54th Inf Brigade counterattacked to regain lost ground - guns cooperated as per Order No. 41 - During night adv^d Bn H.Q. established at J17 b 5.8	HC
	8th		See O.O. 40 and Narrative of Operations (Appendix 70)	HC App 70.
	9th		do	HC
	10		do	
		2 pm	Orders received verbally from 18 Division to withdraw all guns after dusk to Valley C 21 c central	
		9.30 pm	All Coys clear of forward area	
			Major Hibbert DSO returned from leave	HC

D. D. & L., London, E.C. (A7883) Wt W809/M1672 350,000 4/17 Sch. 52a Forms/C/2118/14

Instructions regarding War Diaries and Intelligence Summaries are contained in F. S. Regs., Part II. and the Staff Manual respectively. Title pages will be prepared in manuscript.

WAR DIARY
or
~~INTELLIGENCE SUMMARY~~.
(Erase heading not required.)

Army Form C. 2118.

Place	Date	Hour	Summary of Events and Information	Remarks and references to Appendices
			Tracing showing dispositions of Guns taken over from 47th Bn MGC attached	(App 75)
Valley C21 C	11th		B. C. & D. Coys relieved 47th Bn MGC in the line (Albert Sector) moving from C 21 C by march route. relief complete 1-15 am 12th - A Coy remained in Reserve in Valley C.21.c cent - Dispositions of guns as per attached tracing. - Order No 42 issued (see Appendix 71)	HC app 71.
	12th	8.30 am	Bn HQ. A Coy & Rear Coy HQ-BC&D Coy moved to WARLOY	
WARLOY		4:30 pm	CO attended conference Divnl HQ.	
			Situation in line quiet	HC
	13		do	HC
	14		do	HC
	15		A Coy relieved B Coy (16 guns in line) } B & D Coys ordered to C Coy " D " (12 guns in line) } stand by to be ready to act ~~with~~ advance Guard if required. - S83 issued (see Appendix 72)	HC App 72
	16	5am	Lt-Col Minet DSO MC proceeded on special leave - Major Hebbert DSO assumed command - Major Paterson 2nd in Command.	HC
	17		Operations nil - situation quiet	HC

D. D. & L., London, E.C.
(A7883) Wt. W809/M1672 350,000 4/17 Sch. 52a Forms/C/2118/14

Army Form C. 2118.

Instructions regarding War Diaries and Intelligence Summaries are contained in F. S. Regs., Part II. and the Staff Manual respectively. Title pages will be prepared in manuscript.

WAR DIARY
or
~~INTELLIGENCE SUMMARY.~~
(Erase heading not required.)

Place	Date	Hour	Summary of Events and Information	Remarks and references to Appendices
WARLOY	18th	10am	Conference at 18 DIV. HQ. - Situation in line Quiet	HC
"	19th	2.20pm	O.O. No 43 issued - during night D Coy relieved C Coy in line	
"	~~20~~		2 Coy's (B & C) 50th Bn MGC attached to 18th Bn MGC & billeted in	
			WARLOY OO43 attached - Appendix 73	HC App. 73.
"	20th	10am	Conference of Coy. Cmdrs at Bn HQ. Order No 44 issued (App 74)	App 74.
			During night B Coy 50th Bn MGC relieved 123rd American MG Bn	
			in right Divisional Sector - C Coy 50th Bn MGC relieved A Coy	
			18th Bn MGC - A Coy 18 Bn MGC to Warloy - Reliefs complete	
			12.30 am 21st	
		9.15pm	O.O No 45 issued (See Appendix 76)	HC App. 76.
	21st		Preparations made in accordance with O.O. 45	
		2pm	Advd Bn HQ established at W.25.b 2.7	HC
W.25b 2.7	22nd	2.45am	Division rang up Rear HQ also Bde Maj. 54th Inf Bde	
			informing us that patrols of 54th Inf Bde ~~were on a~~	
			had pushed forward and had encountered no enemy - 54th	
			Inf Bde on line roughly - ALBERT - MEAULTE Road	HC

D. D. & L., London, E.C. (A7883) Wt. W809/M1672 350,000 4/17 Sch. 52a Forms/C/2118/14

Instructions regarding War Diaries and Intelligence Summaries are contained in F. S. Regs., Part II, and the Staff Manual respectively. Title pages will be prepared in manuscript.

18th Battalion Machine Gun Corps

WAR DIARY
or
~~INTELLIGENCE SUMMARY.~~
(*Erase heading not required.*)

August 1918

Army Form C. 2118.

Place	Date	Hour	Summary of Events and Information	Remarks and references to Appendices
	22nd (cont)		This being line of primary barrage line, time table had to altered accordingly – Coys & 58th DIV & 12th DIV. informed and alterations effected by 3.15 am. – Message phoned to this effect to G.S.O.1 Division. Special Order of the day issued (Appendix 77)	HC App 77
		4.45 am	Zero Hour for Operations as per 0045	
			Operations 22nd August – 5th September 1918 See Narrative (app 80) of Operations attached. Lessons Learnt (app 81)	HC App 80 App 81
	23rd		Water Supply Arrangements issued under G121 (Appendix 78)	App 78
	24th		" " " G125 (Appendix 79)	App 79
			List of Casualties during August attached (Appendix 82)	App 82
			Changes of Establishment during month as Appendix 83	App 83
			[signature] Capt for Major Commanding 18th Bn Machine Gun Corps	H Corran Asst Adjt

D. D. & L., London, E.C. (A7883) Wt. W809/M1672 350,000 4/17 Sch. 52a Forms/C/2118/14

SECRET. COPY No. 18.

Reference Map:- 62.d.N.E.
1/10,000 - [illegible] (Local) APPENDIX 68. 4th August 1918

18TH BATTALION M.G.C. ORDER No. 41.

1. INFORMATION. On a date to be notified later the 18th Division will carry out an attack in conjunction with other Divisions on our right. Scheme of attack has been explained to all concerned.

2. ACTION OF M.Gs. The 18th Battn. M.G.C. plus "D" Coy. 58th Battn. M.G.C. will co-operate in two roles :-
(1) Barrage.
(2) Consolidation forward. The Div. on our Left will co-operate by barraging the spur in K.2 and 3.

3. DISTRIBUTION. Guns will be distributed as follows:-
"A" Coy. (16 Guns) for consolidation of the RED and GREEN lines shown on map issued to Coy's.
"B" Coy. (less 8 Guns) consolidation of the BLUE Line.
"C" Coy. (less 8 guns) for consolidation of 55th Infantry Bde's Left flank.
All guns detailed above are allotted to their respective Brigades and will receive Operation Orders from G.O.C.'s concerned.
The remainder of the guns will be grouped in batteries as follows:-

No.1.Bty. 4 Guns "D" Coy. 58th Battn. M.G.Corps.
No.2.Bty. 8 Guns "D" Coy, 18th Battn. M.G.Corps.
No.3.Bty. 8 Guns "D" Coy. 58th Battn. M.G.Corps.
No.4.Bty. { 4 Guns "B" Coy.
{ 4 Guns 58th Battn. M.G.Corps.
No.5.Bty. 4 Guns "C" Company.
No.6.Bty. 4 Guns of "C" Company.
No.7.Bty. 4 Guns "B" Coy. 18th Bn. M.G.C.
No.8.Bty. 4 Guns "B" Coy, 18th Bn. M.G.C.

The remaining guns will be in Divisional Reserve.

4. POSITIONS & TARGETS. Positions and targets are shown on map attached.

5. RATES OF FIRE. Times and rates of fire as shown in Appendix "A" "Fire Organisation Orders" attached.

6. PREPARATION. All preparations for batteries located within present British line as regards, sites, ammunition, supplies, water supply and belt filling arrangements will be completed by dawn 7th inst. Reports being sent to Battn. H.Qrs to this effect.

7. S.A.A. 2,000 rounds in belts, per gun, must be kept at each gun position at all times.
16,000 rounds per gun must be dumped at belt filling positions.
A Machine Gun ammunition dump will be formed at Quarry in K.19.a.3.9. (Bonnay road) of 250,000 rounds. Company Transport Officers will be responsible that 50,000 rounds S.A.A. is dumped at this Quarry by dawn 7th.

8. OIL AND WATER. 2 Petrol tins of water per gun will be dumped at each gun position by dawn 7th, also sufficient supply of flannelette, etc.,
Reserve of oil, water, spare parts etc., will be kept at Battalion Headquarters at J.17.d.3.2. where the Battalion Armourer will be stationed.

9. COMMUNICATIONS.

(a) Telephone lines will be laid direct to Group Headquarters. An adequate system of runners must also be maintained.

(b) Communication with forward guns.

(i) O.C. "B" Company will have placed at his disposal Visual signallers who will go forward with him to 63rd Inf. Bde. H.Q.rs which will be established at approximately [illegible].

(ii) Communications of "B" Company will be through 64th Infantry Brigade.

(iii) Messages of "C" Coy's forward guns will be sent through O.C. "D" Coy. Lines will be laid to Nos. 5 and 6 Batteries.

(iv) "D" Coy's (10th Bn.M.G.C.) forward Btys. will work in conjunction with "A" and "B" Coys. Lines will be laid on to No.1.Battery.

(v) "D" Coy's (64th Bn.M.G.C.), will have a line direct with Battn. H.Q.rs and Batteries.

(c) Runners will only be used as a last resource.

10. PERSONNEL. Battery Commanders will arrange that only those men actually required at the guns should be employed in the gun positions. The remainder should be under cover in the vicinity of the guns ready to replace casualties and refill belts.

11. ACTION ON S.O.S. On S.O.S. signal being sent up (GREEN over GREEN over GREEN) the whole of the Batteries will at once open fire, less No.6 Battery rates of fire being as follows:-

250 rounds per minute for 10 minutes.

50 rounds per minute for a further 10 minutes.

Guns will then cease fire unless another S.O.S. signal is sent up.

12. SYNCHRONISATION OF WATCHES. Watches will be synchronised at Battalion Headquarters in J.17.d. at Zero minus 3 hours and Zero minus 1 hours.

13. ZERO HOUR. Will be notified later.

14. FORWARD MOVEMENT. No.7 and 8 Batteries of "D" Coy, 10th Bn.M.G.C. which are moving forward will be under the orders of Capt. [illegible], M.C.

These Batteries will not move forward - in the case of

(a) No.7. - until half an hour after the BLUE Line is consolidated, and -

(b) No.8. - until half an hour after the RED Line is consolidated

15. AMMUNITION BY AEROPLANE. The R.A.F. are issuing to the Battalion "V" shaped pieces of calico. These will be handed to all sections going forward and will be placed near position. Aeroplanes will then drop two boxes S.A.A. from each plane by parachute.

Aeroplane signals should be taken in as soon as each gun has 10,000 rounds

16. RATIONS. On Zero day all personnel will carry one day's rations plus the Iron Ration

17. SHOVELS. Two shovels per Gun team will be carried.

18. MEDICAL ARRANGEMENTS. Will be notified later by Medical Officer direct.

19. BATTLE SURPLUS. A battle surplus of 1 Officer and 10 men per Company must remain in C.M.G.O. control.

9. A C K N O W L E D G E.

Lieut & A/Adjt.,
18th Battalion Machine Gun Corps.

Issued at .... a.m. 8th Aug.1918.

No.1.Copy C.O.
" 2 " 2nd-in-Command.
" 3 " Adjutant.
" 4 " "A" Coy.
" 5 " "B" Coy.
" 6 " "C" Coy.
" 7 " "D" Coy, 18th Bn.M.G.C.
" 8 " "D" Coy, 58th Bn.M.G.C.
" 9 " T.O. & QMr.
" 10 " Signals, 18th Bn.M.G.C.
" 11 " 18th Division.
" 12 " Corps Machine Gun Officer.
" 13 " C.R.A. 18th Div.
" 14 " 53rd Inf. Bde.
" 15 " 54th Inf. Bde.
" 16 " 55th Inf. Bde.
" 17 " 58th Battn.M.G.C.
" 18/19 War Diary.
" 20 " File.

FIRE ORGANISATION ORDER

Group No.	Commanded by	Battery No.	Composition	Loc	Target	Time	Rate of fire
A.	O.C. D. Coy. 50th Bn. M.G.C.	1	4 guns	J. 18. d. 1. 1	Road K. 8. c. 7. 6 — K. 8. d. 2. 9	Z–Z + 2 hrs 15 mins	50 rounds per min.
		3	8 guns	J. 24. d. 5. 7	K. 14. b. 0. 7. K. 8. d. 9. 5.		
B.	O.C. B. Coy 18th Bn. M.G.C.	4	4 guns B. Coy 18th; 4 guns D. Coy 50th	K. 19. a. 1. 7	K. 15. a. 4. 3 — K. 15. b. 7. 5.		
C	O.C. C. Coy 18th Bn. M.G.C.	5	4 guns	K. 7. c. 4. 7	K. 9. a. 5. 0 — K. 9. b. 7. 0.		
		6	4 guns	K. 13. b. 8. 1	K. 22. c. 7. 2 — K. 28. b. 3. 6.	Z–Z + 2 hrs 15 mins.	50 rounds per min.
D.	O.C. D. Coy. 18th Bn. M.G.C.	2	8 guns	J. 18. d. 4. 9	K. 14. b. 1. 5 — K. 15. a. 4. 5	Z–Z. + 2 hrs. 15 mins.	50 rounds per min
		7.	4 guns	K. 21. a. 2. 5 approx.	K. 17. b. 4. 7 — K. 17. b. 8. 2.	Z + 3.45 – Z + 4.50	
		8.	4 guns	K. 22. d. 5. 5. approx	K. 24. d. 2. 8 — L. 19. c. 2. 4	Z + 5.15 – Z + 6.15	50 rounds per minute.

Identification Trace for use with Artillery Maps.

E K

K

LEGEND
Water & SAA dump ..... Δ
S.O.S. area ..... ▭
Consolidation Guns ..... o→

No. 5

No. 4

No. 2

No. 3

No. 1

BRITISH FRONT LINE

D E J K

J K

DIVL BDY

BDE BDY

NOTE.—(1). These traces are intended to facilitate the communication of information as to the position of targets, which have been located on a squared map.

(2). The squares on this trace are 500 yards in length on the 1/10,000 scale, 1,000 yards in length on the 1/20,000 scale, and 2,000 yards in length on the 1/40,000 scale.

(3). The squares on the trace are fitted to the squares of the map showing the targets, which are then drawn on the trace. Sufficient letters and numbers must also be added to enable the recipient to place the trace in the correct position on his own map. A little detail may also be traced, but this is not essential. The name and scale of the map to which the trace refers must be always given. The trace can be used for the 1/10,000, 1/20,000, or 1/40,000 scale.

G.S.G.S. 5023.

Tracing taken from Sheet 62D NE

of the 20,000 map of FRANCE.

Signature .... Date ....

SECRET. Copy No. 10

Reference Map:- Sheet.
62.d.N.E. 1/20,000.

APPENDIX 69.

6th August 1918.

18th BATTN. M.G.C. ORDER NO. 41.

1. A Counter-attack to re-establish the position lost this morning will be carried out by the 54th Infantry Brigade at a time to be notified later.

2. Action of M.Gs.
18 Guns of 18th Bn.M.G.C. plus 8 guns of "D" Coy, 50th Bn.M.G.C. will co-operate with barrage fire.

3. Distribution.
Guns will be distributed into 5 batteries as follows:-
No.1.Battery ... 4 Guns "C" Company.
No.2.Battery ... 4 Guns "B" Company.
No.3.Battery ... 8 Guns "D" Coy, 18th Battn.M.G.C.
No.4.Battery ... 4 Guns "D" Coy, 50th Battn.M.G.C.
No.5.Battery ... 2 Guns "B" Company.
Batteries will be sited as per the attached tracing.

4. Rates and times of Fire.
At Zero the M.G. barrage will come down on the BLUE Line and remain there for 15 minutes.
Rate of fire Medium, 120 - 150 rounds per minute.
All guns will then cease fire and remain in readiness to put down S.O.S. barrage if required.

5. Ammunition.
An adequate supply of ammunition must be carried up to all battery positions at once, and 8 belts per gun must be maintained for direct targets.

4a. Zero hour must be obtained from 54th Infantry Brigade direct.

6. Action on S.O.S.
Immediately S.O.S. signal is sent up (GREEN over GREEN over GREEN) the whole of the Batteries will open fire. Rates of fire being as follows:-
250 rounds per minute for 10 minutes.
50 rounds per minute for a further 10 minutes.
Guns will then cease fire unless another S.O.S. signal is sent up.

7. Synchronisation of Watches.
Watches will be synchronised as soon as possible at 54th Inf. Bde. H.Qrs at J.23.a.9.1.

8. A C K N O W L E D G E.

Lieut & A/Adjt.,
18th Battalion Machine Gun Corps.

Issued at 9 p.m.

No.1.Copy C.O.
" 2 " 2nd in Command.
" 3 " Adjutant.
" 4 " "B" Coy.
" 5 " "C" Coy.
" 6 " "D" Coy, 18th Bn.M.G.C.
" 7 " "D" Coy. 50th Bn.M.G.C.
" 8 " 18th Division 'G'
" 9 " 54th Infantry Brigade.
" 10/11" War Diary.
" 12 " File.

M

62 D N.E
1/20,000

use with Artillery Maps.

J

K

11

8

No 1
4 Guns
C Coy

No 2
4 Guns
B Coy

No 3.
8 Guns
D Coy

No 4
8 Guns
50th M G Bn

No 5
2 Guns
B Coy

23

1
2
3
4
5

Appendix 70

NARRATIVE OF OPERATIONS SHOWING THE PART PLAYED BY THE 18TH BATTALION M. G. CORPS AND "D" COMPANY, 50TH BN.M.G.C. (Attached) DURING THE PERIOD 7th to 10th AUGUST 1918.

Reference Map:- FRANCE. 62.d.N.E. & N.W. 1/20,000.

MACHINE GUNS.

Organisation. To support the attack guns were organised into :)-

(a) Barrage guns.
(b) Guns for consolidation forward.

They were distributed as follows:-

16 Guns for consolidation of the RED and GREEN Lines shown on attached Tracing "A".

8 Guns for consolidation of the BLUE Line and 8 guns for consolidation of 55th Infantry Brigade's Left Flank

44 Guns grouped in batteries as shown on attached Tracing "A".

ACTION OF M.Gs.

Night of 7th/8th August 1918.

At 8.50 p.m. the S.O.S, signal was answered by 10 minutes rapid and 10 minutes medium fire, many of the guns operating under heavy shell fire.

At Zero minus 25 minutes rapid fire was opened on S.O.S. lines for 5 minutes in accordance with instructions.

At Zero Batteries opened fire on S.O.S. lines at the rate of 250 rounds per minute for 10 minutes, then 50 rounds per minute for a further 10 minutes.

16 Guns of "A" Company which were attached to 53rd Inf. Bde were allocated as follows:-

2 Guns to 8th Royal Berkshire Regiment.
2 Guns to 10th Essex Regiment.
4 Guns to 7th Royal West Kent Regiment.

and the remaining 8 guns for consolidation in depth and overhead fire batteries.

At Zero plus 15 minutes the guns detailed to the above three Units moved forward from the Valley in J.17.b. to the assembling point of their respective Reserve Companies who were moving forward at Zero plus 30 minutes. Owing to the very thick mist the situation became very vague. The guns however eventually pushed forward into the following positions:-

2 Guns at K.20.d.9.9.
2 Guns at K.20.d.1.8.
4 Guns at K.20.b.1.5 and K.20.a.8.8.

and engaged enemy Machine Guns and snipers in the Aerodrome in K.21.a. and on the ridge behind in K.21.Central and K.21.d. also parties of the enemy in K.15.d.

The remaining 8 guns were sent forward and eventually established themselves :-

4 Guns in K.20.c.5.3. and 5.5.
4 Guns in K.20.c.0.5. and 0.0.

The situation was at that time very obscure.

The 8 Guns of "B" Company moved forward shortly after 2 p.m. but found the situation so uncertain that positions were taken up :-

4 Guns in CUMMINS TRENCH and
4 Guns in CROYDON TRENCH,

on left of the BRAY - CORBIE Road.

At 7.30 a.m. the mist having cleared, a further reconnaissance was made and the guns in CUMMINS TRENCH were moved forward to a position at K.25.b.10.70 to protect the left flank.

The 8 Guns of "C" Company moved forward at 8 a.m. and eventually got into positions at :-

4 Guns in CLONCURRY TRENCH.
4 Guns in trench in K.14.c.

These guns obtained several direct targets in MORLANCOURT and inflicted casualties.
During the day intermittent bursts of fire were kept up by the batteries on their S.O.S. lines.

4 Guns were detailed to report to 5th Brigade R.H.A. where they acted as escort to guns moving forward to advanced positions.

<u>Night of 8th/9th August.</u>

In accordance with orders firing was carried out as follows by all S.O.S. guns :-

3.35 a.m. to 4 a.m. Medium Rate.
4.20 to 4.30 a.m. Rapid.

Particular attention being given to the valley in K.10.c. and all roads and tracks East of MORLANCOURT, and throughout the morning direct targets were continuously engaged in MORLANCOURT.

Harassing fire was kept up until 5.30 a.m. when our Infantry again attacked. Numerous casualties were inflicted on the enemy evacuating MORLANCOURT by our guns in K.14.c.

<u>Night of 9th/10th August.</u>

The night passed without incident and after dark on the 15th all guns were withdrawn to rear Battn. H.Qrs at C.21.c. Central in accordance with orders.

<u>Casualties.</u>

Statement showing casualties incurred by Battalion during these operations is attached (Appendix "B")

~~Lessons Learnt.~~

~~Attached. (Appendix "C")~~

(Sgd) E.C.L. Munet. Lieut-Colonel,
Commanding 18th Battalion Machine Gun Corps.

15th August 1918.

APPENDIX "B".

CASUALTIES INCURRED DURING THE
PERIOD 8th to 10th AUGUST 1918.

Officers.

,Lieut. W. RAMAGE, Wounded, Slightly at Duty 7.8.18.

Other Ranks. (18th Battalion Machine Gun Corps)

Date.	Killed.	Wounded,	Wounded at Duty.	Missing.
8th.	3	10	5	1
9th.	-	1	-	-
TOTALS:-	3	11	5	1

(50th Battn. M.G.C. - "D" Coy)

8th.	1	15	-	-
GRAND TOTAL:-	4	26	5	1

--------oOo------

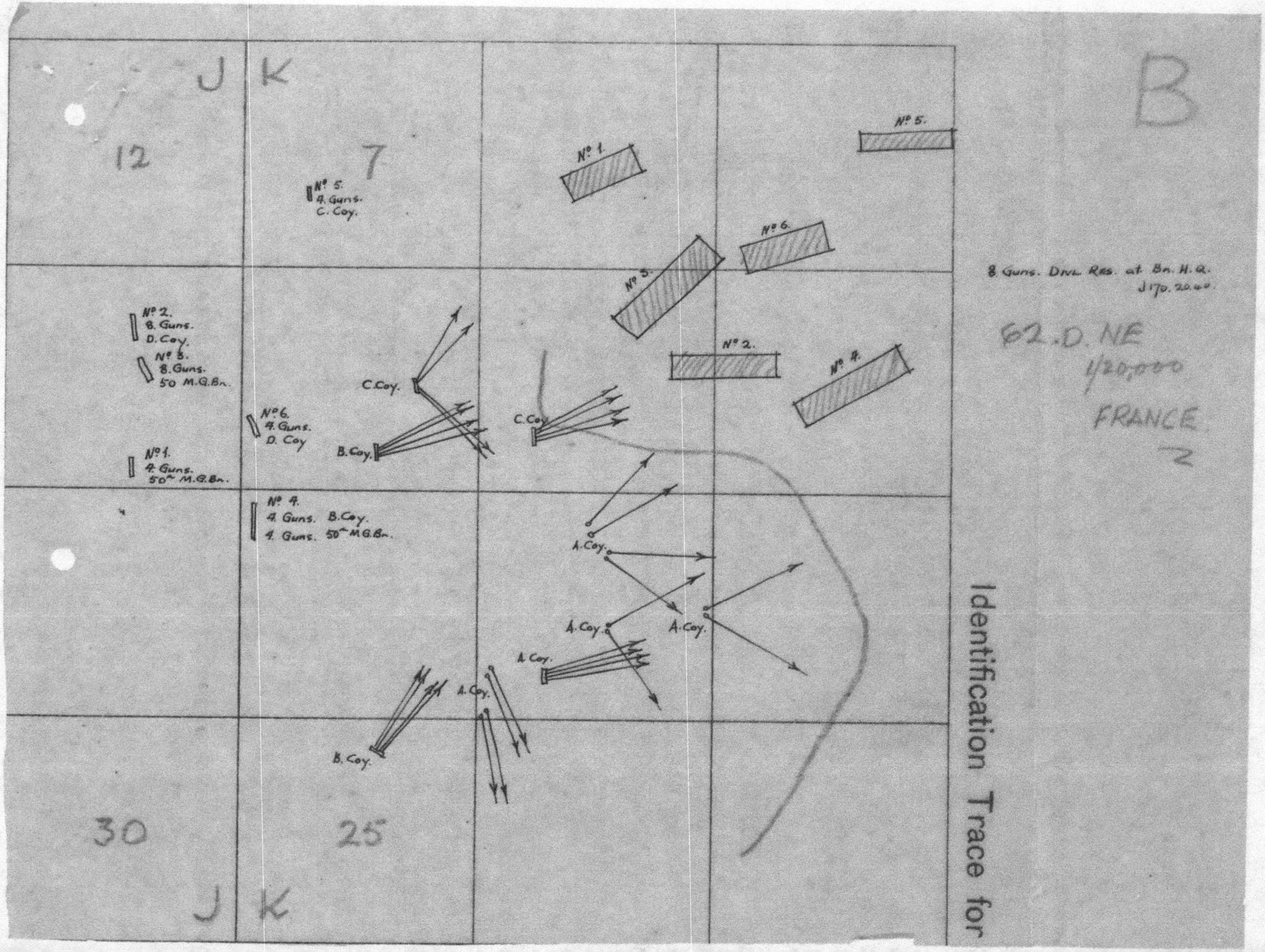

Identification Trace for

B

8 Guns. Divl. Res. at Bn. H.Q.
J170.20.40.

62.D. NE
1/20,000
FRANCE
2

J K

12

7

Nº 5.
4. Guns.
C. Coy.

Nº 2.
8. Guns.
D. Coy.

Nº 3.
8. Guns.
50 M.G.Bn.

Nº 1.
4. Guns.
50th M.G.Bn.

Nº 6.
4. Guns.
D. Coy

Nº 4.
4. Guns. B.Coy.
4. Guns. 50th M.G.Bn.

C.Coy.

B.Coy.

C.Coy.

A.Coy.

A.Coy.

A.Coy.

A.Coy.

A.Coy.

B.Coy.

Nº 1.

Nº 5.

Nº 6.

Nº 3.

Nº 2.

Nº 4.

30

25

J K

SECRET. APPENDIX 71 Copy No. 9....

Reference Map:- SENLIS 1/20,000. 11th August 1918.

18TH BATTN. M. G. C. ORDER No. 42.

1. The 18th Battn.M.G.C. will relieve the 47th Bn. M.G.C. in the line in the Northern sector of the III Corps front.

2. (a) Companies will be distributed as follows:-
"B" Coy will relieve the left Coy, 47th Bn.M.G.C.
"D" Coy will relieve the right Coy, 47th Bn.M.G.C.
"C" Coy will relieve Support Company.
"A" Coy will be in reserve in WARLOY.
(b) 123rd American Machine Gun Battalion will be allotted to the BAIZIEUX Defence system and 123rd American Regtl. M.G. Companies will be responsible for the defence of the Southern sector.

3. Arrangements regarding relief will be made between Company Commanders concerned.

4. Receipts will be ~~xxxx~~ given for all trench stores taken over (including any tents and shelters) and same will be forwarded to Orderly Room, in duplicate, by 12 noon 12th inst.

5. Completion of relief will be reported to Bn. H.Q. by wire using the number of this order.

6. Bn. H.Qrs. will close at C.21.c.Central at 2 p.m. to-day and re-open in WARLOY on arrival.

7. A C K N O W L E D G E.

H. Corran

Lieut & A/Adjt.,
18th Battalion Machine Gun Corps.

Issued at 11.40 a.m. Copies to:-

No.1.Copy C.O.
" 2 " 2nd in Command.
" 3 " Adjutant.
" 4 " "A" Company.
" 5 " "B" Company.
"" 6 " "C" Company.
" 7 " "D" Company.
" 8 " T.O. & QrMr.
" 9 " War Diary.
" 10 " War Diary.
" 11 " File.

SECRET. 18th Battn. M.G.C. No. S.83.

APPENDIX 72

To:- "A", "B", "C", "D" Coys 18th Bn.M.G.C.
18th Division, 53rd and 54th Inf. Bdes.
T.O. Sigs. 123rd M. G. Battn.

15th August 1918.

Amendment to 18th Bn.M.G.C. No.S.81.

1. The following reliefs will take place to-night:-

"A" Company relieve "B" Company.
"C" Company relieve "D" Company.

"B" Company will then stand by at Company H.Qrs. ready to move at half-hour's notice under orders of G.O.C. 54th Inf. Bde.

"D" Company will move to WARLOY and take over billets of "A" Company and stand by ready to move at half-hour's notice under orders of G.O.C. 54th Infantry Brigade.

Completion of reliefs will be notified to Battalion Headquarters using Code word "STARRY"

2. TRANSPORT.
"A" Company Transport remains in WARLOY.
"B" Company Transport moves to "B" Coy. H.Qrs (Fighting limbers and Officers Chargers only)
Where bomb stops not available animals are to be spread out.
"C" Company Transport remains WARLOY.
"D" Company Transport takes over "B" Coy's Lines.
The Companies moving forward, i.e., "B" and "D" will have Pack saddles on all off-side mules, also two spare pack animals per Company.

3. SIGNAL COMMUNICATION.
The Signal Officer will detail at once 5 signallers to each Company going forward equipped with signal apparatus to be carried forward on fighting limbers.

4. Should the move forward take place before the reliefs, Coys. will carry out Orders issued under No.S.81.

5. Advanced Battn. H.Q. will move to dug-out in MAZE V.24.d. 80.55 as soon as the move forward is ordered.

6. O.C. "D" Company will at once detail an Officer for liaison with the 54th Infantry Brigade.

H. Cooper

Lieut & A/Adjt.,
18th Battalion Machine Gun Corps.

Issued at 12.45 p.m.

SECRET. APPENDIX 73. Copy No. 10

Reference Map:- SENLIS 1/20,000. 19th August 1918.

18TH BN. M. G. C. ORDER No. 43.

1. "D" Company, 18th Battn. M.G.C. will relieve "C" Coy. 18th Bn.M.G.C. in the right Sector of the front covered by this Battn, to-night 19/20th August 1918.

2. All details of relief will be arranged between Company Commanders concerned.

3. Completion of relief will be reported to Battalion H.Q. by wire, using the number of this Order.

4. "C" and "D" Coys, 18th Bn.M.G.C. to Acknowledge.

H. Corran

Lieut & A/Adjt.,
18th Battalion Machine Gun Corps;

Issued at 2.20 p.m.

Copies to:-

No.1.Copy C.O.
" 2 " Second-in-Command.
" 3 " Adjutant.
" 4 " "A" Coy.
" 5 " "B" Coy.
" 6 " "C" Coy.
" 7 " "D" Coy.
" 8 " T.O.&.QrMr.
" 9 " 123rd American M.G.Bn.
" 10 " War Diary.
" 11 " War Diary.
" 12 " File.

SECRET. Copy No. 9...

Reference Map:- SENLIS 1/20,000. APPENDIX 74 20th August 1918.

18TH BATTALION M.G.C. ORDER No. 44.

1. The following reliefs will take place to-night:-

2. "B" Company 50th Battn. M.G.C. will relieve 123rd American M.G.Bn. in right Divisional Sector, but will not take over their gun positions. They will, however, take over the Company H.Qrs situated at approximately NINE ELMS, also, all S.A.A. and Fortress Rations (if any) at these quarters.

Battery positions ~~xxx~~ as pointed out by O.C. "B" Company 18th Bn.M.G.C. are to be prepared forthwith and 15,000 rounds S.A.A. placed at each gun position.

Battery positions to be completed by 11 p.m. 21st August 1918, and all lines of fire laid out according to instructions that will be issued later.

The Battery of 4 Guns pointed out as detached from the rest of the Company, will not be placed in these positions. Further instructions as to this Battery will be issued later.

3. "C" Company 50th Bn.M.G.C. will relieve "A" Company 18th Battn.M.G.C. according to verbal instructions given. Battery positions as pointed out by O.C. "A" Coy 18th Bn.M.G.C. will be prepared and 15,000 rounds S.A.A. dumped at each gun position and line of fire laid out according to instructions to be issued later, to be completed by 11 p.m. 21st inst, and Battn. H.Qrs notified to this effect.

4. Completion of relief in both cases to be reported to Battn. H.Qrs by wire using the number of this order.

5. Acknowledge.

H Corran

Lieut & A/Adjt.,
18th Battalion Machine Gun Corps.

Issued at 4 p.m. Copies to:-

No.1.Copy C.O.
" 2 " "A" Company. 18th Bn.M.G.C.
" 3 " "B" Coy, 50th Bn.M.G.C.
" 4 " "C" Coy, 50th Bn.M.G.C.
" 5 " 123rd American M. G. Battn.
" 6 " Signal Officer.
" 7 " QrMr. and T.O.
" 8 " War Diary.
" 9 " War Diary.
" 10 " File.

DISPOSITIONS OF GUNS
TAKEN OVER BY 18TH BATn MGC.
FROM. 47 BAT. MGC.

Identification Trace for use with Artillery Maps.

APPENDIX. 75

SUPPORT GROUP HQ
4 GUNS SUPPORT GROUP
RIGHT GROUP HQ
LEFT COY HQ
RIGHT COY HQ.

B17 B39 B38 B11 B10 B4 B48 B8 B46 B2 B7 B6 B5 B35 B45 B49 B47 A16 A15 A17 A23 B40 A19 A10 A21 A7 A31 A30 A4 A25 A32 A2 A24 A1 A26 A36

V W
D E
D E

RIGHT GROUP	RED
LEFT GROUP	GREEN
SUPPORT GROUP	PURPLE
124 AMERICAN BN. MG. GUNS	
A·B	BROWN
C·D	BLACK
⊙ 2	GUNS
⊙ 4	"

NOTE.—(1). These traces are intended to facilitate the communication of information as to the position of targets, which have been located on a squared map.

(2). The squares on this trace are 500 yards in length on the 1/10,000 scale, 1,000 yards in length on the 1/20,000 scale, and 2,000 yards in length on the 1/40,000 scale.

(3). The squares on the trace are fitted to the squares of the map showing the targets, which are then drawn on the trace. Sufficient letters and numbers must also be added to enable the recipient to place the trace in the correct position on his own map. A little detail may also be traced, but this is not essential. The name and scale of the map to which the trace refers must be always given. The trace can be used for the 1/10,000, 1/20,000, or 1/40,000 scale.

Tracing taken from Sheet SENLIS

of the 1: 20,000 map of FRANCE

Signature .... Date ....

G.S.G.S. 3023.

SECRET. APPENDIX 76 Copy No. 19..

Reference Map:- SHEETS, 1/20.000. 20th August 1918

18TH BATTN. M.G.C. ORDER No. 45.

1. The III Corps will attack the enemy's positions between BRAY and ALBERT at an hour, and on a date to be notified later.

The 18th Division will cover the flank of the main attack by forming a defensive flank East of ALBERT.

The 12th Division will be on our right.

On our Divisional front the 54th Infantry Brigade will attack on the right, the 55th Infantry Brigade on the left.

2. ACTION OF M.Gs.

The 18th Battn. M.G.C. and two Companies of the 50th Battn. M.G.C. will be disposed as follows:-

18th Bn.M.G.C.	("A" Coy. in Reserve attached to 53rd Inf. Bde.	
	("B" Coy. attached to 54th Inf. Bde.	
	("C" Coy. attached to 55th Inf. Bde.	
	("D" Coy. in Divisional Reserve)	Firing covering barrage
50th Bn.M.G.C.	("B" Coy. in Divisional Reserve)	
	("C" Coy. in Divisional Reserve)	

The two Companies with attacking Brigades ("B" and "C" Coys. 18th Bn.M.G.C.) to be used for consolidation of ground captured and to take up defensive positions in depth, vide tracing "A". X When these positions are taken up all guns will be at once laid on S.O.S. lines for a defensive barrage covering the captured position.

X. To be forwarded later.

The two Companies of the 50th Battn.M.G.C. and "D" Company 18th Bn.M.G.C. are providing covering barrage fire on selected areas as shown on Tracing "B"

"D" Company, 18th Battn.M.G.C. is to be prepared, on orders being received, to move up to the approximate line of roadway in E.11.a. and c, to provide a protective S.O.S. barrage in front of right Brigade objective after consolidation

Group C.50 will, after consolidation of objective lay out enfilade S.O.S. protective barrage covering left Brigade front.

One section of 4 guns of 12th Bn.M.G.C. are assisting during the advance, as shown on Tracing "B" and subsequently by moving up two pairs of guns covering the right Brigade front after consolidation of objective.

3. COMPOSITION OF BATTERIES. and

Times and rates of fire are as shown on Fire Organization Chart attached

4. AMMUNITION SUPPLY.

15,000 rounds per gun must be kept at each position.

3,000 rounds per gun will always be kept, in belts, in reserve for S.O.S. and direct targets.

Forward dumps will be established under arrangements to be made by Company Commanders.

5. COMMUNICATIONS.

Communication will be maintained by telephone and visual as shown on the attached Appendix "C".

Five signallers will be allotted to each Company with the attacking Brigades ("B" and "C" Coys. 18th Bn.M.G.C)

Five signallers will also be allotted to "A" Coy. 18th Bn. M.G.C. should it be necessary for this Company to move forward but these will not be detailed until required.

6. ACTION OF S.O.S.

On the S.O.S. Signal (RED over RED over RED) being sent up, all batteries laid on S.O.S. lines will open fire at the rate of:-

250 rounds per minute for 10 Minutes.
50 rounds per minute for a further 10 Minutes.

7. RATIONS.

On "Z" Day all personnel will carry one day's rations plus the iron ration.

Fortress rations, not required, will be returned to Company H.Qrs by Company Transport to-night.

8. SYNCHRONISATION OF WATCHES.

Watches will be synchronised at Brigade Headquarters at Z - 3 and Z - 2 hours.

9. ZERO HOUR.

Zero hour will be notified later.

10. PICKS, SHOVELS and SANDBAGS.

Each Gun team going forward will carry 1 pick and 1 shovel and 2 sandbags per man.

11. MEDICAL ARRANGEMENTS.

Medical arrangements will be notified later.

12. PREPARATIONS.

All Battery positions must be completed; ammunition, oil, water etc., dumped, lines of fire laid out and guns ready for firing by 11 p.m. 21st inst. A notification to this effect being sent to Advanced Battalion Headquarters.

These positions must be carefully camouflaged.

One extra barrel per gun must be taken forward.

13. LOCATIONS.

Battn.H.Q. (Advanced)		W.25.b.2.7.
(Rear)		WARLOY.
"A" Company.)		53rd Brigade H.Qrs.
"B" Company.)	18th	54th Brigade H.Qrs
"C" Company.)	Bn.	55th Brigade H.Qrs.
"D" Company.)	M.G.C.	E.3.c.4.3. + Bn Adv HQ
"B" Company 50th Bn.		QUARRY in E.14.c.
"C" Company 50th Bn.		W.20.d.99.10.

14. Os.C. Companies attached Brigades, will report to Advanced Battn. H.Qrs. the location of their Advanced Coy.H.Qrs when moved forward, also dispositions of their guns.

15. TANKS.

The following signals will be used from Tanks to Infantry:-

(a) A green and white flag to indicate "Come on".

(b) A red and yellow flag to indicate "I have broken down, go on".

(c) A tricolour flag to indicate that the tank is returning out of action and prevent its being mistaken for an enemy tank.

16. BATTLE SURPLUS.

Battle surplus will be retained at Rear Company H.Qrs. which will not move until further orders.

C.Cuthbert Major,
Commanding 18th Battalion Machine Gun Corps.

Issued at ..9:15 p.m. by D.R.L.S. Copies to:-

No.1. C.O.	No.9. T.O.&.Qrmr.	No.15. "B"Coy. 50th.Bn.
" 2 2nd-in-Command.	" 10. 18th Division 'G'	" 16. "C" " 50th Bn.
" 3 Adjutant.	" 11. 53rd Inf.Bde.	" 17. H.Q.50th Bn.M.G.C.
" 4 "A" Company.	" 12 54th Inf.Bde.	" 18. H.Q.12th Bn.M.G.C.
" 5 "B" Company.	" 13. 55th Inf.Bde.	" 19. War Diary.
" 6 "C" Company.	" 14. C.M.G.O.,III Corps."	20. War Diary.
" 7 "D" Company.		" 21. File.
" 8 Signal Officer.		

FIRE ORGANIZATION CHART.

GROUP C.50.

Commanded by O.C. "C" Company, 50th Battn. M.G.C.

Batty.	No.of Guns.	Location Approx.	Task.	Target.	Time.	Rate of Fire.
G.	8	W.22.c.5.8.	1.	E.10.b.0.8. - E.4.d.0.4.	(a) Z - Z plus 10. (b) Z plus 10 - Z plus 20.	250 rds.per min 50 " " "
			2.	W.29.a.2.2 - W.29.c.6.4.	Z plus 30 - Z plus ~~60~~.60	50 r.p.m.
			3.	W.29.a.7.2.- W.29.d.6.0.	Z plus ~~[illegible]~~ -70 Z plus ~~145~~.120	50 r.p.m.
			4.	W.30.a.1.2 - W.30.c.8.5.	S.O.S.	10 mins.250 rpm 10 " 50 rpm
H.	8	W.22.a.9.2.	1.	E.4.d.0.4. - E.4.b.3.3.	(a) Z - Z plus 10. (b) Z plus 10 - Z plus 20.	250 r.p.m. 50 r.p.m.
			2.	W.29.c.6.3.- E.5.a.9.5.	Z plus 30 - Z plus ~~[illegible]~~. 60	50 r.p.m.
			3.	W.29.d.6.0 - E.5.b.3.7.	Z plus ~~[illegible]~~.-70 Z plus ~~145~~.120	50 r.p.m.
			4.	W.29.b.8.2.- W.30.a.1.2.	S.O.S.	10 mins.250 rpm. 10 mins 50 rpm.

-----oOo------

FIRE ORGANIZATION CHART.

GROUP, D.18.

Commanded by Captain N. RYDER, M.C. 18th Battn. M.G.C.

Battery.	No. of Guns.	Location Approx.	Task.	Target.	Time.	Rate of Fire.
D.	8	E.9.a.8.0.	1.	E.10.b.0.2. - E.10.b.0.8.	Z - Z plus 10.	250 rds.p.m.
			2.	E.10.d.6.2. - E.10.d.7.6.	Z plus 15 - Z plus 40.	50 r.p.m.
E.	4	E.3.c.6.0.	1.	E.5.c.4.0. - E.5.c.5.4.	Z - Z plus 60.	50 r.p.m.
			2.	E.5.d.8.6. - E.6.c.2.7.	Z plus 65 - Z plus 90.	50 r.p.m.
F.	4	E.3.a.7.3.	1.	E.5.c.5.4. - E.5.c.6.7.	Z - Z plus 60.	50 r.p.m.
			2.	E.5.d.7.4. - E.6.c.1.3.	Z plus 65 - Z plus 90.	50 r.p.m.

FIRE ORGANISATION CHART.

GROUP B.50.

Commanded by Major. F. H. PASTEUR, M.C.

Battery.	Task.	Location Approx.	Target.	No. of Guns.	Time.	Rate of Fire.
"A"	1	E.15.d.2.0.	E.16.b.0.3.- E.16.b.0.9.	4	Z - Z + 10	250 rds. per min.
	2		E.11.b.0.0 - E.11.b.3.4.	4	Z + 15 - Z + 45	50 " " "
"B"	1	E.15.c.2.2.	E.10.d.0.0.- E.10.d.0.6.	6	Z - Z + 10	250 " " "
	2		E.11.c.5.4.- E.11.c.9.9.	6	Z + 15 - Z + 40	50 " " "
"C"	1	E.15.c.3.6.	E.10.d.0.6 - E.10.b.0.2.	6	Z - Z + 10	250 " " "
	2		E.17.a.2.6 - E.11.c.8.0.		Z + 15 - Z + 60	50 " " "
	3		E.11.c.8.0.- E.11.d.4.4.		Z + 65 - Z + 45	50 " " "

-----------ooo--------

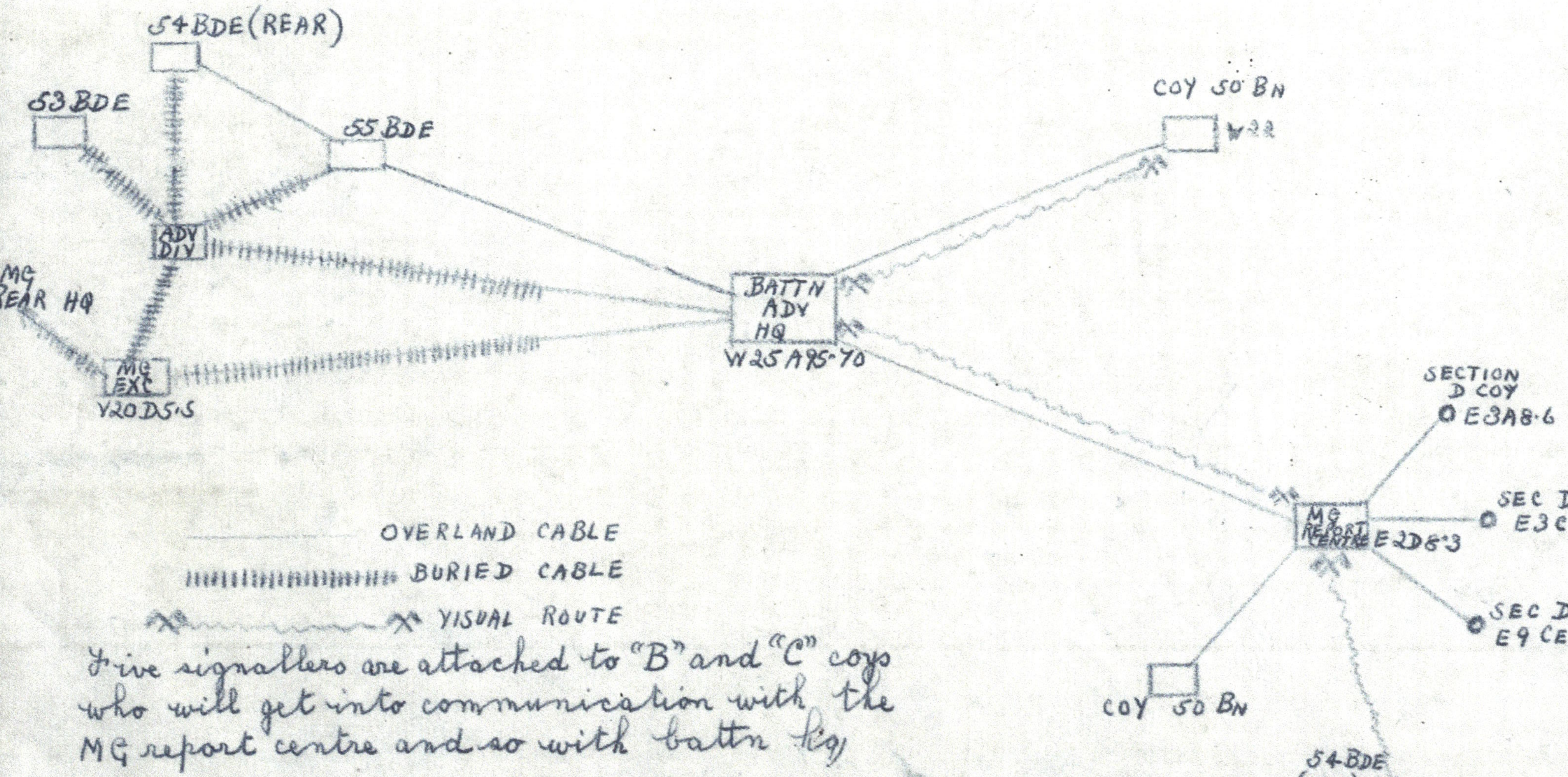
Appendix "C"
18th Bn MACHINE GUN CORPS
COMMUNICATIONS 9·0PM 21st AUG 1918
54 BDE (REAR)
53 BDE
55 BDE
ADV DIV
MG REAR HQ
MG EXC
Y20D5·5
BATTN ADV HQ
W25A95·70
COY 50 BN
W22
SECTION D COY
E3A8·6
SEC D COY
E3C6·1
MG REPORT CENTRE
E2D8·3
SEC D COY
E9 CENTRAL
COY 50 BN
54 BDE (ADV)
OVERLAND CABLE
BURIED CABLE
VISUAL ROUTE
Five signallers are attached to "B" and "C" coys
who will get into communication with the
MG report centre and so with battn hq

A

use with Artillery Maps.

SOME PROPOSED POSITIONS AFTER CONSOLIDATION.

W X

E F

12 M.G. Gn.

12 M.G. Gn.

Note. 2 Guns at W 29 a 86. are forward Consolidation Guns.

E F

… located on a squared map.
…le, and 2,000 yards in length

… on the trace. Sufficient
…own map. A little detail
… always given. The trace

Tracing taken from Sheet SENLIS

of the 1:/20,000 map of

Signature .... Date ....

Identification Trace for use with Artillery Maps.

LEGEND

1st Barrage.
2nd do.
3rd do.

B

DIV BDY

55 BDE

54 BDE

DIV BDY

V W W X

D E E F

D E E F

NOTE.—(1). These traces are intended to facilitate the communication of information as to the position of targets, which have been located on a squared map.

(2). The squares on this trace are 500 yards in length on the 1/10,000 scale, 1,000 yards in length on the 1/20,000 scale, and 2,000 yards in length on the 1/40,000 scale.

(3). The squares on the trace are fitted to the squares of the map showing the targets, which are then drawn on the trace. Sufficient letters and numbers must also be added to enable the recipient to place the trace in the correct position on his own map. A little detail may also be traced, but this is not essential. The name and scale of the map to which the trace refers must be always given. The trace can be used for the 1/10,000, 1/20,000, or 1/40,000 scale.

G.S.G.S. 3025.

Tracing taken from Sheet SENLIS

of the 1: 20,000 map of FRANCE.

Signature .... Date ....

18th Battn. M.G.C. No. S. 124.

To:- All Units. APPENDIX 77

The Divisional Commander directs that attached letter from G.O.C-in-Chief be communicated to all ranks without delay.

H. Corran

Lieut for Major,
24th August 1918. Commanding 18th Battalion Machine Gun Corps.

"General Sir H.S. RAWLINSON,
Commanding Fourth Army., O.A.D.911.

" I request that Army Commanders will, without delay, bring to the notice of all subordinate leaders the changed conditions under which operations are now being carried on and the consequent necessity for all ranks to act with the utmost boldness and resolution in order to get full advantage from the present favourable situation.

" The effect of the two very severe defeats and the continuous attacks to which the enemy has been subjected during the past month has been to wear out his troops and disorganise his plans. Our Second and Fifth Armies have taken their share in this effort to destroy the enemy and already have gained considerable ground from him in the LYS Sector of our front. To-day the Tenth French Army crossed the AILETTE and reports that a Bavarian Division fled in panic, carrying back with it another Division which was advancing to its support. To-morrow the attack of the Allied Armies on the whole front from SOISSONS to NEUVILLE-VITASSE (near ARRAS) is to be continued.

" The methods which we have followed hitherto in our battles with limited objectives when the enemy was strong are no longer suited to his present condition. The enemy has not the means to deliver counter-attacks on an extended scale, nor has he the numbers to hold a continuous position against the very extended advance which is now being directed upon him.

" To turn the present situation to account the most resolute offensive is everywhere desirable. Risks which a month ago would have been criminal to incur ought now to be incurred as a duty. It is no longer necessary to advance in regular lines and step by step. On the contrary, each Division should be given a distant objective which must be reached independently of its neighbour and even if one's flank is thereby exposed for the time being.

" Reinforcements must be directed on the points where our troops are gaining ground, not where they are checked. A vigorous offensive against the sectors where the enemy is weak will cause hostile strong points to fall, and, in due course, our whole Army will be able to continue its advance. This procedure will result in speedily breaking up the hostile forces and will cost us much less than if we attempted to deal with the present situation in a half hearted manner.

" The situation is most favourable. Let each one of us act energetically and without hesitation push forward to our objective".

22nd August 1918. (Signed) D. HAIG.

SECRET.

III Corps. No.E.13218.
18th Div.No.14/31/1"G"
18th Battn.M.G.C.No.S.121.

APPENDIX 78

To:- Os.C. "A", "B", "C", "D" Coys 18th Bn.M.G.C.
T.Os. "A", "B", "C", "D" H.Q. Coys. do.,
O.C. 50th Battalion Machine Gun Corps.
Os.C. "B", "C" Coys 50th Battn.M.G.C.
T.Os. "B", "C" Coys do.,
Quarter-Master, 18th Bn.M.G.C.

WATER SUPPLY ARRANGEMENTS FOR THE FORWARD AREA
FOR 22nd August 1918.

1. Water Point at D.29.b.3.8. Will open at 12 noon 22nd inst. It will consist of:-

1 Water Cart Filler.
1 Chlorinating set with water bottle fillers.
200 F.R. Horse Troughing.

It is fed by pipe line from Pump at BUIRE.

2. Water point at J.22.a.5.8. Will open during morning of 22nd inst. It will consist of:-

1 Water Cart Filler.
2 Chlorinating Sets with Water Bottle Fillers.

It is supplied by pipe line from Pump in J.28.c.
200 F.R. Horse Troughing will be in use here from 6 p.m. 22nd inst.

3. Water Point at I.30.a. This consists of Storage Tanks, 7,000 gallons capacity. Fed by Garford Water Lorries and already in operation.

4. Water Point at J.16.d. This consists of Storage Tanks, 7,000 gallons capacity. Fed by Garford Water Lorries and already in operation.

Chief Engineer, III Corps will move these tanks forward along the BRAY - CORBIE Road if and when requested to do so by the 47th Division. Their erection at the new point will take about 8 hours from receipt of notice.

5. Chief Engineer, III Corps will erect Tanks, total capacity 7,000 gallons, at a point on the ALBERT - AMIENS Road forward of D.19 - 20, when requested to do so by the 18th Division. This work will take approximately 8 hours from receipt of request. Tanks will be filled by Garford Water Lorries night of 22nd/23rd inst.

6. Water Sterilizing Lorry Points are already in operation at:-

(a) RIBEMONT - J.3.Central.
(b) TREUX CHATEAU - J.6.a.4.2.

These each have Cart and Water Bottle Fillers, and an average daily supply of 5,000 gallons.

M. Corran
Lieut.

23rd August 1918.

Act.Adjt, 18th Battalion Machine Gun Corps

SECRET. 18th/Div/No/14/21/2 (Q).
18th Battn. M.G.C. No. [illegible].

APPENDIX 79

To:- **ALL UNITS.**

The following is a resume of all correspondence issued with regard to Water Points in forward area:-

(1) A good well with a windlass in yard of Bellevue Farm.

(2) A well with hand pump at R.10.b.2.8.

(3) A good spring at R.4.a.6.6. (1 scoop of lime to each water cart.)

(4) A well with petrol pump at Cross Roads R.3.c.2.6.

(5) Water Tanks erected at W.30.a.1.7., capacity about 3000 gallons, these will be filled by water lorry each night.

(6) Water point at R.29.b.3.8. petrol pump,(as soon as situation admits, the present pump will be replaced by a steam pump of larger capacity), consists of :-

1 Water Cart filler.
1 Chlorinating set with water bottle fillers.
200 ft. Horse Troughing.

(7) Water sterilising points at :-

(a) RIBEMONT - J.3.central.
(b) TREUX CHATEAU. J.6.a.4.3.

Sterilising lorries, temporarily inactive until amount of poisoning in water is ascertained.

These all have Cart and Water Bottle fillers and an average daily supply of 5000 gallons.

(8) Water Point at W.26.d. Tanks have been erected and 6 lorries detailed to fill to-night.

Water troughs will be erected in the vicinity of running water where required by formations. Application should be made to Division "Q" giving proposed site. Horses should not be taken into the stream to water if it can be avoided.

H. Morran

Lieut. & A/Adjt.
24th August 1918. 18th Battalion Machine Gun Corps.

18th Battn.M.G.C.No.S.132.

APPENDIX 80.

18TH BATTALION MACHINE GUN CORPS.

-NARRATIVE OF OPERATIONS-

22nd August 1918

to

5th September 1918.

PHASE I. Attack of 54th and 55th Inf. Bdes.

PHASE II. Attacks of 53rd Inf. Bde. on TARA HILL and CHAPES SPUR.

PHASE III. Advance of 54th and 55th Brigades to MONTAUBAN.

PHASE IV. Capture of BERNAFAY and TRONES WOODS by 53rd Inf. Bde. with 7th Bn.Queens R.W.S.Regt. attached.

PHASE V. Advance of 54th Inf. Bde. on COMBLES.

PHASE VI. Attack by 55th Bde. on N.W. corner of ST PIERRE VAAST WOOD to capture of SAILLISEL by 7th Royal West Kents.

PHASE VII. Capture of ST PIERRE VAAST WOOD by 53rd Inf. Bde. and subsequent advance to line of TORTILLE RIVER.

----------OOO----------

DISTRIBUTION.

Commanding Officer	1 Copy.
2nd in Command,	1 "
Adjutant.	1 "
"A","B","C","D",Coys	2 Copies each. (18th Bn).
Signals.	1 Copy.
H.Qrs. 50th Bn.M.G.C.	1 Copy.
"B" & "C" Coys 50th.	1 Copy.each.
18th Division.	1 "
53rd,54th,55th I.Bds.	1 " each.
D.I.M.G.U.	1 Copy.
CMGO. III Corps.	1 "
War Diary.	2 Copies.
File.	1 Copy.

-0-0-0-0-0-0-0-0-0-0-0-0-0-0-0-0-

18TH BATTALION MACHINE GUN CORPS.

N A R R A T I V E   O F   O P E R A T I O N S.
22nd August - 5th September 1918.

FIRST PHASE:- Attack of 54th and 55th Infantry Brigades.

(12 midnight 21st - 12 midnight 22nd)

Ref Map:- Sheet SENLIS, 1/20,000.   18th Battn.M.G.C.Order No.45

ORGANISATION.
Battalion Headquarters:- W.25.b.2.7.
The Battalion had at its disposal, 4 Companies 18th Bn.M.G.C. and "B" and "C" Coys. 50th Battn.M.G.C. These were organised into:-

(a) 2 Companies for consolidation forward, co-operating with Infantry Brigades.
(b) 1 Company in Reserve, attached to 53rd Infantry Brigade.
(c) 3 Companies in Divisional Reserve, firing covering barrages.

ACTION OF M.Gs. FIRING BARRAGE.
All guns were in position at 12 midnight 21st.
At 3 a.m. 22nd information was received from 54th Infantry Brigade, that Infantry were on the line of the road E.4.d.0.0 - E.16.b.0.0. Companies firing covering barrage were at once notified and necessary alterations made in barrage scheme.
Zero hour:- 4.45 a.m.
At Zero plus 70 all batteries opened fire at rate of 50 rounds perminute for 50 minutes. Guns of "C" Company, 50th Bn.M.G.C. were then laid on S.O.S. lines to cover left flank of final objective.
At 10 a.m. "D" Coy, 18th Bn.M.G.C. was withdrawn from Battery positions and sections concentrated in E.2.d. ready to move forward with 53rd Infantry Brigade.
At 12 noon, "B" Coy, 50th Bn.M.G.C. was withdrawn from Battery positions and distributed for defence of line of railway in E.9.c. and E.15.a.
1 p.m. to 1.30 p.m. In conjunction with attack of 55th Infantry Brigade "C" Coy, 50th Bn. harassed area W.29.b, W.30.a. and c. to keep down hostile M.G. fire.
9.30 - 11 p.m. "C" Coy, 50th Bn. fired on S.O.S. line at slow rate to cover attack of 7th Queens to gain final objective for the day.

ACTION OF GUNS WITH 55TH INF. BDE.
Distribution.
(a) 8 Guns co-operating with Infantry attack.
(b) 8 Guns in Brigade Reserve, (BRISBANE TRENCH)
No.10.Section (2nd Lieut.A.C.FERRIS) went forward with advanced parties of 8th East Surrey Regt. and assisted in mopping up of ALBERT by neutralising M.Gs. and snipers firing from Strong Points in ruined houses, and finally (about 8 a.m.) took up defensive positions with posts of East Surreys on light railway:-

2 Guns W.29.a.6.4.
2 Guns W.29.c.5.8.

From these positions 2nd Lieut.A.C.FERRIS, in conjunction with O.C. 55th T.M.Battery personally located and engaged nests of enemy M.Gs and snipers in W.29.b., the enemy being driven into the open by the trench mortar bombardment suffered heavy casualties by these machine guns.
At 1 p.m. the two guns at W.29.c.5.8. moved forward to assist an advance of "B" Coy. 7th Buffs. The attack was held up by artillery and machine gun fire and the gun teams suffered six casualties, the survivors bringing back the guns to the point of departure; these

/guns

guns were relieved at 3 p.m. by 2 guns of No.9.Section and withdrawn to Company H.Qrs, there being insufficient personnel to replace casualties.

No.12.Section (Lieut.J.LAURIE) went forward with 7th Buffs to assembly positions on light railway and advanced with leading Coys. to positions at 11.30 a.m.

2 Guns at E.5.b.3.3.
2 Guns at E.5.b.7.5.

from which they engaged the retreating enemy and established defensive positions.

No.11.Section (Lieut.W.RAMAGE) moved forward at 10 a.m. and took up defensive positions in depth at E.5.a.7.3. covering TARA VALLEY and TARA HILL.
These guns were not engaged.

No.9.Section less 2 guns moved to Advanced Brigade Report Centre E.3.b.2.5. and remained in Brigade Reserve.

The above positions were maintained until 7 p.m. 24th when 8 guns occupied defensive positions at W.22.Central. Company, less 8 guns concentrated at DIRTY TRENCH (D.6.d.8.3.)

<u>ACTION OF GUNS WITH 54th INF. BDE.</u> ("B" Coy, 18th Bn.M.G.C.)

2 Sections were detailed to follow close behind Infantry and to consolidate. Guns reached position shortly after capture of final objective:-

2 Guns E.11.Central.
2 Guns E.11.c.3.2.
2 Guns E.11.b.6.7.
2 Guns E.5.d.8.5.

1 German heavy machine gun was captured and turned on to the enemy in the valley E.12.a. and b.; enabling Infantry patrols to push forward and capture a number of prisoners.

Good targets were obtained by all these guns on the retiring enemy.

9 a.m. No.7.Section from Brigade Reserve moved forward and occupied positions in E.5.a. to cover the left flank of the Brigade until 55th Infantry Brigade reached its objective.

No.8.Section remained in Brigade reserve and was not employed.

-------------ooo-----------

<u>SECOND PHASE:-</u> <u>Attacks of 53rd Inf. Bde. on TARA HILL and CHALMES SPUR.</u>

<u>(12 Midnight 22nd - 9.30 p.m. 24th.)</u>

<u>Reference Maps:-</u> <u>57.d.S.E. and 62.d.N.E. 1/20,000</u>

<u>ORGANISATION.</u>

(a) <u>Forward Guns.</u> "A" Company, 18th Battn.M.G.C. attached to 53rd Inf. Bde. for consolidation forward.

"B" and "C" Coys. 18th Bn. M.G.C. disposed in depth for defence of ground East of RIVER ANCRE.

(b) <u>Divisional Reserve.</u> "D" Company, 18th Battn.M.G.C. concentrated in E.2.c.

8 Guns "B" Coy. 50th Bn.M.G.C. at E.17.c.9.1. for protective enfilade barrage on line E.12.b.80 - E.6.d.8.4.

"B" Coy, 50th Bn.M.G.C. less 8 guns, in defensive positions E.9.c. and E.16.a.

"C" Coy. 50th Bn.M.G.C. firing covering barrage

(c)

<u>Action of Forward Guns.</u> (<u>"A" Coy. 18th Bn.M.G.C</u>).

At 4.45 a.m. 53rd Bde, with 7th Queens attached, attacked on a frontage of three Battns.

On orders of G.O.C. 53rd Inf. Bde. Lieut.J.O.R.EVANS,M.C. Commanding "A" Company, detailed 1 section to each attacking Battn, and ordered one section to follow the attack and consolidate strong points in W.30.c. and E.6.a. on Brigade line of Resistance.

/At Zero.

At Zero the 3 Forward sections moved forward close in rear of Reserve Coys of their respective Battalions and took up positions on the objective about half an hour after its capture by the Infantry.

At Zero plus ½ hour Lieut. EVANS went forward and personally co-ordinated the fire of these sections for defence of the front line.

No.2.Section under Lieut. D. J. HUTSON moved forward after a reconnaissance and took up strong positions in depth.

Very shortly after capture of objective, enemy M.Gs. were being engaged and neutralised and suspected areas for forming up of enemy infantry swept with fire.

Guns were disposed in positions:-

No.1.Section	...	4 Guns	...	W.30.a.7.2.
" 3 Section	...	2 Guns	...	W.30.d.4.6.
	...	2 Guns	...	W.30.d.7.5.
" 4 Section	...	4 Guns	...	E.6.a.8.7.
" 2 Section	...	4 Guns	...	in bank between E.6.a.7.1 and E.6.b.2.2.

At 1 a.m. 24th 53rd Inf. Bde. attacked and captured CHAPES SPUR For this operation, 8 guns were detailed to go forward independently and form a defensive flank facing South, taking as their objective the line of a trench running from X.25.a.1.1. to X.19.d.8.6. Owing to Officer casualties these guns were under the Command of 2nd Lieut. J.B.RUSSELL who led them forward at Zero plus 30 minutes straight to their objective, where good fire positions were selected by N.C.Os. and numerous targets engaged. Guns were again co-ordinated for defence by Lieut. EVANS. Valuable information regarding the position of the enemy was furnished by observers with these guns and infantry outpost line was pushed forward to line of railway, X.20.Central.

Disposition of guns at close of operations was:-

2 Guns at X.25.b.6.8.
2 Guns at X.19.d.8.4.
2 Guns at X.25.a.5.8.
2 Guns at X.25.a.3.4.
4 Guns at W.30.d.1.8.
4 Guns at E.6.a.7.1. - E.6.b.2.2.

On 54th Infantry Brigade front, Infantry worked forward as the enemy retired.

"B" Coy, 18th Bn.M.G.C.

No.5. Section pushed guns forward on to spur in E.12.a and c. and engaged numerous targets

Remainder of guns maintained positions and obtained good targets.

Action of Barrage Guns.

"C" Coy. 50th Battn.M.G.C.

23rd. From Zero to Zero plus 64, fired on barrage lines at slow rate.

At 5 p.m. moved to battery positions in W.29.a. and E.5.a.

24th. 1 a.m. to 1.30 a.m. Fired covering barrage at slow rate.

1.45 a.m. to 4.30 a.m. fired bursts of harassing fire on area X.25.d.

6 a.m. deployed into defensive positions on Divisional line of resistance, (B)

25th. 4 a.m. Moved forward to occupy Divisional line of resistance.(C)

"B" Coy, 50th Bn.M.G.C.

O.C. Company was in touch with G.O.C. 54th Inf. Bde.

23rd. Brought harassing fire to bear throughout the day on enemy positions in E.12.b. and E.6.d.

12 noon to 1 a.m. S.O.S. barrage, slow rate of fire on threatened counter attack.

24th. 12 noon. Moved forward 4 Guns from E.17.c.9.1. to F.7.c.8.0. and harassed trenches in F.2.a. and c to assist patrols of 54th Bde. working forward.

Divisional Reserve.

"C" Company, 18th Bn.M.G.C.

Withdrew from positions East of ANCRE. 8 Guns took up positions in W.22.a.

Coy. Reserve 8 guns concentrated at D.6.d.8.3. 5.30 p.m. 23rd.

5 p.m. 24th. Company concentrated at D.6.d.8.3.

"B" Company 50th Bn.M.G.C.

5 p.m. 24th, 8 guns Divisional Reserve concentrated at E.14.c.

"D" Coy, 18th Bn.M.G.C.

Remained concentrated.

9.30 p.m. attached to 55th Infantry Brigade., relieved "A" Company in line.

---------ooo---------

THIRD PHASE:- Advance of 54th and 55th Brigades to MONTAUBAN.

(9.30 p.m. 24th - 10 p.m. 26th August)

Reference Maps:- Sheets, 57.d.S.E., 57.c.S.W., 62.d.N.E., 62.c.N.W

ORGANISATION.

"B" Coy, 18th Bn.M.G.C. with 54th Inf. Bde. right of Divisional Sector.

"C" Coy, 18th Bn.M.G.C. at D.6.d. ready to move forward in support of 55th Inf. Bde.

Divisional Reserve.

"A" Coy, 18th Bn.M.G.C. concentrated,

"B" Coy, 50th Bn.M.G.C. with 8 guns and "C" Coy, 50th Bn.M.G.C with 12 Guns under orders to occupy TARA LINE (C).

Action.

"B" Coy, 18th Battn.M.G.C.

2.30 a.m. No.5.Section followed Infantry and took up positions in F.3.b. and 1.

During the afternoon the Infantry having made considerable progress, No.6.Section moved forward with limbers and occupied positions on spur X.28.d.

2 Sections in Brigade Reserve in F.1.d

"D" Coy, 18th Battn.M.G.C.

O.C. Coy. was given "carte blanche" for employment of guns, maintained close touch with all sections and kept G.O.C. 55th Bde. and O.C. 18th Battn.M.G.C. continually informed of the situation.

25th. At dawn all sections went forward on prescribed lines. Hostile artillery opposition being slight, limbers and pack animals were used boldly, enabling M.Gs. to keep pace with rapid advance of the Infantry

"A" and "B" Sections by 9 a.m. were engaging parties of enemy in X.23.d. from positions in X.28.c.

Enemy having retired from this spur, all sections moved with pack animals towards valley X.23.b. - X.29.d. with scouts in touch with advanced parties of Infantry.

At 6 p.m. "A" Section worked away to the right flank and gained touch with Cavalry patrols in MAMETZ Village, cleared out enemy snipers and engaged good targets of enemy parties retreating in S.25.b. Section then pressed forward to high ground in F.5.d. and brought flanking fire to bear on S. and E. edges of MAMETZ WOOD assisting the advance of our Infantry.

At dusk sections were in positions:-

"B" Section ... X.29.a.6.8.
"C" Section ... X.23.b.2.4.
"D" Section ... X.23.d.3.7.

all in touch with leading Companies of Infantry.

26th. 6 a.m. enemy were still occupying spur in X.24.a. and c. and high ground X.30.a. and c.

Machine guns employing flanking and overhead fire preparatory to Infantry attack.

/10.25 a.m.

10.25 a.m. "A" and "B" Sections moved forward with 7th Buffs, in attack on spur X.30.a. and c.

At 1.30 p.m. "A" Section endeavouring to work along right flank was caught in enemy barrage at F.6.a.5.0. and rendered temporarily immobile through casualties to personnel and pack animals.

From this position, the Section Officer got into touch with Infantry of right flank Division (South of MONTAUBAN ROAD) and rendered valuable assistance by engaging enemy snipers and M.Gs. in spur A.8.a. and c.

On arrival of reinforcements the section moved forward and gained touched with 7th Buffs at S.27.b.1.5.

"B" Section starting after Infantry came up with the front line in S.2.6.a. at 12 noon, moved forward with leading Company into MONTAUBAN S.2.7.d.1.9. at 5 p.m. and engaged a counter-attack developing from direction of LONGUEVAL.

"C" Section at 7.30 a.m. 2 Guns under Sgt. COLLINGWOOD with "B" Company East Surreys was held up in X.20.a. and c. by enemy machine guns. Sgt. COLLINGWOOD organised fire of Lewis and machine guns, silenced the enemy and personally led two platoons of Infantry and two machine Gun teams to the assault of a strong point in Cemetery S.20.d.7.8., afterwards engaging enemy retiring on right with enfilade fire.

7 p.m. The four guns of this section in S.21.c. with Infantry, engaged counter-attacks on spur S.22.b. and S.16.d. and afterwards reorganised in depth with 2 guns at S.20.d.8.8. 2 Guns at S.21.b.1.5.

"D" Section 7.30.a.m. Advanced with Infantry, 2 guns at a time, established a position at S.20.b.9.6. and engaged enemy targets S.27.a. and b.

During the afternoon, the section Officer (2nd Lieut.PETTITT) reconnoitred Infantry outpost line, S.21.b.9.0 - S.16.c.0.0., but before moving forward engaged enemy counter attack by indirect fire on walls of valley S.22.d., and direct fire on S.28.a. and S.22.c., at dusk consolidating Infantry line of resistance about S.21.a.1.5.

At the end of this phase the Infantry were on a line running North and South from Eastern edge of MONTAUBAN with forward guns disposed as under:-

"D" Coy. 18th Bn.	"D" Section	4 Guns, S.21.a.1.5.
	"C" Section	2 Guns, S.21.b.1.4.
		2 Guns, S.20.d.8.8.
	"A" Section	4 Guns, S.27.b.1.5.
	"B" Section	4 Guns, S.27.d.1.9.
"B" Coy. 18th Bn.	4 Guns	X.22.d.6.1.
	12 "	Brigade Reserve, X.29.d.5.6.
"C" Coy. 18th Bn.	In Brigade Reserve concentrated at X.30.a.0.8	

Battalion Headquarters moved simultaneously with Divisional H.Qrs to X.25.d.4.5.

Divisional Reserve.

"A" Coy, 18th Battn. at dawn 25th concentrated in E.2.c. moving forward on the 26th with 53rd Inf. Bde. to X.30.a.8.6.

"B" Coy, 50th Bn.M.G.C. at dawn on the 25th placed 8 guns in position on Divisional line (C), remaining 8 guns concentrated in BECOURT WOOD, F.1.d. in close touch with Battn. H.Qrs.

"C" Coy, 50th Battn.M.G.C. at dawn on the 25th placed 12 guns in position on Divisional line (C), 4 guns concentrated at X.25.d.2.3. in close touch with Battn. H.Qrs.

"C" Coy, 50th Bn.M.G.C. at dawn on the 26th, 16 guns were in position on Divisional Line (D).

"B" Coy. 50th Bn.M.G.C. At 6 p.m. 26th concentrated in readiness to occupy further line of resistance.

-----------ooo-----------

(FOURTH PHASE.

FOURTH PHASE:- Capture of BERNAFAY AND TRONES WOODS by 53rd Infantry Brigade with 7th Queens attd.

(Midnight 26th - 8 p.m. 28th Aug.1918)

Reference Maps:- Sheets 57.c.S.W., 62.c.N.W. 1/20,000.

ORGANISATION.

"A" and "C" Coys, attached to 53rd Inf. Bde.

"D" Company with 55th Inf. Bde. on Divisional line of Resistance.

Divisional Reserve. "B" Company concentrated at X.29.d.4.6. "C" Coy, 50th Bn.M.G.C. on Divisional Line (D); "B" Coy, 50th. Bn. awaiting orders to man Divisional line (E).

ACTION.

"A" Company. 8 Guns went forward following Infantry attack at 4.55 a.m. These guns remained in neighbourhood of Quarry S.22.c.0.5. while situation in front was obscure. No.2.Section eventually arrived on line held by Infantry at 1 p.m.

Positions taken up were:-

2 Guns at S.29.c.3.5.
2 Guns at S.28.a.0.9.

from which hostile movements and machine guns were engaged in TRONES WOOD.

8 Guns in Brigade Reserve in S.30.a.8.8.

No.4.Section under C.S.M. DICKINSON worked forward through successive fire positions to S.23.a.4.0. at 11 a.m. and from these positions engaged enemy in TRONES WOOD and on Western edge where Infantry were driven out. 2,500 rounds were fired and casualties caused to enemy whose advance was effectually stopped.

At 6.45 p.m. this Section engaged with flanking fire enemy trench and strong point, S.29.c.3.7., S.29.d.1.9. for 20 minutes covering the Infantry attack.

After the situation was cleared up, 8 Guns in Brigade Reserve were placed in positions for defence of left flank.

4 Guns at S.22.a.4.3.
4 Guns at S.21.b.8.0.

"C" Company.

Owing to casualties, were at this stage only able to man 12 guns.

4 Guns moved forward following advance of 7th Queens.R.W.S.Rgt. to consolidate in depth at S.29.c.4.6. covering right flank.

7 p.m. 53rd Infantry Brigade attacked and captured TRONES WOOD and at dawn 28th four guns of "A" Company from Brigade Reserve went to Commanding positions at S.22.b.1.5. and 4 Guns of "C" Company moved from S.28.c.4.6. to A.4.a.9.9.

28th. These positions were maintained throughout the day.

Divisional Reserve.

27th. 10 a.m. "B" Coy, 50th Bn.M.G.C. on orders from Division manned Divisional line (E).

"D" Coy 18th Bn.M.G.C. remained in positions taken up on the 26th with reduced teams.

28th. 8 p.m. On relief of the 53rd Inf. Bde. by the 54th. Inf. Bde. "B" Company relieved "C" Coy.

"C" Coy. 50th Bn.M.G.C. concentrated at X.29.b.5.6.

-------oOo-------

FIFTH PHASE:- Advance of 54th Inf.Bde. on COMBLES.

(5 a.m. 29th - midnight 31st)

ORGANISATION.

"A" and "B" Coys. with the 54th Inf. Bde. "D" Coy. in support.

Action of Guns.

"B" Company. All sections starting 5.30 a.m. 29th close behind leading Companies of Infantry were outpaced in rapid advance.

/Limbers

Limbers were sent forward at 10 a.m. and picked up Sections on main road in S.30.b. Advance was carried on in two parallel columns.

Nos. 5 and 6 Sections via ANGLE WOOD to B.3.Central.

Nos. 7 and 8 Sections by main road to T.20.d.9.7. and positions taken up:-

No.6.Section	...	4 Guns	...	B.4.b.1.9.
No.5.Section	...	4 Guns	...	T.27.b.7.7.
No.7.Section	...	2 Guns	...	T.29.a.3.7.
		2 Guns	...	T.28.a.4.9.
No.8.Section	...	4 Guns	...	T.21.d.9.6.covering spur running South from MORVAL.

Enemy in MORVAL - PRIEZ FARM Line were engaged.

11.30 a.m. "A" Company moved forward in support with limbers and occupied positions in depth.

4 Guns at B.4.c.4.7.
4 Guns at B.30.b.2.0.
8 Guns in Brigade Reserve concentrated at T.26.a.1.3.

30th. 5.15 a.m. 54th Inf. Bde. attempted to turn MORVAL - PRIEZ FARM from south.

No.5.Section advanced with the 11th Royal Fusiliers and on attack being held up at PRIEZ FARM dug in at B.5.a.5.0.

From these positions many targets were engaged during 30th and 31st.

29th. "D" Company attached to 55th Inf. Bde. concentrated at X.29.b.5.4.

30th. Moved to S.29.d.9.3.

31st. 6 p.m. moved to B.3.Central and prepared for operations.

Divisional Reserve.

"C" Company. 29th. Concentrated at X.30.a.0.8.

31st. Moved forward to 55th Inf. Bde. rendezvous for attack.

"C" Coy, 50th Bn.M.G.C.

31st. 4.30 a.m. occupied Divisional Line (F).

"B" Company, 50th Bn.M.G.C. Remained in occupation of Divisional line (E).

Battalion Headquarters.

1.30 p.m. 30th. Moved to S.24.c.2.1.

--------ooo-------

SIXTH PHASE:- Attack by 55th Bde. on N.W. corner of ST PIERRE VAAST WOOD to capture of SAILLISEL by 7th Royal West Kent Regiment.

(Midnight 31st - 8 p.m. 1st Sept)

ORGANISATION.

"C" Company and "D" Company, less 8 guns, attached to 55th Inf. Bde.

8 Guns "B" Company)
8 Guns "D" Company) Firing flank barrage.
8 Guns "C" Coy.50th.Bn)

"A" Company, "B" Coy, less 8 guns, "B" and "C" Coys. 50th Bn.M.G.C. - Divisional Reserve.

ACTION OF GUNS FIRING BARRAGE.

These guns were in position along North and Eastern edge of COMBLES at dusk 31st, organised in batteries of 8 guns and ordered to harass the whole area, bounded on the North by Grid line through T.17.Central - T.18.Central. (Divisional boundary) and on the South by COMBLES - FREGICOURT - SAILLISEL Road, for six hours starting at Zero, cross fire was also brought to bear by guns of "C" Coy. from captured high ground from South of valley.

/Infantry.

Infantry of 55th Brigade were ordered to enter valley from South and East to mop up the area after Zero plus 8 hours.

The scheme was highly successful, large numbers of the enemy on being dislodged from the high ground on North and South ran down into the valley and were heavily engaged by those guns at ranges of 1,500 - 2,800 yards. Many casualties being observed.

The remainder then fled towards the East and found their retreat cut off by the 7th Buffs, who captured in this operation alone, nearly 500 prisoners.

Shortly after Zero, 8 guns of "D" Company at S.29.c.7.4. were fired on from an enemy strong point at S.29.d.2.5. and 2 guns put out of action be rifle and machine gun fire. 2 Guns were detailed to deal with this while the remainder continued on barrage lines.

At 11.30 a.m. the strong point still causing trouble, six guns were trained on the point and the slightest movement engaged with intense bursts of fire.

At 1 p.m. a white flag was displayed and 100 Germans surrendered to the senior Officer on the scene - a Captain of the 47th Division -

ACTION OF FORWARD GUNS.

"C" Company. No.12.Section with 8th East Surrey Regiment advanced with leading Company to PRIEZ FARM were outpaced owing to casualties and worked forward to T.30.d.3.3. from which guns worked in conjunction with Reserve Company in clearing FREGICOURT, keeping down enemy fire and subsequently obtained good targets in the valley S.24.a. and b.

Nos 9 and 11 Sections with 7th Buffs moved forward close behind Infantry and took up positions:-

No.9.Section	...	4 Guns	...	U.19.d.7.5. firing N.
No.11.Section	...	4 Guns	...	U.26.a.3.5. firing N.E. and S.E.

No.9.Section obtained many targets of enemy retreating out of valley towards SAILLY - SAILLISEL and observed many casualties.

No.10.Section Brigade Reserve, occupied positions at B.5.a. 7.7.

8 Guns "D" Company, Brigade Reserve took over from "A" Coy. defensive positions:-

4 Guns	...	...	B.4.a.4.7.
4 Guns	...	...	B.3.b.2.0.

7 p.m.

No.13.Section "D" Company was detailed to follow attack of 7th Royal West Kents and consolidate objective.

2nd Lieut.W.H.G.CURTIS went forward to reconnoitre and report to Infantry Battalion Commander who gave orders as to siting of guns and moved them about during that night and following day. Final positions occupied was:-

U.14.c.8.2. firing N.E.

Divisional Reserve.

8.p.m. "B" Company, 50th Bn.M.G.C. occupied Divisional Line (G). "B" Coy, 18th Bn.M.G.C. withdrew all guns to B.8.a.9.9. "C" Coy, 50th Bn.M.G.C. on Divisional Line (F). "A" Coy, 18th Bn.M.G.C. concentrated B.3.b.8.2.

------ooo------

SEVENTH PHASE:- Capture of ST PIERRE VAAST WOOD by 53rd Inf. Bde. and subsequent advance to line of TORTILLE RIVER.

(8 p.m. 1st Sept - midnight 4.9.18)

ORGANISATION.

"A" Company forward with 53rd Inf. Bde.

"C" Company.) with 55th Infantry Brigade in Defensive
"D" Coy.4 Guns.) positions.

Divisional Reserve.

"B" and "C" Coys, 50th Battn. on Division lines (G) and (F).

"B" Company 18th Bn.M.G.C. and "D" Coy,less 4 guns, concentrated in valley B.3. and 3.

/Action of Forward Guns.

ACTION OF FORWARD GUNS.

2nd. "A" Company. Nos. 2 and 4 Sections detailed for forward consolidation were given approximate objectives and formed up before Zero on line of BAPAUME - PERRONNE Road in U.20. a. and U.26.a.

Advance was made with Support Coys of 10th Essex and 8th Royal Berks.

No.2.Section placed :-
2 Guns at U.21.c.6.0.)
2 Guns at U.22.c.1.5.) For defence of Right Flank.

Good targets were obtained on enemy retiring in front of Infantry mopping up parties.

No.4.Section met with considerable resistance and engaged the enemy N.E. of ST PIERRE VAAST WOOD from U.20.b.7.5.

No.3.Section in Brigade Reserve was moved forward after capture of objective to U.15.b.5.3. for defence of left flank.

No.1.Section was in Brigade Reserve at FREGICOURT.

3rd. On withdrawal of enemy to East bank of TORTILLES River guns of "A" Company advanced in echelon behind patrols of 53rd Infantry Brigade and took up positions.

No.2.Section ... 2 Guns ... U.24.d.5.5. firing S.E.
2 Guns ... U.22.d.3.3.
No.4.Section ... 2 Guns ... U.16.d.2.7.)
2 Guns ... U.17.c.4.7.) firing N.E.

7.30 p.m.
No.2.Section having been subjected to heavy H.E. and gas bombardment was withdrawn from positions in U.24.d. and relieved in U.22.d. by 4 guns of No.1.Section. Section came into Brigade Reserve at U.19.a.2.1.

4th. Line of Left Flank Division having been advanced, No.4. Section moved across and placed 4 Guns at U.24.a.2.5. from which enemy M.Gs. firing from U.19.d.8.2. were engaged and silenced.

6.30.p.m. Heavy gas bombardment of trench U.22.a. and d. causing 24 casualties (gas) in No.1.Section.

12 midnight. M.Gs. of 12th Division being in position, all guns were withdrawn to U.19.a.2.1. and Company marched out on morning of the 5th.

Action of Guns of 55th Inf. Bde.

2nd. Remained in Defensive positions all day.
9.p.m. Were organised to meet possible counter-attack from N.E.
3rd. Withdrew from positions and concentrated.
"C" Company ready to move forward with Advance Guard from FREGICOURT.
"D" Company, 4 Guns to Divisional Reserve, B.3.Central.

Divisional Reserve.

2nd. 8 p.m. "C" Coy, 50th Bn. occupied Divisional Line (H).
3rd. "B" Coy, 18th Bn.M.G.C. was detailed to operate with advance guard of 55th Inf. Bde. and moved to FREGICOURT.
"D" Company remained in Divisional Reserve and moved to PRILZ FARM.
3rd Sept. 10 a.m. Battn. H.Qrs moved to T.29.c.2.6.
4th. Relief of Coys. by Coys. of 12th Battn.
5th. Relief of "B" and "C" Coys. 50th Bn. by 2 Coys of 100th Bn.
9 a.m. 18th Battn. H.Qrs handed over to 12th Bn.H.Qrs.

Battalion concentrated S.W. of TRONES WOOD, T.29.d.2.3.

C Corbett
Major,
Commanding 18th Battalion M. G. Corps.

12th September 1918.

APPENDIX "A".

KEY TO DIVISIONAL LINES.

(A) Line of Railway West of ALBERT. W.22.d. - E.15.c.
(B) Eastern outskirts of ALBERT - BELLEVUE FARM - S. to MEAULTE.
(C) TARA HILL, ridge and spur - E.12.a.Central.
(D) Ridge X21.b. - X.28.a. - Western edge of FRICOURT WOOD. - F.4.c.Central.
(E) Eastern outskirts of BAZENTIN-LE-GRAND - QUARRY S.22.c. - S.28.c. - BRIQUETTERIE A.4.b. (inclusive).
(F) BOULEAUX WOOD, T.22.b. - LEUZE WOOD - FALFEMONT FARM (All inclusive.
(G) High Ground T.17.d. - HAIE WOOD - FREGICOURT - PRIEZ FARM, (all inclusive)
(H) U.14.c.7.0. - Western edge of ST PIERRE VAAST WOOD - U.27.c.0.0.

-------ooo-------

APPENDIX "B".

CASUALTIES.

O.Rs.

Date & Coy.	Killed.	D of W.	Wounded.	Wounded (Gas)	Missing.	TOTAL.
22nd Aug.						
"A" Coy.	-	-	-	-	-	-
"B" Coy.	1	1	5	-	1	8
"C" Coy.	1	-	6	6	-	13
"D" Coy.	-	-	1	-	-	1
23rd Aug.						
"A" Coy.	2	-	11	-	-	13
"C" Coy.	-	-	-	1	-	1
26th Aug.						
"C" Coy.	-	-	1	-	-	1
"D" Coy.	-	-	5	-	-	5
27th Aug.						
"A" Coy.	-	-	5	-	-	5
"C" Coy.	1	-	7	-	-	8
"D" Coy.	7	1	8	-	-	16
28th Aug.						
"D" Coy.	-	-	1	-	-	1
29th Aug.						
"A" Coy.	-	-	2	-	-	2
"C" Coy.	-	1	-	-	-	1
30th Aug.						
"A" Coy.	-	-	1	-	-	1
"B" Coy.	1	-	2	-	-	3
1st Sept.						
"B" Coy.	1	-	2	2	-	5
"C" Coy.	-	-	8	-	-	8
2nd Sept.						
"A" Coy.	-	-	1	-	-	1
"B" Coy.	-	-	1	-	-	1
"D" Coy.	-	1	-	-	-	1
3rd Sept.						
"A" Coy.	-	-	3	-	-	3
4th Sept.						
"A" Coy.	-	-	1	32	-	33
TOTALS:-	14	4	71	41	1	131

OFFICERS:-

22nd Aug.	Lieut.J.R.Godfrey (Wounded)
23rd Aug.	2nd Lt.D.J.Hutson.(Wounded) 2/Lts A W Billbrough & W P Nash
25th Aug.	Lieut.J.H.G.Clark.(Wounded)
27th Aug.	Lieut.E.H.Maddox.R.E.(K.in A), 2nd Lt.H.W.Burden (Wnd) 2nd Lieut. J. B. Russell (Wounded at Duty).
4th Sept.	Major.E.Wigley, 2nd Lt.J.L.Charlton, (Wounded Gas).

-o-o-o-o-o-o-o-o-o-o-o-

APPENDIX 8.1

SUMMARY OF LESSONS LEARNT
DURING RECENT OPERATIONS.

1. The principle of a main Divisional line of resistance given by Divisional Headquarters from day to day during the advance worked admirably. Two Companies were earmarked for these lines and concentrated in a suitable position with limbers packed.

The Battalion Commander and Officers of Companies detailed, had time to reconnoitre the line to be taken up and on no occasion was there any delay at all in taking up those lines.

As a general rule the advance were placed on a one Brigade front with two Machine Gun Companies working forward, one Company right forward with one section or more, as circumstances required, in Brigade Reserve; one Company following up with same reserve, occupying intermediary support line positions in depth, and when the days objectives had been gained, and these two Companies passed through what had become the Main line of Resistance laid down by Division for resisting counter attacks, a Divisional reserve Company was at once moved on to this line. Three Companies were then deployed in defensive positions in depth, with, in the case of the two forward Companies, ample Brigade reserves.

I would point out that throughout the operations, there were six Companies available, but by cutting down the Companies at the disposal of the Brigade forming the Advance Guard to one Company instead of Two as were employed throughout these operations, the same system could similarly be carried out. This would however leave no surplus under the hand of the Battalion Commander to provide rest and reliefs during operations extended over any prolonged period and the loss of the 2 extra Companies would have been felt very considerably during those operations

2 Method of disposal of Coys throughout Operations.

Two Companies allotted to the Brigade forming Advance Guard. (This would appear to be a somewhat extravagant use of Machine Guns on a narrow Brigade front, but as the forward machine guns undoubtedly took on a great deal of the work usually laid down for the Lewis Guns; this was really on occasions necessary to obtain adequate superiority of fire power)

One Company detailed to operate with the Brigade in Support.
One Company concentrated with Brigade in Reserve.
One Company manning Main Divisional Line of Defence.
One Company. In Divisional Reserve concentrated ready to bound forward to next main line of resistance.

The Companies available were detailed for their different roles from day to day according to their condition at the time for the particular work to be done.

Two Companies were always kept concentrated ready to move forward, either to a Divisional line of resistance, or to go forward with a Brigade ordered to form the advance Guard at shortest notice.

3. It was particularly noticeable that throughout the operations the gun Teams never allowed enemy machine guns or rifle fire to silence their guns, on the contrary, were immensely eager to reverse the case, which they almost invariably did. Every day direct enemy targets were continually presenting themselves from very short to extreme ranges which were always eagerly taken on and afforded the men the keenest satisfaction. So much in-direct fire had been done in the past, the results of which could never be perceived, that direct targets afforded the greatest pleasure to all ranks.

These remarks are amply supported by the testimony of Prisoners

The necessity and value of control of guns by Officers has proved every day. The initiative shown by the machine gun section Officers was very marked in most cases but in a battle of continual movement, 2 Gun Teams are about as much as one Officer can handle really well and boldly, and he will usually go further and afford more assistance to the Infantry with these two, than endeavouring to manoeuvre four.

5. More liaison between Company Commanders operating forward with Brigades might have been an advantage on occasions, in order to avoid duplicating tasks and in some instances enabling them to hold more reserve.

6. The closest liaison between companies and the Battalion operating with Brigades during whatsoever tasks may be assigned to them by the Brigadier, is in my opinion, absolutely essential. The location of every gun should be regularly reported in order that Battalion Commander may co-ordinate his Divisional Reserve with the guns operating forward and keep in touch with the sections of these Companies.

Battalion H.Qrs maintained adequate signal communication throughout, to enable this to be done with the minimum trouble for those concerned and a system of mounted Orderlies duplicated every time when signals failed.

7. SET PIECE ATTACKS.
When guns are attached to Infantry Brigades for purposes of consolidation on objectives being gained, the Machine Gun Officer, should only be given the details of the task his guns are to undertake; i.e., Defence of flanks, likely avenues of approach for the enemy etc., It must be left to the Machine Gun Officer to site and place his own guns.

In an operation of this kind tasks should invariably be set by the Infantry Commander in consultation with the machine gun Officer co-operating in his attack.

Machine guns should not necessarily move forward with the Infantry or their movement in any way hampered. It must be remembered that they carry heavier loads and must be fresh to fight their guns on reaching their objectives

8. In open warfare with more or less unlimited objectives entailing use of Advanced Guards.
When machine guns are attached to an Infantry formation for co-operation, the Machine Gun Officer must obtain from the Infantry Commanders the plans and general method of advance on which he can base his own dispositions. He should then be given a free hand to move and handle his guns to the best of his ability as he thinks fit to meet the general situation.

On no account must individual guns be detailed to Infantry Companies etc., or the control of the guns taken from the Machine Gun Officer.

The Machine Gun Officer is responsible for keeping in close touch with the Infantry Commander on the spot, so that close co-operation between the two arms may be continually maintained. On meeting enemy posts of resistance, the Infantry Officer will explain the method of attack and the M.G. Officer will then state how best he can support it and place his guns accordingly

9. It was fully realised that the old method and rules for advancing machine guns, i.e., by bounds, are absolutely sound.

On several occasions targets were engaged very rapidly by getting forward only the gun, tripod and three or four belt boxes, the remaining belt boxes and gear being brought up by spare numbers later.

Scouts were found essential and did excellent work.

10. In the attack recorded in Narrative, the operations from the machine gun point of view proved highly satisfactory. Forty guns in batteries of 8 and 4, were allotted areas to harass for six hours, after this time the Infantry went forward and mopped up the whole tract, on Direct Targets which our Artillery barrage had not been directed throughout the operation. Direct Targets were seen and engaged throughout this time and prisoners testify to the efficacy of the fire.

11. COMMUNICATION.

Under the system of Communication adopted by the Battalion during these operations the whole of the Signalling personnel were placed at the disposal of the Signalling Officer, Lieut. E. H. MADDOX, R.E. and controlled from Battalion Headquarters.

A single line was laid and maintained from Rear Battn. H.Qrs through Battn. Adv. H.Q. to a forward exchange on the line of advance of Battn. H.Qrs.

From these three exchanges, lines were laid by shortest routes to Divisional Advanced H.Qrs, nearest Brigade H.Qrs and to all Companies.

This scheme ensured a progressive line of communication which was both quick and reliable, avoiding blocking of Divisional and Brigade lines, and providing an alternative line for the Infantry should occasion arise.

Rigid economy in cable was practised and salvage encouraged.

Visual Signalling was employed with success:-

(a) During a rapid advance as a temporary measure before lines could be laid.

(b) F.O.O. Forward Stations signalling back over a heavily shelled area.

On these occasions Signallers went forward with Company H.Qrs and were very quickly in touch with exchanges.

The R.E. Signal Section and Battalion Signallers performed their duties with keenness and resource, being very ably Commanded by Lieut. E. H. MADDOX. After this Officer was killed in action, Command was taken over by Sergt. L. TUNGATE who carried on with energy and efficiency throughout the operations.

Cyclists and mounted Orderlies were used between Battn. H.Qrs and Companies. Companies depended for forward communication entirely on runners and mounted Orderlies, an adequate number of picked men and a good supply of cycles proving thoroughly reliable.

In order to facilitate Communication, orders were issued to Companies to keep Battn. H.Qrs promptly notified of every move and for Coy. Rear H.Qrs to move with Battn. Rear H.Qrs with which they were always in closest touch.

12. SUPPLIES.

Rations were issued from Refilling Point to Battn. QrMr. and then issued to Coy. Rear H.Qrs. This showed the great advantage of keeping Coy. Rear H.Qrs and Battn. Q.M. Stores together.

This scheme worked very satisfactorily as Company Advanced H.Qrs were always able to advise Company Rear as to location at which rations were to be brought.

C. Webbert [signature]

Major,

Commanding [illegible] Battalion, Machine Gun Corps.

[illegible] September, [illegible]

APPENDIX. 82.

CASUALTIES INCURRED BY THE
18th Battn. M. G. Corps.
DURING THE MONTH OF AUG.1918.

O F F I C E R S.

Lieut. E. P. Sunderland.	Wounded in Action	6.8.18.
2nd Lieut. C. Horton, M.C.	do.,	6.8.18.
Lieut. W. Ramage.	Wounded at Duty,	7.8.18.
Lieut. J. R. Godfrey.	Wounded in Action	22.8.18.
2nd Lieut.A.W.Billbrough	do.,	23.8.18.
2nd Lieut.W.P.Nash.	do.,	23.8.18.
Lieut. D. J. Hutson.	do.,	23.8.18.
2nd Lieut. J. H. G. Clark.	do.,	26.8.18.
2nd Lieut. H. W. Burden, M.C.	do.,	27.8.18.
Lieut. E. H. Maddox, R.E.	Killed in Action,	27.8.18.
2nd Lieut. J. B. Russell.	Wounded at Duty,	27.8.18.

--------ooo-------

O T H E R   R A N K S.

Date.	Killed.	Died of Wds.	Wounded.	Wounded (Gas)	Missing.	TOTAL.
1st.	-	-	2	-	-	2
2nd.	-	-	2	-	-	2
5th.,	-	-	-	1	-	1
6th.	-	-	6	-	1	7
8th.	3	-	15	-	1	19
9th	-	-	1	-	-	1
21st.	-	-	1	-	-	1
22nd.	2	1	7	-	2	12
23rd.	2	-	12	6	-	20
24th.	-	-	3	-	-	3
26th.	2	-	9	-	-	11
27th.	2	-	6	-	-	8
28th.	4	-	14	-	-	1
29th.	-	-	1	-	-	1
30th.	-	-	1	-	-	1
31st.	1	-	2	-	-	3
TOTALS:-	16 :	1 :	82 :	7 :	4 :-	110

----------ooo----------

CHANGES IN ESTABLISHMENT AND STRENGTH OF BATTN., DRAFTS RECEIVED, CHANGES IN OFFICERS ETC., DURING MONTH OF AUG.1918.

-0-0-0-0-00-0-0-0-0-0-0-0-0-0-

Paper Strength of Battalion, (excluding attached):-

1st August 1918:- 47 Officers 922 Other Ranks.

DECREASES.

For Casualties in Officers during month see Appendix 82.

Other Ranks.

Evacuated to C.C.S.	36.
In Hosp.over 7 days,	3.
To Course at GRANTHAM,	1.
To Base, Inefficient,	2.
Candidate for Commission,	1.
TOTAL DECREASES:-	43.
Casualties in Action,	110.
TOTAL:-	153.

INCREASES.

Lieut. G. H. Brownrigg-Jay. Joined Bn. from M.G.C. Base Depot and taken on strength, 4.8.18.

Lieut (A/Capt) E.L.BIRD.M.C.)
2nd Lieut.A.E.Ferguson.)
2nd Lieut.R.S.Robertson.)
Lieut. G. D. Loup, M.C.)
Lieut. J. Bryce.)
Joined Battn. as Reinforcements from M.G.C. Base Depot and taken on strength, 29.8.18.

3 O.Rs. joined Battn. from M.G.C. Base Depot & taken on strength 12.8.18
21 O.Rs. ------------------------do.,------------------------15.8.18.
11 O.Rs. ------------------------do.,------------------------23.8.18.
40 O.Rs. ------------------------do.,------------------------29.8.18.

TOTAL INCREASE (Other Ranks):- 75.

Strength 1st:-	47	Officers	922	Other	Ranks.
Decreases:-	8	"	153	"	"
	39	"	769	"	"
Increases:-	6	"	75	"	"

Paper Strength of Battalion
31st August 1918:- 45 Officers,844 Other Ranks.
(Less attached)

----------000---------

Vol 9

··Confidential··

···War Diary···

of

···18th Battn. Machine · Gun · Corps···

From 1st Sept. 1918. ··· Appendices ···

To 30th Sept 1918. ··· 80 · to · 92 · Attached ···

VOL. VIII

18th Battalion Machine Gun Corps

Instructions regarding War Diaries and Intelligence Summaries are contained in F. S. Regs., Part II. and the Staff Manual respectively. Title pages will be prepared in manuscript.

WAR DIARY
or
~~INTELLIGENCE SUMMARY.~~

(*Erase heading not required.*)

Army Form C. 2118.

September 1918

Place	Date	Hour	Summary of Events and Information	Remarks and references to Appendices
			Ref Map Sheet SENLIS 1/20,000	
TRONES WOOD			For Operations 1st – 5th September 1918 see Narrative of Operations submitted with War Diary with August appendix 80.	
	2nd		Captain J W K Wareham rejoined Battalion from M G Course Camiers	[illegible]
MONTAUBAN STATION	6th		Coys resting and cleaning up	[illegible]
	7th		Coys at disposal of Coy Cmdrs repacking limbers refitting etc	[illegible]
	8th		Church Parade 11 am & resting	[illegible]
	9th		Company Training	[illegible]
	10th		do	[illegible]
	11th		do	[illegible]
	12th		do Mayor C B Hibbert DSO attended conference at Divnl H.Qrs at 9 pm for discussion of future operations	[illegible]
	13		Company Training	
	14.		Preparations for move – reconnaissance of new area and Coy Commdrs conference. Order No 47 issued	App 84. [illegible]
SAULCOURT.	15.		A. & B Coys proceeded by march route to new area – bivouaced vicinity of SAULCOURT. Order No 48 issued	App 85. [illegible]
	16.		H.Q., C & D Coy proceeded by bus to LIERAMONT. 2 sections 'A' Coy relieved. Order No 49 issued	appendix 86.

D. D. & L., London, E.C.
(A7883) Wt. W809/M1672 350,000 4/17 Sch. 52a Forms/C/2118/14

Instructions regarding War Diaries and Intelligence Summaries are contained in F. S. Regs., Part II. and the Staff Manual respectively. Title pages will be prepared in manuscript.

WAR DIARY
or
INTELLIGENCE SUMMARY.
(Erase heading not required.)

Army Form C. 2118.

Place	Date	Hour	Summary of Events and Information — REF. MAP. SHEET 62 C. NW	Remarks and references to Appendices
			2 sections 'B' Coy of 74th Div. in line.	[initials]
RONNSOY.	17		The following battle positions were taken up for dawn attack on RONNSOY on 18th	
			'A' Coy 18th Battn, one section 'B' Coy 18th Battn 2 Coys 100th Battn. battery positions	[initials]
			neighbourhood of ST EMILLIE. 'B' Coy - 3 sections rendezvous at 54th Bde.	
			'C' Coy. rendezvous with 55th Bde and D Coy bivouaced SAULCOURT WOOD	
	18.		Dawn attack launched. 'B' Coy 3 sections went forward with 55th Bde and	[initials]
			occupied positions assigned to them in 1st objective. 'C' Coy went forward	
			with 55th Bde. 'D' Coy followed through with a view of going ~~through~~ to	
			Blue line of exploitation. 'C' & 'D' Coy were both held up short of their	[initials]
			objective owing to attack not being entirely successful.	
	19.		Guns worked forwarded according to Infantry movement. Battn H Bloc	[initials]
			moved to SAULCOURT WOOD. LT COL MINET returned from leave.	
	20.		LT COL MINET DSO MC. assumed command of Battalion. Guns in line stationary. Order No 50 issued	[initials] App. 87.
	21.		No M.G. change. Divisional conference near ST EMILLIE.	
	22.		Attack resumed. - guns in line co-operated with harassing fire partially	[initials]
			successful but RONNSOY not entirely cleared.	

D. D. & L., London, E.C. (A7883) Wt. W809/M1672 350,000 4/17 Sch. 52a Forms/C/2118/14

Instructions regarding War Diaries and Intelligence Summaries are contained in F. S. Regs., Part II. and the Staff Manual respectively. Title pages will be prepared in manuscript.

WAR DIARY
or
INTELLIGENCE SUMMARY.
(Erase heading not required.)

Army Form C. 2118.

Place	Date	Hour	Summary of Events and Information	Remarks and references to Appendices
			REF MAP. SHEET 62 C NW.	
	23.		Positions stationary with exception of inter-Coy reliefs. Harassing fire night and day.	SRP
	24		Night of 24th/25th 18th M.G. Battn was relieved by 27th American Div. Order No. 52 issued.	SRP App. 88
	25		Battn marched to COMBLES and billeted there.	
	26 27		Refitting and baths. 5133 issued-	SRP App 89.
	28		Battn proceeded by march route to SAULCOURT and at dusk took up battle positions. Order No. 53 issued.	SRP app 90
	29		At dawn the Div. attacked at VENDHUILLE. Gun positions and orders attached. Order of battle for M.G. as follows. 2 sections 'B' Coy with 54th Bde. 2 sections 'D' Coy with Liason force. 2 sections 'C' Coy with 55th Bde. Remainder of Battn firing covering barrage.	SRP
	30.		Attack of previous day successful. Gun positions stationary. Statement of Casualties attached - see appendix 91 Statement showing changes in Establishment and strength attached - see appendix 92	SRP app 91 app 92

[signature]
Lieut.-Col.
Cmdg. 18th Bn. Machine Gun Corps.

A5834 Wt. W4973/M687 750,000 8/16 D. D. & L. Ltd. Forms/C.2118/13.

18 DIV.
18 MG CORN

COPY.

2028 B

SUMMARY OF LESSONS LEARNT
DURING RECENT OPERATIONS

1. The principle of a main Divisional line of resistance given by Divisional Headquarters from day to day during the advance worked admirably. Two Companies were earmarked for these lines and concentrated in suitable positions with limbers packed.

The Battalion Commander and Officers of Companies detailed, had time to reconnoitre the line to be taken up and on no occasion was there any delay at all in taking up these lines.

As a general rule the advance took place on a one Brigade front with two Machine Gun Companies working forward, one Company right forward with one section or more, as circumstances required, in Brigade Reserve: one Company following up with same reserve, occupying intermediary support line positions in depth, and when the days objectives had been gained, and these two Companies passed through what had become the Main Line of Resistance laid down by Division for resisting counter attacks, a Divisional reserve Companyw was at once moved on to this line. Three Companies were then deployed in defensive positions in depth, with, in the case of the two forward Companies, ample Brigade reserves.

I would point out that throughout the operations, there were six Companies available, but by cutting down the Companies at the disposal of the Brigade forming the Advance Guard to one Company instead of two as were employed throughout these operations, the same system could similarly be carried out. This would however leave no surplus under the hand of the Battalion Commander to provide rest and reliefs during operations extended over any prolonged period and the loss of the two extra Companies would have been felt very considerably during these operations.

2. METHOD OF DISPOSAL OF COYS. THROUGHOUT OPERATIONS. Two Coys. allotted to the Brigade forming Advance Guard. (This would appear to be a somewhat extravagant use of Machine Guns on a narrow Brigade front, but as the forward machine guns undoubtedly took on a great deal of the work usually laid down for the Lewis Guns; this was really on occasions necessary to obtain adequate superiority of fire power).

One Company detailed to operate with the Brigade in support.
One Company concentrated with Brigade in Reserve.
One Company manning Main Divisional Line of ~~Resistance~~. Defence
One Company In Divisional Reserve concentrated ready to bound forward to next main line of resistance.

The Companies available were detailed for their different roles from day to day according to their condition at the time for the particular work to be done.

Two Companies were always kept concentrated ready to move forward either to a Divisional line of Resistance, or to go forward with a Brigade ordered to form the advance Guard at shortest notice.

3. It was particularly noticeable that throughout the operations the gun teams never allowed enemy machine guns or rifle fire to silence their guns, on the contrary, were immensely eager to reverse the case, which they almost invariably did. Every day direct enemy targets were continually presenting themselves from very short to extreme ranges which were always eagerly taken on and afforded the men the keenest satisfaction. So much indirect fire had been done in the past, the results of which could never be perceived, that direct targets afforded the greatest pleasure to all ranks.

These remarks are amply supported by the testimony of prisoners.

4. The necessity and value of control of guns by Officers was proved every day. The initiative shown by the Machine gun section Officers was very marked in most cases but in a battle of continual movement, 2 guns teams are about as much as one Officer can handle really well and boldly, and he will usually go further and afford more assistance to the Infantry with these two, than andeavouring to manoeuvre four.

5. More liaison between the two Company Commanders operating forward with the Brigades forming advance guard might have been an advantage on occasions, in order to avoid duplicating tasks and in some instances enabling them to hold more reserve.

6. The closest liaison between companies operating with Brigades, and the Battalion Commander during whatsoever tasks may be assigned to them by the Brigadier, is in my opinion, absolutely essential. The location of every gun should be regularly reported in order that the Battalion Commander may co-ordinate his Divisional Reserve with the guns operating forward and keep in touch with the sections of these Companies.

Battalion H.Qrs. maintained adequate signal communication throughout, to enable this to be done with the minimum of trouble and delay for those concerned and a system of mounted orderlies duplicated every line when signals failed.

7. SET PIECE ATTACKS. In my opinion when guns are attached to Infantry Brigades for purposes of consolidation on objectives being gained, the Machine gun officer, should only be given the details of the task his guns are to undertake, i.e., Defence of flanks, likely avenues of approach for the enemy, etc., . It must be left to the Machine gun Officer to site and place his own guns.

In an operation of this kind tasks should invariably be set by the Infantry Commander in consultation with the machine gun Officer co-operating in his attack.

Machine guns should not necessarily move forward with the Infantry or their movements in any way hampered. It must be remembered that they carry heavier loads and must be fresh to fight their guns on reaching their objectives.

8. In open warfare with more or less unlimited objectives entailing use of advanced guards, when machine guns are attached to an Infantry formation for co-operating, the Machine gun officer must obtain from the Infantry Commanders the plans and general method of advance on which he can base his own dispositions. He should then be given a free hand to move and handle his guns to the best of his ability as he thinks fit to meet the general situation.

On no account must individual guns be detailed to Infantry Companies etc., or the control of the guns taken from the Machine Gun Officer.

The Mahine Gun Officer is responsible for keeping in close touch with the Infantry Commander on the spot, so that close co-operation between the two arms may be continually maintained. On meeting enemy posts of resistance, the Infantry Officer will explain the method of attack and the M.G. Officer will then state how best he can support it and place his guns accordingly.

9. It was fully realised that the old method and rules for advancing machine guns, i.e., by bounds, are absolutely sound.

On several occasions targets were engaged very rapidly by getting forward only the gun, tripod and three or four belt boxes, the remaining belt boxes and gear being brought up by spare numbers later.

Scouts were found essential and did excellent work.

10. In the attack recorded in Narrative, Page 7, VI Phase, the operations from the machine gun point of view proved highly satisfactory. Forty guns in batteries of 8 and 4, were allotted areas to harass for six hours, after this time the Infantry went forward and mopped up the whole tract,, on the whole of which area our Artillery Barrage had not been directed throughout the operation. Direct targets were seen and engaged throughout this time and prisoners testify to the efficacy of the fire.

11. COMMUNICATION. Under the syatem of communication adopted by the Battalion during these operations the whole of the signalling personnel were placed at the disposal of the signalling Officer, Lieut. E.H. MADDOX, R.E. and controlled from Battalion Headquarters.
A single line was laid and maintained from Rear Bn. H.Q. through Bn. Adv. H.Q. to a forward exchange on the line of advance of Bn.H.Q.
From these three exchanges, lines were laid by the shortest routes to Divisional Advanced H.Qrs., nearest Brigade H.Qrs. and to all Companies.
This scheme ensured a progressive line of communication which was both quick and reliable, avoiding blocking of Divisional and Brigade lines, and providing an alternative line for the infantry should occasion arise.
Rigid economy in cable was practised and salvage encouraged.

Visual signalling was employed with success :-
(a) During a rapid advance as a temporary measure before lines could be laid.
(b) Forward stations signalling back over a heavily shelled area.
On these occasions signallers went forward with Company H.Q. and were very quickly in touch with exchanges.

The R.E. signal section and Battalion signallers performed their duties with keenness and resource, being very ably commanded by Lieut. A.H. MADDOX. After this Officer was killed in action, Command was taken over by Sergt. L. TUNGATE who carried on with energy and efficiency throughout the operations.

Cyclist and mounted orderlies were used between Bn. H.Q. and Companies. Companies depended for forward communication entirely on runners and mounted orderlies, an adequate number of picked men and a good supply of cycles proving thoroughly reliable.

In order to facilitate communication, orders were issued to Companies to keep Bn. H.Q. promptly notified of every move and for Coy. Rear H.Q. to move with Bn. Rear H.Q. with which they were always in closest touch.

12. SUPPLIES. Rations were issued from Refilling Point to Bn. Q.Mr. and then issued to Coy. Rear H.Q. This showed the great advantage of keeping Coy. Rear H.Q. and Bn. Q.M. Stores together.
This scheme worked very satisfactorily as Company Advanced H.Q. were always able to advise Company Rear as to location at which rations were to be brought.

(Signed) C.B. HIBBERT, Majr.
Commdg. 18th Battalion Machine Gun Corps.

18th September, 1918.

SECRET. APPENDIX 84 Copy No. 8.

Reference Maps:- Sheets.
62.d.N.E., & 62.d.N.W. 1/20,000

14th September 1918.

18TH BATTN.M.G.C. ORDER NO. 47.

1. "A" and "D" Companies, 18th Battalion Machine Gun Corps will move to neighbourhood of LIERAMONT to-morrow the 14th inst.

2. Hour of departure from Camp:- 10 a.m.

3. The above Companies will make their own arrangements as regards billeting in forward area. Advance parties should therefore be sent forward to arrange accommodation.

4. RATIONS.
Battn. Quartermaster will arrange to despatch rations for 15th under arrangements to be made with Transport Officer.
Details of rationsupply for the 17th and onwards will be notified later.

5. WATER.
Serious difficulty is anticipated as regards water supply in the forward area. Every available receptacle travelling with Transport will be filled before departure from this area.
Men will be specially warned not to waste water on any account.

7. COMMUNICATION.
On arrival in forward area Companies will ascertain nearest Signal Office and advise Battalion Headquarters Location of their Coy. H.Qrs.

8. Acknowledge.

Asst. ~~Capt &~~ Adjt.,
18th Battalion Machine Gun Corps.

Issued at 6.45 p.m. Copies to:-

No.1. Copy C.O.
" 2 " 2nd-in-Command.
" 3 " Adjutant.
" 4 " O.C. "A" Company.
" 5 " O.C. "D" Company.
" 6 " Quartermaster.
" 7 " Transport Officer.
" 8/9 " War Diary.
" 10 " File.

SECRET. Copy No. 10

appendix 85

Reference Maps:- Sheets:- 15th September 1918.
62.d.N.E. & 62.d.N.W. 1/20,000.

18TH BATTN.M.G.C. ORDER NO. 48.

1. MOVE.
(a) The 18th Battn.M.G.C. (Less "A" and "B" Coys) will move by bus and march route to AIZECOURT-le-BAS - LIERAMONT Area to-morrow 16th inst.
(b) Transport of above will move by road to new area under orders of Battn. Transport Officer, to be clear of this Camp by 8 a.m.

2. EMBUSSING.
(a) Head of lorry column:- S.30.c.0.8.
Hour of embussing:- 9 a.m.
Debussing Point:- NURLU
(b) Embussing strengths will be rendered to Orderly Room by 8 a.m.
(c) Coys. and Battn. H.Qrs will each detail 3 Other Ranks to report to the Adjutant at Bn. Orderly Room at 8.30 a.m.
(d) Coys. will parade on Company Parade Grounds at 8.30 a.m. and await orders from Adjutant as to numbers of busses allotted etc.,

3. KITS, BAGGAGE, etc.,
1 Lorry will report to Bn.H.Qrs at 8 a.m. 16th for conveyance of Qr.Mrs Stores etc.,
Officers Kits of Bn.H.Qrs will be stacked outside H.Qrs Mess by 7.30 a.m.

4. LOCATION.
On arrival in new area Companies will at once advise Adv. Bn.H.Qrs location of Company H.Qrs.
Location of Battalion Headquarters will be notified later.

5. MOVEMENT.
There will be no movement forward of LIERAMONT until dusk.
All troops on the march, will, on the approach of hostile aircraft, halt on the side of the road. There will be no movement until the enemy aircraft have disappeared.

6. WATER.
Serious difficulty is anticipated as regards water supply in the forward area. Every available receptacle travelling with Transport will be filled before departure from this area.
Men will be specially warned not to waste water on any account.

7. ACKNOWLEDGE.

[signature]
Capt & Adjt.,
18th Battalion Machine Gun Corps.

Issued at 6.10 p.m. Copies to:-
No.1.Copy, C.O.
" 2 " 2nd-in-Command.
" 3 " Adjutant.
" 4 " O.C. "C" Coy.
" 5 " O.C. "D" Coy.
" 6 " Transport Officer.
" 7 " Quartermaster.
" 8 " H.Qrs.
" 9/10" War Diary.
" 11 " File.

SECRET. Copy No. 26

Ref. Maps:- Sheets 62.c.N.E. and 62.c.S.W. 1/20,000. *appendix 86.* 16th September 1918.

18TH BATTN.M.G.C. ORDER NO. 49.

General Situation. 1. An attack on a wide front will be carried out on a date and at an hour to be notified later, with a view to securing a position affording good observation over the HINDENBURG LINE

2. The III Corps will attack with the 74th Division on the right, 18th Division on the right centre and the 12th Division on the Left Centre.

3. There will be three objectives:-

FIRST OBJECTIVE:-	GREEN LINE.
SECOND OBJECTIVE:-	RED LINE.
Line of Exploitation:-	(BLUE LINE, in which (GUILLEMONT FARM and the (KNOLL are of special (importance on the Div. front

General Plan of Attack as regards 18th Div. 4. The 18th Division will attack as follows:-
54th Inf. Bde. will capture and consolidate the First Objective (The GREEN Line);
55th Inf. Bde. with attached troops will capture and consolidate the Second Objective (RED Line) and exploit success to the Line of Exploitation.
Boundaries of Division and Objectives are shown on attached tracing (marked "A").

Action of M.Guns. 5. The machine guns available to support this Operation on the Divisional front are as follows:-

4 Companies 18th Battn.M.G.C.)
2 Companies 100th Battn.M.G.C.) These will be employed as follows:-

"A" Coy, 18th Bn.M.G.C.) "4 Guns "B" Coy 18th Bn.M.G.C.) "C" and "D" Coys, 100th Bn.M.G.C.)	Will provide initial covering barrage.
8 Guns "B" Coy, 18th Bn.M.G.C.	Operating forward with 54th Inf. Bde., taking up positions for defense on GREEN LINE.
4 Guns "B" Coy, 18th Bn.M.G.C.	Moving to F.14.c.3.5. (Approx)
"C" Coy, 18th Bn.M.G.C.	Operating with 55th Inf. Bde. forward of the GREEN LINE.

"D" Coy, 18th Bn.M.G.C. | Will support advance of 55th Inf. Bde. from the GREEN LINE.

Detailed Tasks. 6.

(a) O.C. "C" Coy, 100th Bn.M.G.C. will detail two gun teams under an Officer to take up position in trench in F.13.b.8.7. on the forward slope. Those guns to be in position, well dug in and camouflaged on "Y"/"Z" night.

The Officer detailed will arrange for an Infantry patrol to ascertain if this trench is occupied by the enemy, first and will report to O.C. Sector for this purpose.

These guns are to be ready from Zero onwards to take on direct targets East and N.E.. These two guns will withdraw at Zero plus 60.

(b) Companies firing the initial barrage will, on cessation pack up and concentrate ready to move forward on orders being received

(c) "D" Coy, 18th Bn.M.G.C. (less 4 Guns in Reserve) will be in position in F.10.d. and F.16.d. ready to assist the advance of the 55th Inf. Bde at Zero plus 190. O.C. "D" Coy. will keep in touch with G.O.C. 55th Inf. Bde. and follow the Brigade closely to their assembly positions

(d) The 8 Guns of "B" Coy, 18th Bn. operating with the 54th Inf. Bde. for capture of GREEN LINE will also be ready to assist the advance of the 55th Inf. Bde at Zero plus 190.

(e) Targets and areas to be harassed; rates and times of fire and approximate location of batteries will be as shown on attached tracing "B".

Group Organization Cahrts attached (Marked "C")

(f) The GREEN LINE, when captured, will become the main line of Resistance.

Os.C. "D" and "B" Coys, 18th Bn.M.G.C. will organise their gun positions accordingly.

Ammunition Supply. 7. 15,000 rounds per gun will be got forward to each battery position for guns firing initial barrage.

A sufficient supply of ammunition for gun positions established forward of our present front line will be got into position as soon after Zero as possible.

3,000 rounds per gun will always be kept in belts in reserve for S.O.S. and direct targets.

Forward dumps will be established and arrangements will be made by Company Commanders. A dump of 200,000 rds. S.A.A. is being established at Rear Bn.H.Qrs and will be available for use of Coys.

Communication. 7. The forward line of Communication will be:-
Advanced Bn.H.Qrs
Forward R.C. SAULCOURT WOOD at E.15.b.8.7.
with a further station
at E.17.c.0.4.
It is proposed to establish a visual station in F.19.b. as soon as the situation permits, to be in communication with SAULCOURT WOOD.
Lines will be laid forward to Company H.Qrs as soon after Zero as possible.

S.O.S. Signals. 8. The following S.O.S. signals are at present in use:-
Australian Corps (On right) RED over RED over RED.
III Corps. RED over RED over RED.
V Corps (On Left) GREEN over RED over GREEN.
On S.O.S. signal being sent up all batteries laid on S.O.S. lines will open fire at the rate of 250 rounds per minute for 10 minutes; 50 rounds per minute for a further 10 minutes.

Picks, Shovels and Sandbags. 9. Each gun team going forward will carry, one pick, one shovel and two sandbags per man.

Medical Arrangements. 10. To be notified later.

Preparations. 11. All battery positions must be completed; ammunition oil and water dumped; lines of fire laid out and guns ready for firing by 11 p.m. 17th inst. A notification to this effect being sent to Advanced Battn. H.Qrs using code word "PLUM".
These positions must be carefully camouflaged. One extra barrell per gun must be taken forward.

Aeroplanes. 12. A Counter-attack aeroplane will be up continuously from daylight onwards in order to detect the approach of enemy counter attacks, notice of which it will give by flying towards the counter attacking troops, dropping a white parachute flare as near to the counter attacking troops as possible.

Synchronisation of Watches. 13. Watches will be synchronised at 54th Inf. Bde. H.Qrs at 2 p.m. on "Y" Day. Each Company will arrange to have an Officer at this H.Q. at that hour.

"Z" Day & Zero Hour. 14. Will be notified later.

Headquarters.	15.	Adv: Bn: H.Qrs.	D.12.d.2.2.
		"B","C","D" Coys 18th Bn.	SAULCOURT WOOD, E.16.b.0.7.
		"A" Coy, 18th Bn.M.G.C.	To be notified later.
		"C" & "D" Coys 100th Bn.	To Be notified later.
		53rd Inf. Bde.	To be notified later.
		54th Inf. Bde.	} E.15.b.0.7. Command post
		55th Inf. Bde.	} at E.15.b.7.7.

55th Inf. Bde. will probably move later to F.15.Central. "C" and "D" Coys, 18th Bn.M.G.C. will move accordingly.

Reports. 16. Coys. are again reminded of the importance of sending back reports to Battn. H.Qrs of dispositions of guns, moves of H.Qrs etc., These should be notified by runner without delay.

Accurate daily casualty reports will be wired to Rear Bn.H.Qrs as usual.

Secrecy. 17. The necessity of Secrecy is to be impressed on all concerned. Listening sets are probably already installed in the HINDENBURG LINE. All reference on the telephones to units, moves or operations is prohibited. All telephone circuits are to be metallic.

Tanks. 18. Four tanks are co-operating with 54th Infantry Brigade for capture of RONSSOY. Special efforts will be made to put out of action any anti-tank guns employed by the enemy.

19 ACKNOWLEDGE

Capt & Adjt.,
18th Battalion M. G. Corps.

Issued at ...... p.m. Copies to:-

No.1.Copy C.O.
" 2 " 2nd-in-Command.
" 3 " Adjutant.
" 4 " "A" Coy 18th Bn.
" 5 " "B" Coy 18th Bn.
" 6 " "C" Coy 18th Bn.
" 7 " "D" Coy 18th Bn.
" 8 " H.Q. 100th Bn.M.G.C.
" 9 " "C" Coy 100th Bn.
" 10 " "D" Coy 100th Bn.
" 11 " Signals.
" 12 " Transport Officer.
" 13 " Quartermaster.
" 18 " 18th Division.

No.19.Copy 53rd Inf. Bde.
" 20 " 54th Inf. Bde.
" 21 " 55th Inf. Bde.
" 22 " C.M.G.O. III Corps.
" 23 " 12th Bn.M.G.C.
" 24 " 74th Bn.M.G.C.
" 25/26" War Diary.
" 27 " File.

Nos 14 & 15 18th Division. Spare.
" 16 & 17 18th Bn.M.G.C. Spare.

No. 2. Group. Commanded by O.C. "C" Coy, 100th Bn.M.G.C.

Composition.	No. of Guns.	Targets.	Times. From.	To.	Rate of Fire.
14 Guns "C" Coy, 100th Bn.M.G.C.	14	1. Trench System- F.8.d.2.7 - F.14.b.9.4.	Z	Z plus 114.	Z plus 5 Rapid. Z plus 5 to Z plus 114 Slow.
		2. Crest Line F.8.d.7.7 - F.15.a.5.7.			

Location:- Trenches in E.13.c.

----------oOo----------

Reference:- Map 62.c.N.E.   No. 1. Group.   Commanded by:- Capt. J. H. GOOD.
18th Battn.M.G.C.

Composition.	No. of Guns.	Targets.	Times. From.	Times. To.	Rate of Fire.
16 Guns "A" Coy. 18th Bn. M.G.C. 4 Guns "B" Coy. 18th Bn.M.G.C.	4	1. Trench F.14.d.0.3 – F.14.d.7.0.	Z	Z plus 10	Rapid.
	16	1. Trench F.14.d.7.0.– F.20.b.8.0.	Z	Z plus 10	Rapid.
			Z plus 10	Z plus 23	Slow.
	12	2. Trench F.21.a.7.0. – F.21.a.6.7.	Z plus 23.	Z plus 35.	Slow.
	4	2. Trench F.21.a.6.7. – F.15.d.1.2.	Z plus 23.	Z plus 35.	Slow.
	4	2. Trench F.15.d.1.2 – F.15.d.4.6.	Z plus 23	Z plus 40.	Slow.
	20	3. Trench F.16.c.0.0. – F.22.a.0.0.	Z plus 40.	Z plus 65.	Slow.

-------ooo-------

GROUP ORGANIZATION CHART.

No.3. Group. Commanded by O.C. "D" Coy, 100th Bn.M.G.C.

Composition.	No of Guns.	Location.	Targets.	Times. From.	Times. To.	Rate of Fire.
16 Guns "D" Coy. 100th Bn.M.G.C.	16.	Sunken Road. E.18.b.	F.14.b., F.15.a. All fire North of line F.14.c.O.8. - F.15.b.O.8.	Z	Z plus 114.	Z plus 5 Rapid. Z plus 5 to Z plus 114 Slow.

-----ooo-----

No.4.Group. Commanded by O/C B & D Coys. 18th Bn

Composition.	No of Guns.	Location.	Targets.	Times. From.	Times. To.	Rate of Fire.
12 Guns "D" Coy, 18th Bn.M.G.C. 8 Guns "B" Coy, 18th Bn.M.G.C.	20	F.10.d.	Valley F.10.b., F.11.a. F.5. c. and d.	Z plus 190	Z plus 277.	Slow. (To engage direct targets and harass whole area).
		F.16.d.	Bounded on S. by TOMBOIS ROAD, & on North by Divl. Boundary.			

-----ooo-----

APPENDIX "D".
(To accompany
Order No.49.)

MEDICAL ARRANGEMENTS.

1. Location of Medical Posts.
R.A.P's. Sites as arranged by G.O's.C.
Ford Car Post. VILLERS FANCON.
A.D.S. LONGAVESNES - E.25.d.6.8.
M.D.S. TEMPLEUX la FOSSE - J.4.b.4.6.

2. Routes of Evacuation.
For Walking Wounded.
Walking wounded will proceed to A.D.S. thence by Horse ambulance and lorries to the Corps Walking Wounded Collecting Station. Horse ambulances will be pushed forward towards ST EMILIE as the situation permits.
Lying Cases.
By hand carriage and wheeled stretchers to nearest car post; thence by Ford Cars to the A.D.S. and thence by large cars to M.D.S. From the M.D.S. by M.A.C. Cars to C.C.Ss, DOINGT and MARICOURT. Ford Cars will be pushed forward as far as the situation permits along the line VILLERS FANCON - ST EMILIEE - LEMPIRE.

----------oOo-------

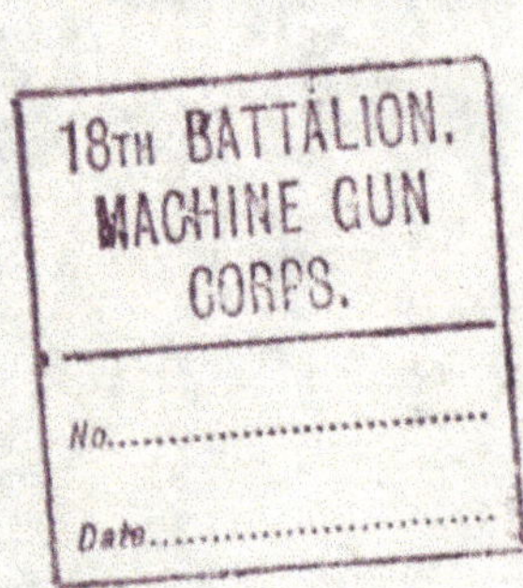

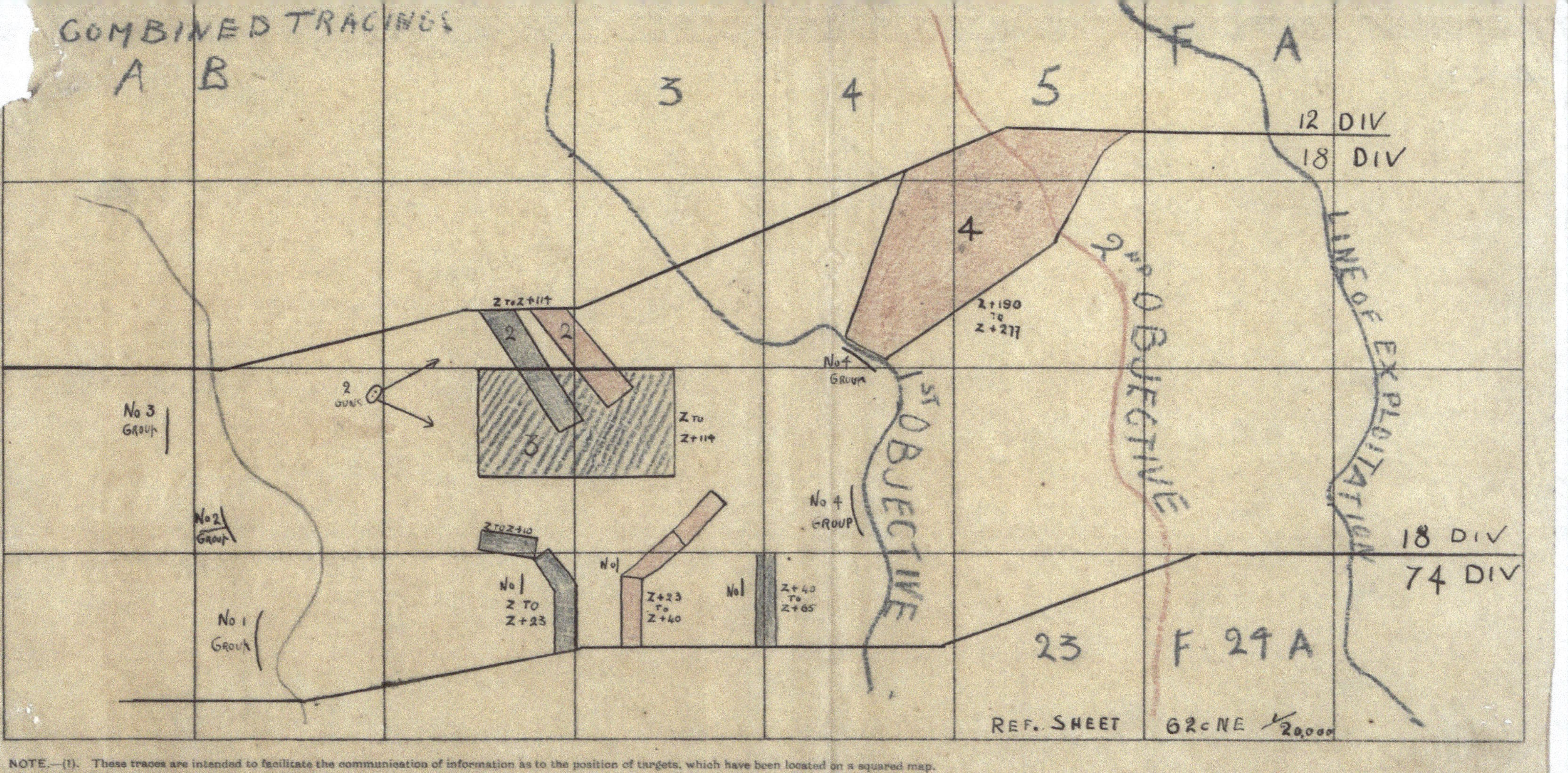

NOTE.—(1). These traces are intended to facilitate the communication of information as to the position of targets, which have been located on a squared map.

(2). The squares on this trace are 500 yards in length on the 1/10,000 scale, 1,000 yards in length on the 1/20,000 scale, and 2,000 yards in length on the 1/40,000 scale.

(3). The squares on the trace are fitted to the squares of the map showing the targets, which are then drawn on the trace. Sufficient letters and numbers must also be added to enable the recipient to place the trace in the correct position on his own map. A little detail may also be traced, but this is not essential. The name and scale of the map to which the trace refers must be always given. The trace can be used for the 1/10,000, 1/20,000, or 1/40,000 scale.

G.S.G.S. 3023.

Tracing taken from Sheet ....

of the 1: .... *map of* ....

Signature .... *Date* ....

SECRET. *appendix 87* Copy No. 14...

Reference Maps:- 62.c.N.E.
62.b.N.W. 1/20,000. 20th September 1918.

18TH BATTN. M.G.C. ORDER No. 50.

1. The 18th Division will attack and capture the BLUE LINE between F.6.a.9.3. and A.7.b.9.2.
The attack will be carried out in conjunction with Divisions on right and left.

2. ACTION OF M.Gs. Guns will be organised for the attack as follows:-
(a) 4 Guns "D" Coy 18th Bn.) From present positions will
6 Guns of "C" Coy do.,) bring harassing fire to bear
6 Guns "B" Coy.) on THE KNOLL, F.12.a. From
8 Guns "A" Coy.) Zero to Z plus 55.
(b) 4 Guns of "A" Coy, will follow attack of 53rd Inf. Bde. on the left and take up positions in the neighbourhood of THE KNOLL under arrangements with G.O.C. 53rd Inf. Bde.
4 Guns of "B" Coy. will follow attack of 54th Inf. Bde. on right and take up positions at F.12.c.80.00 (Approx), commanding MACQUINCOURT VALLEY and the slopes to the North.
4 Guns "D" Coy, 18th Battn. M.G.C. will occupy DOLEFUL POST, organised for defence in depth.
(c) S.O.S. Barrage.
"C" and "D" Coys. 100th Bn.M.G.C. will each place 12 guns on the line of SART FARM and HOLLAND POST and lay on S.O.S. lines to cover the front of the objective as per attached tracing.
"C" and "D" Coys. *100th Bn* will concentrate East of ST EMILIE and will stand to at Zero and move forward on receipt of orders.

3. DEFENCES.
The line when captured will be maintained at all costs.

4. AMMUNITION SUPPLY.
Coys. firing S.O.S. barrage will have 10,000 rounds S.A.A. per gun in positions and will maintain this amount.
Os.C. all Coys. 18th Bn.M.G.C. will arrange for an adequate supply of ammunition to be maintained with all sections.

5. COMMUNICATIONS.
Forward Report Centre and group H.Qrs for barrage guns will be at QUID POST. As soon as the tactical situation permits a line will be run from here to SART FARM. N.C.O. i/c Signals will notify nearest battery of the location of this station as soon as it is established. O.C. Battery will be responsible for circulating this information.

6. S.O.S.
S.O.S. Signal is RED over RED over RED.
On S.O.S. Signal being sent up all batteries laid on S.O.S. lines will open fire at the rate of 250 rounds per minute for 10 minutes; 50 rounds per minute for a further 10 minutes.

7. TANKS.
6 Tanks are allotted to the Division to take part in the atta[ck] and will move forward at Zero plus 1 hour.

8. Z DAY and ZERO hour will be notified later.

9. Location.
Adv. Bn.H.Qrs will be F.14.b.8.1.

10. A C K N O W L E D G E.

J W K Warne [signature]
Capt & Adjt.,
18th Battalion Machine Gun Corps.

Issued at ..5.15.. p.m.

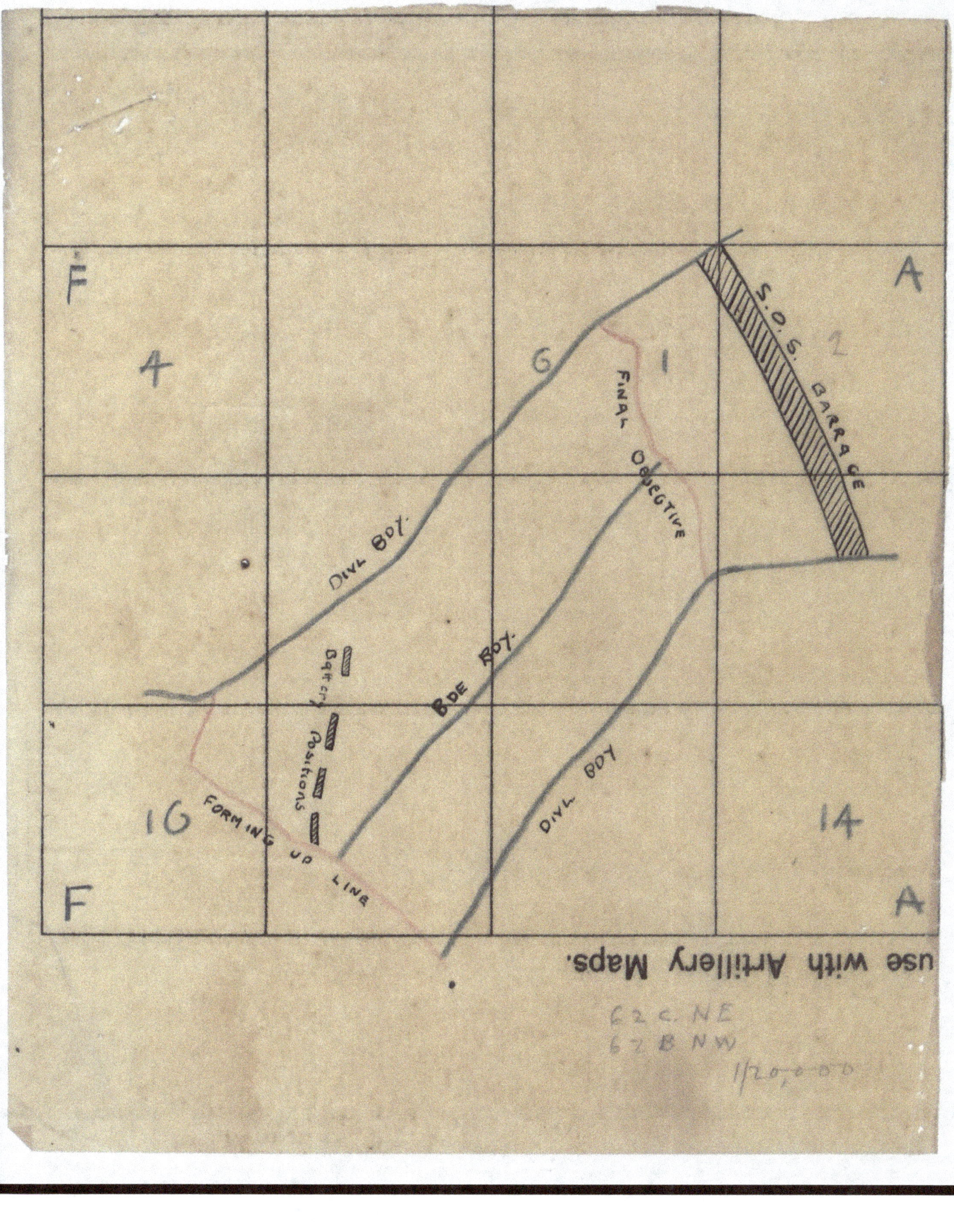

F

4

6

1

A

2

S.O.S. BARRAGE

FINAL OBJECTIVE

DIVL BDY.

BDE BDY.

Battery Positions

DIVL BDY

16

FORMING UP LINE

14

F

A

use with Artillery Maps.

62 C. NE
62 B NW
1/20,000

Appendix 89.

SECRET. 18th Battn. M.G.C. No.S.133.

TO:-x Os.C. "A", "B", "C", H.Q. Coys.
R.S.M. Quartermaster.

---

1. The 18th Battn. M.G.C. (Less "D" Company) will move by route march to the LIERAMONT Area to-morrow 28th inst.
Route:- COMBLES - RANCOURT - BOUCHAVESNES - MOISLAINS - NURLU - LIERAMONT.

2. Companies and Bn.H.Qrs will move independently leaving their present billets at 10.30 a.m.
It is suggested that a halt be made midday and dinners served.

3. Each Coy. and Bn.H.Qrs will send on ahead about 9 a.m. an advance party to secure bivouacing ground for night 28th/29th September.

4. Areas selected must be in the close neighbourhood of LIERAMONT.

5. Locations of Company Headquarters will be forwarded as soon as selected to 18th Divisional H.Qrs LIERAMONT with whom Battalion Headquarters will keep in close touch.

[signature]
Capt & Adjt.,
18th Battalion Machine Gun Corps.

27th September 1918.

SECRET. Copy No. 2

Appendix 88.

Ref. Corps Maps:- 57.c. & 62.c.1/40,000. 26th September 1918.

18TH BATTN.M.G.C. ORDER No. 88.

1. The 27th American Division will relieve the 18th Division in the line on the night 26th/27th September 1918.

2. (a) 18th Bn.M.G.C. will be relieved in the line accordingly on night 26th/27th September as follows:-

"A" Coy 18th Bn.M.G.C. by "B" Coy 27th Bn.
"B" Coy do., by "C" Coy do.,
"D" Coy do., by "D" Coy do.,

(b) All details as regards relief will be arranged between Company Commanders concerned. The following points will be observed:-

(i) Company Commanders will remain in forward Coy. H.Q. during night of 26th/27th and ensure that relieving Company Commanders are conversant with gun positions, etc.,

(ii) The No.1. of each gun in position will remain in the line until after "stand down" on morning of 27th inst.

(iii) Runners and signallers will remain in position until 27th inst.

3. On relief all Coys. in the line will proceed to their Transport lines for night 26th/27th inst.,

4. On the 27th inst. the Battalion will move to the [illegible] area as follows:-

(a) Transport "H" and H.Q.rs - "A" - "B" - "D" Coys. at ½ hour intervals starting at 9.15 a.m.

(b) Personnel. "H" and H.Q.rs - "A" - "B" - "D" Coys at ½ hour intervals leaving camp at 10.30 a.m.

Transport and Personnel H.Q.rs Coy. will move under

command of O.C. "C" Coy.

(e) Route. [illegible] – [illegible] – [illegible] – [illegible] – [illegible] – [illegible].

(f) Billets etc. Each company will detail 1 officer to report to Lieut. H. [illegible] at Battn Hq. [illegible] at 8 a.m. This party will jump lorries to [illegible] and arrange billets. Each Coy. will also send on ahead two Cyclist orderlies to report to Lieut. [illegible] and party at [illegible] HUT about 400 yards north of [illegible] on [illegible] – [illegible] Road. These cyclists will be on [illegible] – [illegible] Road in [illegible] by 1 p.m. for transport and 2 p.m. for personnel to guide Coys. to billets.

Note:- Cookers will move with personnel of Coys. A halt in vicinity of [illegible] should be made and midday meals served. Orders as regards relief of signallers will be issued later.

5. ACKNOWLEDGE.

H. Corran

Lieut & A/Adjt.,
100th Battalion Machine Gun Corps.

Issued at 11.[illegible] p.m. Copies to:-

No.1.copy C.O.
" 2 " 2nd-in-Command.
" 3 " Adjutant.
" 4 " "A" Company.
" 5 " "B" Company.
" 6 " "C" Company.
" 7 " "D" Company.
" 8 " R.S.O. i/c Signals.
" 9 " Quartermaster.
" 10 " War Diary.
" 11 " War Diary.
" 12 " File.

SECRET. appendix 90 Copy No. 17..

Reference Maps:- MONTBREHAIN, 62.c.N.E. & 57.c.S.E. 1/20,000. 28th September 1918.

18TH BATTALION M.G.C. ORDER No. 53.

1. An attack will be carried out on a date, and at an hour, to be notified later along the Fourth Army front.

The III Corps will cover the left flank of the main attack which is being carried out by the Australian Corps and by the II American Corps (Affiliated) on our right.

2. The attack on the III Corps front will be carried out by the 18th Division with two objects in view:-

(a) The protection of the left flank of the 27th American Division by gaining complete observation over VENDHUILE and the Canal and by keeping constant pressure on the enemy in this Vicinity.

(b) The Mopping-up of VENDHUILE and preparation of a way through for the passage of Divisions of the V Corps at the first possible opportunity.

Objective (a) is allotted to the 54th Infantry Brigade.
Objective (b) is allotted to the 55th Infantry Brigade and a Liaison Force of 54th Inf. Bde. detailed to work with the 107th American Infantry Regiment.

3. The 27th American Division will be attacking on our right at Zero under a creeping barrage. Direction of attacks are shown by red arrows; times of arrival will be issued later.

The 12th Division on our left will launch a small subsidiary attack under a creeping barrage later in order to secure the high ground in F.6.a. and X.30.c.

It is estimated that if the operation is carried out according to programme, sufficient simultaneous pressure should be brought to bear on VENDHUILE at 11 a.m. by the Liaison Force, 55th Brigade, 54th Brigade, and 12th Division to enable them to enter the town and mop it up.

4. ROLE OF M.Gs.

For this operation, Machine guns of the 18th Battn. M.G.C. will be employed as follows:-

(a) ½ Company allotted for co-operation with 54th Inf. Bde.
(b) ½ Company allotted for co-operation with the Liaison Force.
(c) ½ Company for co-operation with the 55th Inf. Bde.
(d) Indirect fire will also be brought to bear on THE BIRDCAGE in X.29.d. and also on exits to VENDHUILE.

5. Detailed Tasks.

"A" Company. 18th Battn. M.G.C. will be in Divisional Reserve and will be concentrated in Divisional Concentration Area W.28. W.29.a. and c. E.4 and E.5.a. and c.

"B" Company. 18th Bn.M.G.C.

8 Guns "B" Company are allotted for co-operation with 54th Inf. Bde. as per para 4.a.

These 8 guns will consolidate position captured by 54th Inf. Bde. in A.1.b. and A.2.c. (MACQUINCOURT TRENCH and TINO TRENCH). These guns in selecting positions will keep in view the "Strafing" by direct fire of the Bridges in S.25.b. and S.26.b. and d.

Immediately targets present themselves they will be engaged.

The remaining 8 Guns of "B" Company will be in Battalion Reserve and situated in vicinity of QUID POST.

"C" Company, 18th Bn.M.G.C. will take up indirect fire positions in vicinity of HOLLAND POST and SART FARM in F.17.a. to bring fire to bear on the BIRDCAGE in X.29.d. and also on the Northern exits to VENDHUILE.

Particular attention must be paid in selecting Battery positions to site them up the reverse slope and to keep out of the bottom of the valley on account of gas.

"D" Company. 18th Bn.M.G.C.

8 Guns of "D" Coy are allotted for co-operation with liaison force as per para 4.b.

These guns will go forward with the fourth Company of the 107th American Infantry Battalion and will take up positions as follows:-

4 Guns will cross CANAL and take up positions about A.3.d.9.9. (Approximately)

4 Guns to A.3.c.7.6.

Section Officers must use their initiative to the full extent in selecting these positions.

The task of the 4 guns at A.3.d.9.9. will be to bring direct enfilade fire to bear on bridge in A.3.a.8.4. and gun positions should be chosen accordingly.

Similarly, 4 Guns in A.3.c will dig in as soon as the main bridge in S.26.b. and d. is in enfilade.

The remaining 8 guns of "D" Coy. are allotted for co-operation with the 55th Infantry Brigade. They will not move forward until it is absolutely certain that the high ground in S.28.d, RICHMOND COPSE and RICHMOND QUARRY have been captured by the American Div. Gun positions will be selected at approximately:-

4 Guns ... ... A.2.b.3.0.
4 Guns ... ... A.2.b.9.3.

If serious opposition is encountered 55th Inf. Bde. are not to be involved in a direct attack on VENDHUILE but to bring pressure to bear upon its defences from the spur A.2.c., A.2.a.Central and A.2.b. and take every advantage of a slackening in the enemy's resistance in order to push into the town West of the CANAL. Machine guns will co-operate accordingly.

6. COMMUNICATION.
Will be notified later.

7. SIGNALS.

Success Signal	No. 32 Grenade, WHITE over WHITE over WHITE.
S.O.S. Signal	RED over RED over RED.

8. HEADQUARTERS.

18th Division	LIBRAMONT D.12.d.Central.	
18th Div. Report Centre .	Sunken Road, F.10.c.2.3.	
27th American Div. Adv...	ST EMILIE Quarries, E.18.d.0.7.	
54th Infantry Brigade ...	Sunken Road F.10.c.4.6.	
55th Infantry Brigade ...	EPEHY.	)
18th Battn.M.G.C.Adv. ...	Vicinity QUID POST	) Exact locations
"A" Coy, 18th Bn.M.G.C...	To be notified later	) will be
"B","C",& "D" Coys, ...	Sunken Road in F.10.c	) notified as soon as selected.

9. "Z" DAY & ZERO HOUR.
Will be notified later.

10. TRANSPORT. The III Corps Dry weather track runs as follows:-
CROPPER POST in F.1.d. - F.8.a.0.7 - F.8.a.7.7. - F.8.b.0.1. - F.9.a.0.0. - F.9.b.3.2. - F.10.c.35.55 to F.16.a.9.6.
No other road in American Corps area will be used by Infantry of the 18th Div.
American Corps area is area South of a line drawn on grid line between E.4. and E.10. to F.6. F.12.

11. Medical Arrangements. Location of Medical Posts:-
Forward Car Post ... ... DEELISH POST, F.8.d.3.6.
Rear Car Post ... ... ST.EMILIE, E.18.d.3.0.
Main Dressing Station ... VILLERS FAUCON
All cases will be evacuated along the road TOMBOIS FARM - LOMPIERE POST - RONSSOY - Cross Roads at F.15.d.6.8.- Cross Roads at F.8.a.6.3 - ST EMILIE.

12. Synchronisation of Watches.
Officers will synchronise watches at nearest Brigade H.Qrs.

13. Secrecy.
Attention is again drawn to the great danger of referring direct to operations over the telephone. This will be minimised as much as possible.

14. A C K N O W L E D G E.

Capt & Adjt.,
18th Battalion Machine Gun Corps.

Issued at ..6.. p.m. Copies to:-

No.1. C.O.
" 2 2nd-in-Command.
" 3 Adjutant.
" 4 "A" Company.
" 5 "B" Company.
" 6 "C" Company.
" 7 "D" Company.
" 8 Signals.
" 9 Quartermaster.
" 10 18th Division 'G'
" 11 53rd Inf. Bde.
" 12 54th Inf. Bde.
" 13 55th Inf. Bde.
" 14 C.M.G.O. III Corps.
" 15 27th American M.G.Battn.
" 16 107th American Infantry Bn.
" 17 War Diary.
" 18 War Diary.
" 19 File.

APPENDIX 91.

CASUALTIES INCURRED BY THE
18th Battn. M. G. Corps.
DURING THE MONTH OF
SEPTEMBER 1918.

OFFICERS.

Major E. Wigley.	Wounded (Gas) 4th Sep:1918.
2/Lt. J. L. Charlton.	Wounded (Gas) 4th Sep:1918.
2/Lt. R. S. Clark.	Wounded in Action. 12th Sep:1918
2/Lt. W. H. G. Curtis.	Wounded (At Duty) 12th Sep:1918.
2/Lt. E. S. Hope.	Wounded 18th Sep:1918.
2/Lt. C. W. Buckley.	Wounded (Gas) 20th Sep:1918.
Lt. G. H. Brownrigg-Jay.	Killed in Action 21st Sep:1918.
2/Lt. D. Hancock.	Wounded in Action 21st Sep:1918.
2/Lt. C. Pettitt.	Wounded in Action 22nd Sep:1918.
Lt. C. H. Ffolliott.	Wounded in Action 29th Sep:1918.
Lt R. B. Sisson.	Wounded in Action 29th Sep:1918.

OTHER RANKS.

Date.	Killed.	Died of Wds.	Wounded.	Wounded(Gas)	Missing	TOTAL.
1st	1	-	11	1	-	13
2nd	-	-	1	-	-	1
3rd	-	-	2	-	-	2
4th	-	-	4	-	-	4
5th	-	-	1	32	-	33
7th	-	-	1 (S.I.)	-	-	1
18th	2	-	17	-	-	19
19th	1	1	5	2	-	9
20th	2	-	4	3	-	9
21st	9	-	9	-	-	18
22nd	-	-	4	1	-	5
23rd	-	-	5	-	-	5
24th	-	-	3	9	-	12
25th	-	-	1	6	-	7
29th	2	-	5	-	-	7
30th	-	-	5	-	-	5
TOTALS	17 :	1 :	78 :	54 :	- :	150

-----------0000000-----------

APPENDIX 92.

CHANGES IN ESTABLISHMENT AND STRENGTH OF BATTALION: DRAFTS RECEIVED, CHANGES IN OFFICERS ETC. DURING MONTH OF SEPTEMBER.

Paper Strength of Battalion (Excluding attached):-

1st September 1918:- 45 Officers 844 Other Ranks

DECREASES.

For casualties in Officers during month see Appendix **91.**

Other Ranks.

Evacuated to C.C.S.	30
In Hosp. over 7 days	7
Candidate for Commission	1
Appointment as Sergt Cook	1
TOTAL DECREASES	39
Casualties in action	153
TOTAL	192

INCREASES.

2nd Lieut. D. Hancock.)
2nd Lieut. J.L. Charlton.)
2nd Lieut. E.S. Hope.)
Lieut. C.W. Buckley)
Joined Battalion from M.G.C. Base Depot and taken on strength 31.8.1918.

2nd Lieut. E.C. Boughton)
2nd Lieut. H.J. Burr)
Joined Battalion from M.G.C. Base Depot and taken on strength 19.9.18

Major P. Mathisen)
Lieut. C.L. Davey.)
2nd Lieut. H. Campbell Davies)
Joined Battalion from M.G.C. Base Depot and taken on strength 22.9.18.

Lieut. R.B. Sisson,)
2nd Lieut. L. Jordan.)
Joined Battalion from M.G.C. Base Depot and taken on strength 27.9.18

86 O.R's joined Batt. from M.G.C.Base Depot..	31.8.18
13 O.R's ---------------Do----------------	11.9.18
10 O.R's ---------------Do----------------	19.9.18
43 O.R's---------------Do----------------	22.9.18
3 O.R's---------------Do----------------	26.9.18
50 O.R's---------------Do----------------	27.9.18
11 O.R's rejoined from C.C.S.	-----

TOTAL INCREASE (Other Ranks):- 216

Strength 1st:-	45 Officers	844 Other Ranks
Decreases:-	7 "	192 " "
	38 "	652 " "
Increases:-	11 "	216
Paper Strength of Battalion 30th September 1918:- (Less attached)	49 Officers	868 Other Ranks

... Confidental ...

..War..Diary..

of

... 18th ... Battalion ... Machine ... Gun ... Corps ...

... From ... 1st October ... 1918 ...
... To ... 31st October ... 1918 ...

... Appendices ...
... 93 to 106 ... Attached ...

... Volume ... IX ...

9829

Map Ref. 57B NE
Scale 1/20,000.

Instructions regarding War Diaries and Intelligence Summaries are contained in F. S. Regs., Part II. and the Staff Manual respectively. Title pages will be prepared in manuscript.

18th Bn Machine Gun Corps

WAR DIARY
or
~~INTELLIGENCE SUMMARY.~~
(Erase heading not required.)

October 1918

Army Form C. 2118.

Place	Date	Hour	Summary of Events and Information	Remarks and references to Appendices
RONSSOY WOOD	1st		In line – VENDHUILLE.	
		11a	Visited by OC 50 B MGC and details of relief arranged to take	
			place during afternoon 1st and night 1/2 Oct. as per O.O. 54	app.93
			"C" Coy already in bivouacs in E 8 c r d	
			A Coy on relief concentrated in E 4 a 4.9	
			B do AIZECOURT	
			D do E 8 c r d	
			Reliefs were complete by 3.30 am 2nd Oct. . Order No 55 issued	app.94 JD
	2nd		Advd Bn HQ relieved in RONSSOY WOOD and proceeded to Embussing Point.	
	"	9am	Whole Battalion, (less Transport) concentrated at Cross Road E4 b 9.4	
			to embuss – Lorries late – embussing complete 12.30 pm – proceeded	
			by bus to CONTAY and by march route to MONTIGNY	
			where whole Battalion in billets by 6 pm. – Transport moved	
			by road	JD
MONTIGNY	3rd		Owing to unsatisfactory state of billets – Battalion given permission	
			to move to WARLOY	

D. D. & L., London, E.C.
(A7883) Wt. W809/M1672 350,000 4/17 Sch. 52a Forms/C/2118/14

Instructions regarding War Diaries and Intelligence Summaries are contained in F. S. Regs., Part II. and the Staff Manual respectively. Title pages will be prepared in manuscript.

Army Form C. 2118.

18th Battn Machine Gun Corps WAR DIARY or ~~INTELLIGENCE SUMMARY.~~ October 1918

(Erase heading not required.)

Place	Date	Hour	Summary of Events and Information	Remarks and references to Appendices
MONTIGNY	3rd (Cont)	2 pm	Battalion moved by march route to WARLOY and in billets by 4 pm. – very comfortable	JD
WARLOY	~~3rd~~ 4th		Resting & cleaning up	JD
"	5th		do – Baths at VADENCOURT	JD
"	6th		Sunday – Rest	JD
"	7th		Company Training on Battalion Parade Ground	JD
"	8th		do	JD
"	9th		do	JD
"	10th		do	JD
"	11th		do	JD
"	12th		do Baths.	JD
"	13th		Sunday – Rest – Owing to bad weather No Parade Service	
		10 pm	Warning Order received to be ready to move at 24 hrs notice	JD
"	14th		A C & D Coys on range work – B Coy tactical scheme with 55th Bde	JD
"	15th		All Battalion less Transport on Route March	
		11 am	Orders received from Division for Battalion to be ready to move at once. Warning Order for move issued	JD App 97.

D. D. & L., London, E.C. (A7883) Wt. W809/M1672 350,000 4/17 Sch. 52a Forms/C/2118/14

Instructions regarding War Diaries and Intelligence Summaries are contained in F. S. Regs., Part II. and the Staff Manual respectively. Title pages will be prepared in manuscript.

Army Form C. 2118.

WAR DIARY
or
~~INTELLIGENCE SUMMARY.~~
(Erase heading not required.)

18th Battalion Machine Gun Corps

October 1918

Place	Date	Hour	Summary of Events and Information	Remarks and references to Appendices
WARLOY	15 (cont)		Battalion "standing to" during afternoon – Orders to move on 16th received – Coy Cmdrs A B & D Coys went forward by car to reconnoitre forward area 7 pm. O.O. 56 issued	appendix 95
do	16		Battalion embussed as per O.O. 56	
			C Coy & Bn H.Q. remained at MARETZ & ~~billeted there~~ arriving 6 pm.	
			A B & D Coys proceeded on to MAUROIS where Coy Cmdrs awaited them	
LE CATEAU	[illegible]		"A", "B" and D Coys assisted 66th Div in attack on LE CATEAU and took up barrage position S.W. of this town.	
	17		The attack of 66th Div launched. 18th Battn. M.G.C. H.Qtrs together with C Coy moved to REUMONT. The attack was continued in the evening and these Coys again assisted in barrage fire.	
	18.		"D" Coy was withdrawn to billets in HONECHY. A & B Coys relieved 2 Coys of 25th Battn. M.G.C. for defence of line. Order No 57 issued.	App 96
	19		C.O. attended conference at 18th Divl H.Qtrs. No movement of guns.	

D. D. & L., London, E.C. (A7883) Wt W809/M1672 350,000 4/17 Sch 52a Forms/C/2118/14

Instructions regarding War Diaries and Intelligence Summaries are contained in F. S. Regs., Part II. and the Staff Manual respectively. Title pages will be prepared in manuscript.

WAR DIARY
or
INTELLIGENCE SUMMARY.
(Erase heading not required.)

Army Form C. 2118.

Place	Date	Hour	Summary of Events and Information	Remarks and references to Appendices
LE CATEAU.	20.		No change. Order No 58 issued	R. App 98.
	21.		"Ditto" Order No 59 issued	App 99
	22.		On night of 22nd all Coys moved to their assembly positions for attack Order No 60 issued 2215	App 100 R.
			on BOUSIES as per narrative (App. 102) Battn HQrs moved together with all Coys Order 61 issued	App. 101 App 102.
	23.		Attack of 18th Div. launched at 0120 hrs. See narrative as to actions of M.G.s to LE CATEAU	R.
BOUSIES	24		Battn HQrs moved to BOUSIES. Re organization of gun positions in	
			connection with Divl defence scheme. Order No 62 issued	App 103
	25		Harassing fire programme arranged as per attached tracing to assist	R.
			in 53rd Bde's attack on MT. CARMON. Order No 63 issued	App 104
	26		Attack of 53rd Bde launched. Partially successful.	
			Corps commander visited Battn HQrs and congratulated ~~the~~ the Battn on its	R.
			work during the attack on 23rd & 24th inst.	
	27.		Divl line of resistance slightly altered and gun positions moved to conform.	R.
	28.		Harassing fire programme carried out continuously. 20,500 rds. fired. Tracing attd	R.
	29		As for 28th. Rounds fired. 25000	R.
	30.		'A' Coy 50th Battn M.G.C. relieved our guns in right sector. 8 gun teams withdrawn to BOUSIES	R.

D. D. & L., London, E.C.
(A7883) Wt. W809/M1672 350,000 4/17 Sch. 52a Forms/C/2118/14

Instructions regarding War Diaries and Intelligence Summaries are contained in F. S. Regs., Part II. and the Staff Manual respectively. Title pages will be prepared in manuscript.

WAR DIARY
or
INTELLIGENCE SUMMARY.
(Erase heading not required.)

Army Form C. 2118.

Place	Date	Hour	Summary of Events and Information	Remarks and references to Appendices
BOUCIES	30		Selected targets harassed. Rounds fired 25 500.	P.
	31		As for 30th inst.	P.
			For statement of casualties during month see appendix 105	App 105
			For statement giving changes in Establishment & strength see appendix 106	App 106

E. Ellwort .... Lieut.-Col.
Cmdg. 18th Bn. Machine Gun Corps.

D. D. & L., London, E.C.
(A7883) Wt. W809/M1672 350,000 4/17 Sch. 52a Forms/C/2118/14

SECRET. Appendix 93 Copy No. 10.

Reference Maps:- 57.c.N.E. 57.b.N.W. 1st October 1918.
[illegible] 1/20,000.

18TH BATTN.M.G.C. ORDER No. 54.

1. The 50th Battn. M.G.C. will relieve the 18th Bn. M.G.C. in the line on the night 1st/2nd October.

2. "B" Coy. 50th Battn.M.G.C. will relieve "B" and "C" Coys. 18th Battn.M.G.C. and "D" Coy. 50th Bn. will relieve "A" Coy. 18th Bn.M.G.C.
"B" Coy 50th will take over following positions:-

A.3.a.9.7.	2 Guns.
A.2.b.9.4.	2 Guns.
A.2.b.3.5.	2 Guns.
A.8.c.1.9.	2 Guns.
F.22.d.3.5.	2 Guns.

Remaining 6 guns will be in support in dug-outs about F.16.c.4.6. and will take up positions in QUARRIES AVENUE and SMALL Support in F.12.b. and A.7.a.
Company Headquarters in F.10.c.3.4.
"D" Coy. 50th Bn.M.G.C. will take over following positions:-

[illegible] POST F.5.c.	4 Guns.
X.26.c.1.3.	2 Guns.
X.30.a.4.6.	2 Guns.
X.30.c.6.9.	2 Guns.
X.29.a.9.5.	2 Guns.
SUNKEN Road, F.16.b.Central,	4 Guns.
Company H.Qrs.	F.9.c.1.9.

3. All arrangements as regards relief will be arranged between Company Commanders concerned.

4. All guns not being relieved will withdraw at dusk to-night.

5. Concentration areas will be notified later.

6. Completion of relief will be reported to Adv. Bn. H.Qrs using code word "BULGARIA".

7. Acknowledge.

Capt & Adjt.,
18th Battalion Machine Gun Corps.

Issued at 2.30 p.m. Copies to:-

No.1. C.O.
" 2 2nd in Command.
" 3 Adjutant.
" 4 "A" Company.
" 5 "B" Company.
" 6 "C" Company.
" 7 "D" Company.
" 8 50th Bn.M.G.C.
" 9 War Diary.
" 10 War Diary.
" 11 File.

SECRET. Copy No....9

appendix 94

Reference Map:- AMIENS 1/100,000. 1st October 1918.

18TH BATTN. MACHINE GUN CORPS. ORDER No.55.

1. The Battalion will move to-morrow to AGNICOURT and BAVELINCOURT area; personnel by bus; transport by road.

2, Busses Nos 143 to 172 (inclusive) are allotted to the Battalion and are re-allotted to Coys as follows:-

Battn. H.Qrs.	143 - 146.
"B" Coy.	147 - 152.
"C" Coy.	153 - 158.
"D" Coy.	160 - 165.
"A" Coy.	166 - 171.

Numbers 159 and 172 are spare. Capacity of each lorry 25.

3. (a) Embussing Point:- Front lorry allotted to 18th Bn M.G.C. E.14.b.6.6. (approximately). Column facing West on the SAULCOURT - LIERAMONT Road.
(b) Time of embussing:- 9.15 a.m. (Ready to move off 9.30 a.m. sharp.
2 O.Rs. per Company will report to Adjutant at Cross Roads E.15.a.0.4. at 9 a.m. to act as markers for lorries allotted to Coys.
(c) Debussing Point:- On Contay - WARLOY Road on outskirts of CONTAY.

4. Personnel proceeding by bus will carry packs etc., Dixies will also be carried on the lorries.

5. Transport will move by road under Coy. arrangements. Instructions etc., have already been issued verbally to Coy. representatives.

6. Rations for consumption 3rd inst., will be issued in new area.

7. Coys. should send on ahead to new area an Officer representative to meet Lieut. H. CORRAN who is arranging billets. This Officer should jump lorries to enable him to reach destination before the Battalion.

8. Acknowledge.

Capt & Adjt.,
18th Battalion Machine Gun Corps.

Issued at 8.40 p.m.
Copies to:-

No.1. C.O.
" 2 2nd-in-Command.
" 3 Adjutant.
" 4 "A" Company.
" 5 "B" Company.
" 6 "C" Company.
" 7 "D" Company.
" 8 QrMr.
" 9/10 War Diary.
" 11 File.

all. Batteries 8 Guns

·15

16

K L

4 Guns 33 Bn

A+B. 1.

A+B. 2

A+B. 3

F. 1.

F. 2.

G. 1.

E. 1.

H. 1.

H. 2

G. 2

D. 2.

C. 2

C. 3.

C. 1

E. 2

D. 2.

33 Bn

33 Bn

C. Coy 100 Bn H G.

B. Coy 100 Bn F E

A. Coy 100 Bn D. C.

B. Coy 18 Bn B

D. Coy 18 Bn A.

34

K L

33

NOTE.—(1). These traces are intended to facilitate the communication of information as to the position of targets, which have been located on a squared map.

(2). The squares on this trace are 500 yards in length on the 1/10,000 scale, 1,000 yards in length on the 1/20,000 scale, and 2,000 yards in length on the 1/40,000 scale.

(3). The squares on the trace are fitted to the squares of the map showing the targets, which are then drawn on the trace. Sufficient letters and numbers must also be added to enable the recipient to place the trace in the correct position on his own map. A little detail may also be traced, but this is not essential. The name and scale of the map to which the trace refers must be always given. The trace can be used for the 1/10,000, 1/20,000, or 1/40,000 scale.

G.S.G.S. 3023.

Tracing taken from Sheet 57 B.N.E

of the 1: 20,000 map of

Signature Date

GROUP "Z".

Commanded by..........................

Battery.	Tasks.	No. of Guns.	Time.	Rate of Fire.
H. C Coy. 10th Batt.	Location (approx) & Targets as per Tracing.	8.	Task 1. 2 to 2 plus 60 Task 2. 2 plus 60 to 2 plus 80.	125 rounds per Minute.

33rd DIVISION.

BATTERIES OF FOUR GUNS AT (APPROX)

Targets as per Tracing.

Times.

Task No. 1 Target 2 to 2 plus 20.
Task No. 2 Target. 2 plus 20 to 2 plus 35.

Distribution:-

.O.
2nd in Command.
.B.C.&.D. Coys. 18th Batt.M.G.C.
.0th Batt. M.G.C. (6 Copies)
.rd Division (2 Copies)

GROUP "Y".

Commanded by........................

Battery.	Tasks.	No. of Guns	Time.	Rate of Fire.
E. B. Coy. 100th Batt.	Location (approx) & Targets as per Tracing.	8	Task 1. 2 to 2 plus 50. Task 2. 2 plus 50 to 2 plus 70.	125 rounds per minute

GROUP "Y".

Commanded by..........................

Battery.	Tasks.	No. of Guns.	Time.	Rate of Fire.
F. B Coy. 100th Batt.	Location (approx) & Targets as per Tracing.	8	Task 1. 2 to 2 plus 70. Task 2. 2 plus 70 to 2 plus 80	125 rds. per Min.

GROUP "Z".

Commanded by..........................

Battery.	Tasks.	No. of Guns.	Time.	Rate of Fire.
G. D. Coy. 100th Batt.	Location (approx) & Targets as per Tracing	8	Task 1. 2 to 2 plus 35 Task 2. 2 plus 35 to 2 plus 70	125 rds. per Min.

GROUP "W".

Commanded by..............................

Batteries	Tasks.	No. of Guns.	Times.	Rate of fire.
A. & B. 18th Batt. M.G.C. 8 Guns B. Co. 8 Guns D. Co.	Location (approx) & Targets as per Tracing.	A Batty. [illegible] B.Batty. 8	Task 1 2 to 2 plus 15. Task 2 2 plus 15 to 2 plus 40 Task 3 2 plus 40 to 2 plus 56.	125 rds per Min.

GROUP "Y"

Commanded by...........................

Batteries.	Tasks	No. of Guns.	Time.	Rate of Fire.
C. A. Coy. 100th Batt.	Location (approx) & Targets as per Tracing.	8	Task 1. 2 to 2 plus 50 Task 2. 2 plus 50 to 2 plus 65 Task 3. 2 plus 65 to 2 plus 80.	125 rounds per minute.

GROUP "Z".

Commanded by.........................

Battery.	Tasks.	No. of Guns.	Time.	Rate of Fire.
D. A Coy. 100thBatt.	Location (approx) & Targets as per Tracing.	[illegible]	Task 1. 2 to 2 plus 50 Task 2. 2 plus 50 to 2 plus 80	125 rounds per minute.

10. The Tracings and Fire Orders referred to in Order No. 58 will be issued separately and as early as possible.

11. A C K N O W L E D G E.

Issued at:-..........

Major,
for Lieut. Col.
Commanding 18th Battalion M.G.C.

P.T.O.

Distribution:-

To all Recipients of Order No. 58.

Appendix 99

SECRET. COPY NO...3...

18th BATTALION MACHINE GUN CORPS ORDER NO. 59.

Reference Maps:-
57B.N.E. and 57B.S.E.
1/20,000.

21st Octr.1918.

1. SIGNALS.
During the advance Wireless Stations will be formed by Tanks at the following places:-
K. 23.d.5.8.
K. 18.d.3.0.
L. 7.d.8.2.
L. 9.c.2.6.
In addition to this a Battalion Line will be laid forward as company H.Q. advance under Battalion orders.

2. MACHINE GUNS.
Reference para. 10. Order No. 58., under heading "Barrage Guns" for 2 Companies 100th Battalion M.G.C. read 4 Companies.

3. The additional two Companies of the 100th Battalion M.G.C. on completion of Barrage Shoot will pack up and concentrate in suitable positions in vicinity of Battery positions and await further orders.

4. O.C. "D" Coy. will command the 16 Guns going forward with 55th Brigade.

5. O.C. "A" Coy. will form his Company H.Q. in vicinity of 53rd Brigade.

6. Reference para. 3 of Order No. 58, a fresh Map is attached to replace the previous one issued shewing new objectives and halts. All Maps should be altered accordingly at once.

7. The attack of the 53rd and 54th Brigades will most probably take place very early, so that the attack of the 55th Brigade on the third objective will take place at dawn.

8. The 55th Brigade will capture the third, fourth and fifth objectives.

9. The attack of the 18th Division will start before Zero in order to allow the 18th Division, whose starting line is behind that of the 33rd Division, to arrive on the first objective simultaneously.
At present the opening line of the creeping barrage is K.36.a.2.7 to K.23.c.7.9. This line will be advanced according to the ground gained by Troops of the 53rd and 54th Brigades before "Z" day. The right flank of the barrage will be ~~a~~ line drawn from K.36.a.2.7. to L.26.a.0.7. The Copse in L.25.c. will be treated with a standing barrage until the hour fixed for the joint attack on this Copse and Garde Mill.

"A" Form.
Army Form C. 2121.
(In pads of 100.)

MESSAGES AND SIGNALS.

No. of Message..........

Prefix..........Code..........m. | Words. | Charge.
Office of Origin and Service Instructions.

This message is on a/c of: ....Service.
(Signature of "Franking Officer.")

Sent
At..........m.
To..........
By..........

Recd. at..........m.
Date..........
From..........
By..........

TO: A B C + D Coys. 18th M G Bn
A B C + D Coys. 100th M G Bn

Sender's Number.	Day of Month.	In reply to Number.	AAA
* AB143	21st		

Ref para 9 of 18th M G Bn Order No. 59 the Zero time given to those companies will be the time the 18th Division commences the attack.

From 18th Bn MGC.
Place
Time

The above may be forwarded as now corrected. (Z) (Sd) C B Hibbert Major for C.O.

Censor. Signature of Addressor or person authorised to telegraph in his name.

* This line, except AAA, should be erased if not required.

Wt. W 3252/P511. 500,000 Pads. 1/18. B. & S. Ltd. (E2389.)

14. SYNCHRONISATION OF WATCHES.

An Officer of each Company will report to Battalion H.Q. at Zero Minus 4 hours for purpose of above.

15. HEADQUARTERS.

18th Battalion Machine Gun Corps (Advanced) LE CATEAU., No. 16 Rue Marche de Chevaux. K.35.a.2.4.

"A" "B" "C" and "D" Companies and 2 Companies of the 100th Battalion Machine Gun Corps in LE CATEAU. Exact locations to be notified later.

16. Zero will be notified later.

17. A C K N O W L E D G E.

Issued at..17.30....

Cmdg [signature] Major, for Lt Col
18th Battalion M. G. C.

Distribution.
Copy No. 1 C.O.
2 2nd in Command.
3 Adjutant.
4. "A" Coy.
5. "B" Coy.
6. "C" Coy.
7. "D" Coy.
8. Signals.
9/10. 2 Coys. 100th Batt. M.G.C.
11. O.C. 100th Battn. M.G.C.
12. 18th Division.
13. 53rd Brigade.
14. 54th Brigade.
15. 55th Brigade.
16. 25th Division.
17. 33rd Division.
18/19. War Diary.
20. File.

(a) BARRAGE GUNS.

Approximate Battery positions, Targets, and rates of fire are as shewn on attached tracing and fire organisation charts respectively.

1 Company of the 100th Battalion M.G.C. on completion of its barrage shoot, and when the second Objective is captured, will move to a line 1500 yards back from the 2nd Objective and take up positions ready to answer S.O.S. calls for the defence of that line.

The other Company of the 100th Battalion, will, after completion of its barrage shoot, pack up and be ready to move forward with its Limbers to an intermediary Line between the final and second Objectives for purpose of answering S.O.S. calls to cover the final objective line. This Company will, however, not move forward until orders are received from Battn. H.Q.

(b) FORWARD CONSOLIDATION GUNS.

8 Guns of "B" Coy. with 54th Brigade.
1 Section will proceed to the first Objective and consolidate.
1 Section will go right through to second Objective and consolidate.

16 Guns of "A" Coy. with 53rd Brigade.
Same as for "B" Coy. with the exception that for 1 Section read 2 Sections in each case.

Note 1. Map shewing approximate defensive positions to be taken up will be issued to Company Commanders separately.
Note 2. Pack animals will be used going forward.
Note 3. Guns will follow the rear waves of Infantry in each case.

8 Guns of "C" Coy.)
8 Guns of "D" Coy.) with 55th Brigade.

These guns will go right through to final objective with 55th Brigade for consolidation of that line.
Fighting Limbers will be used going forward.

12. PREPARATIONS.

All Battery positions will be dug and lines laid out ready for fire as soon after dusk as possible on evening of 21st inst. Ample Reserve Dumps of S.A.A. are to be made at Battery positions by the two Companies of the 100th Battalion M.G.C.

Sections of 18th Battalion going forward will arrange for Dumps under Company arrangements, to be made East of the Railway Embankment. Gun Teams going forward should carry the usual complement of Picks, Shovels and Sandbags.

13. DIRECTION.

The greatest care should be taken not to lose direction, and Compass Bearings must be taken by Officers and Section Sergeants to this end.

14. /

SECRET. appendix 98 COPY NO. 18

18th BATTALION MACHINE GUN CORPS.

Reference Maps:-
57B.N.E. and 57B.S.E.
1/20,000.

ORDER NO. 58.

20th October 1918.

1. At Zero hour on "Z" Day the Third and Fourth Armies will attack. The Fourth Army is to form a defensive flank, facing Eastwards, to protect the major operation which will be carried out by the Third Army.

2. The attack of the XIII Corps will be carried out by the 25th Division on the Right and the 18th Division on the Left; on the left of the 18th Division the 33rd Division of the V Corps will attack.

3. BOUNDARIES AND OBJECTIVES.
Inter-Divisional and Inter-Brigade Boundaries and objectives will be as shewn by Maps already issued.

4. GENERAL PLAN.
The attack og the 25th Division, 18th Division and 33rd Division will be frontal and simultaneous up to the capture of the first objective; the 25th Division will not advance through the BOIS L'EVEQUE to the 2nd objective, but will send troops immediately in rear of the right of the 53rd Brigade to picquet the N.W. face of the wood and work round it of it.

5. TASKS OF BRIGADES.
The 53rd Brigade on the right and the 54th Brigade on the left will capture the first and second objectives on the front of the 18th Division. The 55th Brigade will capture the third objective. One Battalion 54th Brigade will be held in Divisional Reserve.

6. ARTILLERY.
The attack will be carried out under a creeping barrage which will move at the rate of 100 yards in 4 minutes.

7. TANKS.
16 Tanks are allotted to the Division for the operation. The Infantry will follow the barrage and the Tanks will follow the Infantry to deal with any point where the Infantry have been held up.
The 1st Echelon of Tanks for the first objective will number 4; for the second 8; and in reserve for the final objective 4.

8. COMMUNICATIONS.
A Battalion Line is being laid to Advanced H.Q. From Advanced H.Q. onwards, the Divisional Lines will be utilised and details of arrangements issued later.

9. SIGNALS.
(a) Red Flares will be carried as well as tin discs to be shewn when the contact aeroplane calls.
(b) The S.O.S. Signal is GREEN
GREEN
RED.

10. MACHINE GUNS.
The Machine Guns assisting the advance of the Division are as follows:-
(a) BARRAGE GUNS.
8 Guns of B. Coy.
8 Guns of C. Coy.
8 Guns of D. Coy.
2 Coys of 100th Battalion M.G.C.

(b) FORWARD CONSOLIDATION GUNS.
8 Guns "B" Coy. operating with 54th Brigade.
16 Guns of "A" Coy. operating with 53rd Brigade.
8 Guns of "D" Coy. operating with 55th Brigade.
8 Guns of "C" Coy. Do. Do.

.v 10.18 ✓ Secret

O/c H.Q. & A B C & D Coys

Reference 18th Hy Batt order No 58 Para 112
for Dusk 21st inst
Read 22nd inst
Operations are postponed
24 hours

C B Wethered? Major
for O/c 18th Batt

Group No.5. Commanded by Coy.Comdr. 100th Bn. Battery "E"

Approximate Positions.	Targets and Tasks.	No.of Guns.	Zero time.	Rate of fire.
F.18.c.90.95	Task.1. from Width of(A.15.a.10.80.to Target (A.15.a.10.20. CREEP TO A.15.a.95.80 to A.15.a.95.20.	8	Z to plus 45.	130 rpm.
	Task 2. from Width of(A.10.c.50.35 to Target. (A.16.a.40.20. CREEP TO A.10.c.90.40 to A.16.a.90.20.	8	Z plus 45 to Z plus 180.	

Group No.6. Commanded by Coy. Comdr. 100th Bn. Battery "F"

Approximate Positions.	Targets and Tacks	No.of Guns.	Zero time.	Rate of fire.
F.18.c.75.40.	Task.1. from Width of(A.15.d.60.60.to Target. (A.15.d.60.00 CREEP TO A.16.d.10.60 to A.16.d.10.00.	8	Z to plus 90. (see remarks).	

Remarks:- From Z to plus 90 creep 100 yards every 5 minutes for 500 yards, then remain stationary on remainder of target to Z plus 174.

Group No.4. Commanded by Lieut. LEITH. Battery "D"

Approximate positions	Targets and tasks.	No.of Guns.	Zero time.	Rate of fire.
F.30.a.1.4	Task 1. From Width(A.20.d.1.4 of (to Target(A.26.b.1.7 CREEP TO A.20.d.8.3 to A.26.b.8.7	6	Z to plus 130.	130 r.p.m.
	Task 2. From A.20.d.15.45 to A.20.d.50.65	2	Z to plus 150.	130 r.p.m.
	Task 3. From Width(A.21.d.50.75 of (to Target(A.21.d.60.35 CREEP TO A.21.b.95.05 to A.22.c.20.80.	6	Z plus 130 to Z plus 150.	

Remarks:- On completion of Task 1. these guns will lay on to, and fire Task 3. from Z plus 130 to Z plus 150.

Group No.3. Commanded by Capt. Llewellyn. Battery "C".

Approximate Positions.	Targets and Tasks.	No.of Guns.	Zero Time.	Rate of Fire.
F.24.a.4.2. to F.24.c.4.9.	Task 1. From A.26.b.8.6. to A.27.a.4.2.	4	Z to plus 54	130 rpm
	Task.2. From A.21.d.2.8. to A.21.d.8.7.	4	Z to plus 155.	
	Task.3. From Width (A.21.d.70.65 of (to Target (A.21.d.80.20. <u>CREEP TO</u> A.22.c.50.60 to A.22.c.55.25.	4	Z plus 54 to Z plus 155.	

Remarks:- On completion of Task 1. these guns will lay on and fire Task 3. to Z plus 155.

Group No. 2. Commander:- Lieut. G. Young. Battery "B"

Approximate Positions.	Targets and tasks.	No. of. Guns.	Zero Time.	Rate of Fire.
F.17.c.9.4.	Task 1. from A.14.b.10.95. to A.8.d.60.00.	2	Z to plus 12.	130 r.p.m.
	Task 2. from A.9.c.0.2. to A.9.c.6.4.	2.	Z to plus 36.	130 r.p.m.
	Task 3. from Width (A.14.d.7.8. of (to Target (A.14.d.7.4. CREEP TO A.15.c.3.8. A.15.c.3.2.	4.	Z to plus 30.	130 r.p.m.
	Task 4. from Width (A.21.a.15.95 of (to Target (A.21.a.15.50. CREEP TO A.21.a.9.8. to A.21.a.9.4.	8.	Z plus 36 to Z plus 125.	130 r.p.m.

Remarks:- Task 1

These guns will cease fire at Z plus 12 and superimpose No. 2. Task.
On completion of tasks Nos. 1, 2, and 3 all guns lay on to and fire Task. 4.

FIRE ORGANISATION CHART.

Group No.1. Commander:- Lieut. Campbell Davies. Battery "A"

Approximate Positions.	Targets and Tasks.	No. of Guns.	Zero Time.	Rate of Fire.
F.12.a.3.3. to F.12.a.1.4.	Task.1. Barrage. from A.20.b.0.8. to A.20.b.4.3.	2	Z to plus 130.	130 R.P.M.
	Task.2. from A.20.b.45.65 to A.20.b.85.15	2	Z to plus 130.	130 r.p.m.
	Task 3. from A.15.c.15.45. to A.15.c.60.	4	Z to plus 50.	

Remarks:- No.3.Task will superimpose Nos. 1 and 2 Tasks at Z plus 50 to Z plus 130.

SECRET.

MEDICAL ARRANGEMENTS!
(To accompany 18th Bn.M.G.C.Order No.64)

1. O.C. 55th Field Ambulance is in charge of Advanced Evacuation. Hd.Qrs. BOUSIES. L.3.b.8.8.
He will have at his disposal the Bearer divisions, horsed ambulances, motor ambulances and wheeled stretcher carriers of 54th and 56th Field Ambulances.

2. O.C. 56th Field Ambulance will be in charge of Divisional Sick station, INCHY.

3. R.A.Ps. will be selected by Brigades concerned.
Ford Car Loading Post:- F.29.c.4.4.
Walking Wounded Collecting Post.) Near Station BOUSIES
Advanced Dressing Station.) L.3.b.8.8.
Corps Main Dressing Station.)
Corps Walking Wounded Post.) LE CATEAU, K.34.a.8.8

4. METHOD OF EVACUATION.
Lying cases by hand carriage and wheeled stretchers to Ford Car post thence by cars to A.D.S.
Walking wounded will be directed through ROBERSART to A.D.S. horsed ambulances will meet them as far forward as possible.
It is proposed to push Ford Cars as far forward as possible.

S. R. Doggett. Capt.
for Lieut-Colonel,
Commanding 18th Battalion Machine Gun Corps.

2nd November 1918.
Copies to recipients of 18th Bn.M.G.C.Order No.64.

10. ZERO HOUR. Will be notified later.

11. ACKNOWLEDGE.

Elliott

Lieut-Colonel,
Commanding 18th Battalion Machine Gun Corps.

Issued at ...... p.m.
Copies to:-

No.1.Copy C.O.
" 2 " Adjutant.
" 3 " "A" Company.
" 4 " "B" Company.
" 5 " "C" Company.
" 6 " "D" Company.
" 7 " Signals.
" 8 " 18th Division "G".
" 9 " 53rd Inf. Bde.
" 10 " 54th Inf. Bde.
" 11 " 55th Inf. Bde.
" 12 " C.M.G.C.
" 13 " 50th Division.
" 14 " 38th Division.
" 15/16" War Diary.
" 17 " File.

7. **TANKS.** 10 Tanks are allotted to the Division. These are reallotted:-

4 to 54th Infantry Brigade.
6 to 53rd Infantry Brigade.

two of the latter taking part in the clearing of the Eastern end of PREUX before advancing with 53rd Inf. Bde.

8. **MACHINE GUNS.**

(a) Barrage Guns.

8 Guns of "A" Company.
8 Guns of "B" Company.
8 Guns of "C" Company.
8 Guns of "D" Company.

(b) Consolidation Guns.

8 Guns of "B" Company) Operating with 53rd Inf.
8 Guns of "D" Company) Brigade.
8 Guns of "A" Company) Operating with 55th Inf.
8 Guns of "C" Company) Brigade.

O.C. "B" Company and O.C. "C" Coy. will be in Command in each case respectively.

(a) Barrage Guns.

Battery positions, targets, rates of fire are as shown on attached tracing, and fire Organisation Charts respectively.

Barrage guns will be grouped in Batteries of 8 under an Officer.

Battery positions will be dug and lines laid out ready for fire by dusk on 2nd inst.

S.A.A. dumps have already been formed at Battery positions.

(b) Forward Consolidation Guns.

Tracing showing approximate final defensive positions issued to Company Commanders herewith. Guns will go forward with auxilliary mountings and 6 belt boxes to enable guns coming into action quickly.

Every effort must be made to help Infantry forward by bringing enfilade fire to bear on any point holding out.

Mules will take forward tripods and extra belt boxes.

Sections going forward will arrange for dumps under Company arrangements.

GunTeams going forward should carry usual complement of picks, shovels, etc.,

9. **SYNCHRONISATION OF WATCHES.**

An Officer of each Company will report to Battn. H.Qrs at Zero minus 4 Hours for purpose of above.

SECRET.

Copy No. 9...

Reference Map:- 57.A.N.W. 1/20,000.

1st November 1918.

18th BATTN. M.G.C. ORDER NO. 64.

1. GENERAL. At Zero hour on "Z" Day the 18th Division will attack in conjunction with the 50th Div. on its right and the 38th Div. on left.

2. PLAN OF ATTACK.

Map "A" was issued to all Coys. giving boundaries, objectives and the proposed plan of attack of the 18th Division in Detail. Referring to this map, tasks were allotted as follows:-

RED. 54th Inf. Bde. to be withdrawn into Div. Reserve as early as possible after clearing up PREUX.

BLUE. 53rd Inf. Bde. to consolidate the RED LINE and to thin out as soon as the Green Brigade has passed through.

GREEN. 55th Brigade to capture the GREEN LINE and exploit success.

3. SECRECY. The strictest secrecy is to be observed, only such as are immediately concerned with preparations for the attack being told of its intention.

4. ARTILLERY. The creeping barrage will open on the initial line at Zero where it will remain for 4 minutes and will then lift at the rate of 100 yards in 6 minutes.
The barrage will halt on the grid between A.9., and 10., 15 and 16., 21 and 22., for one hour. It will halt on the protective barrage line clear of the Red Line for half an hour and then die down.

Through those parts of the forest where high trees are still standing the Barrage will be of H.E. Troops should be warned not to follow within 200 yards of it.

There will be a cessation of fire for 5 minutes prior to the hour fixed for the commencement of the barrage in front of the Red dotted line and four minutes intense fire before it moves on in order to indicate to the Infantry the hour for the next advance.

5. COMMUNICATION.

A Battalion line has been laid to F.29.b.2.9 and F.16.b.7.7. A line will be laid into PREUX as soon as possible and Adv. Bn. H.Q. will move to approx. A.15.c.4.3. Tank will lay cable along the ROUTE DE PREUX.

6. SIGNALS. (a) Red Flares will be carried as well as tin discs, to be shown when the contact aeroplane calls.
(b) S.O.S. Signal is GREEN over GREEN over RED.
(c) Aeroplanes will indicate signs of a counter attack to the Infantry by flying in the direction of the counter attack dropping white lights.

appendix 97

M.G.C.No.584.

18th Battalion Machine Gun Corps.

WARNING ORDER.

The Battalion will be moving to the MARETZ area either this afternoon or to-morrow morning, the exact time to be notified later.

Personnel will move by bus - transport by road.

Guns and 8 belt boxes of S.A.A. per gun will be carried in the lorries. Each Company is being allotted one lorry for this purpose.

Companies should accordingly collect at their Q.M. Stores or some central spot near the road, all necessary guns and gun kit required.

Each man will move in full marching order, leather jerkins to be worn and blankets to be carried.

[signature]

Capt. & Adjt:
18th Battalion Machine Gun Corps.

15th October 1918.

Issued to:-

All Companies.
Q.M.
R.S.M.
H.Qrs.
Signals.
WAR DIARY

appendix 96

SECRET

Copy No. 10

18th Octr 1918

18th Batt Machine Gun Corps

ORDER No 57

1. The 18th Batt M.G.C will take over the Machine Gun Defences in the Line from 25th Division on the night 18/19th and assume command at 09.00 on 19th Octr.

2 "A" & "B" Coys have already relieved the guns of the 25th Batt. M.G.C in the Line.

"C" Coy will be in support

"D" Coy in reserve

3. Advanced Batt H.Q. will be for the present at REUMONT. Rear Batt H.Q. at MAUROIS.

4. "C" Coy will be billetted at REUMONT

"D" Coy at MAUROIS

All Rear Coy H.Q. at MAUROIS

2

5. O.C. "C" & "D" Coys will send on advance parties tomorrow to arrange Billets for their Coys in REUMONT and MAUROIS respectively.

Coys will move independently, but will arrange to be in new Billets by 13.00

6. Until exact location of advanced Batt H.Q. is known, – after 10.00 19th inst all reports will be sent to late H.Q. of 25th Batt. M.G.C at MAUROIS.

7. ACKNOWLEDGE.

[signature]
Capt & adjt.
18th Bn. M.G.C.

Issued at 20.30.

Copies to:–

No. 1	"A" Coy	No. 7	Q.M.
2	"B" "	8	R.S.M.
3	"C" Coy	9	Signals
4	"D" Coy	10/11	War Diary
5	18th Div	12	File.
6	25th Bn. M.G.C.		

SECRET. Copy No........

15th October 1918.

ADDENDA TO 18TH BATTN: MACHINE GUN CORPS ORDER NO.56.

Reference 18th Battn: M.G.C. Order No.56 - para.2.

Embussing arrangements are as follows:-

Companies will be ready to embus by 06.00. Lorries will form up on HEADAUVILLE-WARLOY ROAD, head of column at V.19.a.7.5 heading N.E.

Each Company and Battalion Headquarters will detail 4 O.Rs. to report to Adjutant at Orderly Room at 05.50. These men will be used as follows:-

1 O.R. to return to Company and guide it to lorries.

2 O.Rs will be posted 1 at each end of lorries allotted to Company.

1 O.R. to guide lorry to Company Stores to pick up gun material.

Companies will remain in billets until lorries are allotted and guides return with necessary information.

DEBUSSING.

The Battalion will debus on MARETZ-CLARY ROAD.

Guides and transport detailed by Corps will meet Battalion about O.36.d.5.2. with information re billets, etc.

LORRIES FOR QUARTERMASTER.

In addition to above one lorry will also report to Q.M. Stores at 0.5.30.

W K Wenham

Capt. & Adjt:
18th Battalion Machine Gun Corps.

Issued at 21.25.

Copies to:-

All recipients of Order No.56.

7. **BILLETS**. - As the Battalion is moving by bus, it is impossible to leave behind large rear parties. Companies will therefore ensure that billets are left in a clean condition before the Battalion moves off.

Transport Officers will be responsible for obtaining certificate from the Town Major to this effect for billets occupied by their respective Companies before they move off in the morning.

8. ACKNOWLEDGE.

W K Wernham

Capt. & Adjt:
18th Battalion Machine Gun Corps.

Issued at 20.00.

Copies to:-

No.1. C.O.
" 2. 2nd-in-Command.
" 3. Adjutant.
" 4. "A" Company.
" 5. "B" Company.
" 6. "C" Company.
" 7. "D" Company.
" 8. A/B.T.O.
" 9. Q.M.
" 10. Signals.
" 11. R.S.M.
" 12. War Diary.
" 13. War Diary.
" 14. File.

appendix 95.

SECRET.

Copy No...12...

15th October 1918.

18th BATTN: MACHINE GUN CORPS ORDER NO.56.

1. The Battalion will move to-morrow, 16th instant, to MARETZ - personnel by bus - transport by road.

2. The Battalion will embus on WARLOY-CONTAY ROAD at 06.00. Exact details will be notified later.

3. Transport will move by road staging night 16th/17th at COMBLES and night 17th/18th at VENDHUILLE.
Hour of Starting - 08.30. Order of March - "C" Coy: B.H.Q., "A" "B" and "D" Coys: Lieut. B.H.EBBUTT "C" Coy: will act as Battalion Transport Officer and will be responsible for whole transport.
He will arrange for representatives to be sent on ahead daily to Town Majors, COMBLES and VENDHUILLE, to obtain billets.
Town Majors concerned have been advised of move.
Battalion Headquarters transport will move with "C" Coy:
The usual distances will be observed on the line of march.

4. GUN KIT, ETC. Guns and 20 Belt Boxes per gun and necessary gun kit will move with the Battalion by lorry. These should be dumped at Company Stores ready to be loaded at once. One lorry per Company is being detailed for this purpose.

5. KITS, BAGGAGE, ETC. Men must move in full marching order. Leather Jerkins to be worn. Blankets to be carried.
Officers must get necessary kit forward with them in the lorries. Quartermaster is allotted one lorry for moving Battalion Stores.

6. RATIONS. Dismounted personnel moving by bus -
Rations for 16th - Unexpended portion carried on man.
Rations for 17th - Being issued to Companies to-night and will be carried on the man.
Rations for 18th - In possession of Battalion and will be moved in bulk with Battalion under Quartermasters arrangements, by lorry being detailed for that purpose.

Transport -
Rations for 16th - Unexpended portion carried on man.
Rations for 17th - Being issued to Companies to-night and will be carried on man.
Forage ~~Rations~~ for 16th & 17th - Carried with Company Transport.
Rations & Forage for 18th - Carried on the three supply wagons and will be issued on line of march under directions of Battalion Transport Officer.

Appendix 100

SECRET. COPY NO. 20..

18th BATTALION MACHINE GUN CORPS ORDER NO. 60.

Reference Maps:-
57 B.N.E. and 57 B. S.E.
1/20,000.

22nd Octr.1918.

1. BRIDGES.

4 Bridges will be constructed by the Sappers over the RICHEMONT RIVER in the vicinity of the BOILLERS WOOD FARM.

2. Troops of Units operating with 55th Brigade that the Brigadier General Commanding 55th Infantry Brigade wishes to march along the main MONTAY FOREST ROAD, will be clear of MONTAY by Zero plus 60 Minutes. After this hour troops of this force will be moved by the Road LE CATEAU - BOILLERS WOOD FARM - CORBEAU.

3. S.O.S.
The S.O.S. of the V Corps is
GREEN
RED
GREEN.

4. The Advanced Divisional H.Q. will move to Q.4.c.9.6. after 2nd Objective is captured. The advance of Brigade H.Q. will be along the central line of communication.

5. The central runners and communication route will be
F.24.a.0.0.
L. 4.c.4.9.
L. 9.c.2.5.
thence to Valley about L.14.c., thence down Valley to RICHEMONT MILL.

6. As soon as the 4th Objective has been made good 55th Inf. Brigade H.Q. will move to L.4.a.5.0. When final Objective has been made good it will move to F.29.c.0.5., with an O.P. at RENUART FARM.

7. MACHINE GUN POSITIONS.

The following are approximate positions. Guns going forward are to consolidate.

B. Coy.	2 Guns.	L.7.d.6.5.
B. Coy.	2 Guns.	L.7.d.7.7.
B. Coy.	4 Guns.	L.3.a.10.50.
A. Coy.	2 Guns.	L.13.d.5.8.
A. Coy.	2 Guns.	L.13.d.5.9.
A. Coy.	2 Guns.	L.14.c.4.0.
A. Coy.	2 Guns.	L.20.d.00.8.
A. Coy.	2 Guns.	L.15.a.6.5.
A. Coy.	2 Guns.	L.15.c.3.8.
A. Coy.	2 Guns.	L.9.a.9.0.
A. Coy.	2 Guns.	L.9.d.99.10.
C. Coy.	4 Guns.	F.27.b.2.7.
C. Coy.	2 Guns.	F.23.a.2.2.
C. Coy.	2 Guns.	F.29.a.5.8.
D. Coy.	2 Guns.	L.4.c.6.3.
D. Coy.	2 Guns.	L.4.d.7.7.
D. Coy.	2 Guns.	L.5.b.7.7.
D. Coy.	2 Guns.	L.6.a.2.3.

On completion of Barrage Shoot the 8 Guns of B. Coy. and 8 Guns of D. Coy. detailed will pack up and be ready, on orders received from Battalion H.Q. to relieve Guns of C. and D. Coys. on 3rd and 4th Objective Lines. These guns of C. and D. Coys. will then march forward and consolidate in depth the final objective line.

8. The guns of the 100th Battalion will only be used for Barrage, and will not move forward. All four Companies will be used in three Groups,- "X", "Y", "Z",- each Group consisting of 2 Batteries of 8 Guns each.

Major,
For Lieut. Colonel,
Commanding 18th Battalion M.G.Corps.

Issued at.........

Distribution:-

Copy No 1. C.O.
2. 2nd in Command.
3. Adjutant.
4. "A" Coy.
5. "B" Coy.
6. "C" Coy.
7. "D" Coy.
8. Signals.
9/12. 4 Coys. 100th Batt. M.G.C.
13. O.C., 100th Batt. M.G.C.
14. 18th Division.
15. 53rd Brigade.
16. 54th Brigade.
17. 55th Brigade.
18. 25th Division.
19. 33rd Division.
20/21. War Diary.
22 File.

appendix 102.

NARRATIVE DESCRIBING THE PART PLAYED by the 18TH BATTN. MACHINE GUN CORPS DURING THE OPERATIONS LEADING UP TO THE CAPTURE OF BOUSIES & ROBERSART.

22.10.1918.

1. Disposal of Machine Guns of 18th Battn. M.G.C. and 2 Companies 100th Bn.M.G.C.

On the night of 22nd inst, the following guns were utilized for barrage fire and moved into position.
All guns were laid by 22.00.
Tracing showing gun positions and barrage lines attached. (marked "A")

2 Coys. 100th Bn.M.G.C.
2 Sections,"B" Coy, 18th Bn.M.G.C.
2 Sections, "D" Coy, 18th Bn. M.G.C.

23.10.18.

2. The attack was launched at 01.20 on the 23.10.18 and was a complete success.

"A" Company, 18th Bn.M.G.C. co-operating with the 53rd Infantry Brigade sent two sections forward for consolidation of first objective and reached there without casualties. In the afternoon the remaining two sections of this Company moved forward for the consolidation of the Second Objective and after reaching there, the guns of this Company were then in the following positions:-

2 Guns	K.13.b.80.10.		
2 "	K.14.c.30.00.	2 Guns	L.10.c.10.10.
2 "	K.20.a.80.00.	2 Guns	L.9.a.90.10.
2 "	K.20.c.80.70.	2 Guns	L.15.c.20.75.
2 "	L.15.a.45.50.		

"B" Company. 18th Bn.M.G.C. (Less 2 Sections), were attached to the 54th Infantry Brigade for consolidation purposes.
1 Section operating with the 11th Royal Fusiliers.
1 Section with the 7th Bedford Regiment.
Both these Sections reached their objectives with very slight casualties to personnel, but 4 mules were knocked out en route.
The Section operating with the 7th Bedfords formed a defensive flank Northwards during the interval that touch was lost with the Division on our left. These guns were then on the FAHT FARM - EPINETTE FARM road just in rear of BOUSIES.

"C" Company, 18th Bn.M.G.C. (Less 2 Sections) operated with the 53rd Infantry Brigade but did not deploy until the following day after the village of BOUSIES had been mopped up. They then took up positions for consolidation of our front line:-

1 Section in the vicinity of BOUSIES WOOD. and FAHT FARM
1 Section on the high ground S.W. of ROBERSART.

"D" Company, 18th Bn.M.G.C. (Less 2 Sections) also operated with 53rd Infantry Brigade, and 2 sections of this Company together with 2 Sections of "C" Company were under the command of Major. H. S. PATERSON, (O.C. "D" Coy). Positions were taken up by these two sections in L.20.a. and L.9.d. The Section in L.9.d. successfully engaged a party of the enemy in L.10.a.9.6.

24.10.18.

3. On the 24th the attack was continued and our line advanced to just East of ROBERSART. A Divisional line of Resistance was then given and a complete re-organisation of gun positions effected. Tracing "B" showing these positions is attached.

A Harassing fire Programme was also arranged and selected targets such as enemy machine gun nests, Regtl. and Bn. H.Qrs. Snipers posts etc., were continually harassed.

4. Headquarters.
The Battalion and Company H.Qrs on the night of the attack (22.10.18) were in LE CATEAU and moved the following day to BOUSIES.

5. In every case limbers and pack animals were used with success.

6. Approximate positions for consolidation were chosen before-hand from the map for every gun going forward. This proved entirely successful.

7. From statements of prisoners the initial barrage appeared to be very effective and must have considerably facilitated the advance of our Infantry.

8. Throughout the operations Battn. H.Qrs were in closest touch with Brigades and M.G. Company Commanders.

9. Casualties are shown on attached (Appendix "C").

[signature]
Lieut-Colonel,
Commanding 18th Battalion Machine Gun Corps.

Secret. appendix 101 22-10-18.

18th Machine Gun Battn Order
No. 61.

1. There will be a cessation of fire for 5 minutes prior to the hour fixed for commencement of the barrage in front of the first and succeeding objectives and four minutes intense fire before the barrage moves on in order to indicate to the Infantry the hour for the next advance.

2. Fire organisation orders.
Cancel the times of fire on charts issued with order No 59 and read the following:–

A + B Batteries
Task 1 Z to Z+3 rapid
" 2 Z+3 to Z+20
" 3 Z+20 to Z+35.

C. Battery
Task 1 Zero to Z+40
" 2 Z+40 to Z+65
" 3 Z+65 to Z+80.

2 Contd

D Battery
Task 1 Zero to Z + 40
2 Z+40 to Z + 80

E Battery
Task 1 Zero to Z + 30
2 Z+30 to Z + 70

F Battery
Task 1 Zero to Z + 50
2 Z+50 to Z + 70

G Battery
Task 1 Zero to Z + 20
2 Z+20 to Z + 65.

H Battery
Task 1 Zero to Z + 60
2 Z+60 to Z + 80.

Alterations for guns of 38 Div assisting have been issued separately

Issued to:-

A B C D. 18th Bn M Gc
A B C D 100th Bn M Gc
O.C. 100th Bn M Gc

[illegible] Major
Commdg 18th Bn M Gc

Identification Trace for use with Artillery Maps.

"A"

All Batteries & Guns

57B NE

15

16

33

34

K L

K L

Opening line of Arty Barrage

A+B.1

A+B.2

A+B.3

C.1

C.2

C.3

D.1

D.4

E.1

E.2

F.1

F.2

G.2

H.1

H.2

35 Bn

35 Bn

4 Guns of 35 Bn

C Coy 100 Bn H G

B Coy 100 Bn F E

A Coy 100 Bn D C

B Coy 18 Bn B A

D Coy 18 Bn

APPENDIX "C"

STATEMENT OF CASUALTIES INCURRED
by the
18th Battalion Machine Gun Corps.
for period 22.10.18 - 24.10.1918.

22nd October 1918.	Killed.	Wounded.	TOTAL.
"A" Company.	3	5 (1 at Duty)	8
"B", "C", "D" Coys.		-- Nil --	
23rd October 1918.			
"B" Company.	1	6	7
"A", "C", "D" Coys.		-- Nil --	
24th October 1918.			
"B" Company,	-	1	1
"C" Company.	-	2	2
"D" Company.	-	1	1
"A" Company.		-- Nil --	
TOTAL OTHER RANKS.	4	15	19.

O F F I C E R S.

Major. H. S. PATERSON. Wounded 24.10.1918.

-------ooo------

Appendix 103.

18th BATTALION MACHINE GUN CORPS.

ORDER NO. 62. 24.10.18

The following moves will takex place, gun positions in every case being approximate only.

Guns in the Line:-

"A" Coy.	8
"B" "	8
"C" "	6
"D" "	10

"A" Coy. positions:-

L. 11.a.6.4.	4 Guns.
F. 29.c.9.2.	Do.
Reserve.	8 Guns.

"B" Coy positions:-

F. 28.b.9.4.	2 Guns.
F. 22.c.4.8.	4 "
F. 27.b.4.7.	2 "
Reserve.	8 "

"C" Coy. positions:-

F. 17 b.3.4.	2 Guns.
F. 17 c. 8.4.	4 "
Reserve.	2 "

"D" Coy. positions:-

L. 5.b.7.8.	2 Guns
L. 6.a.3.3.	2 "
A.26.c.1.4.	2 "
F.24.c.3.4.	2 "
A.19.c.2.7.	2 "

These positions are only to be taken up when the final objective has been captured.

All Reserve Guns must be accommodated East of the Richemont River and locations given to Batt. H.Q.

All Coy. Advcd. H.Q. will be East of 2nd Objective.

Battalion Adv. H.Q. moves today to vicinity of L.3.b.

ACKNOWLEDGE.

(Sgd.) C.B. Hibbert,
Major,
for Lieut. Colonel
Commandg. 18th Battalion M. G. Corps.

NOTE:-

All Guns within range, when in position, are to lay out line for protection of final objective.

Appendix 104.

SECRET.

18th BATTALION MACHINE GUN CORPS.

ORDER NO. 63. 25.10.18

Third Army continue to attack tomorrow (26th inst.)
18th Division will co-operatein forming their right flank, will capture MOUNT CARMEL, and will establish a combined post with 33rd Division at A.2.c.3.8. ZERO HOUR 01.00

The 18th M.G. Battalion will co-operate by firing the programme as per attached tracing.

TIMES OF FIRE.

All Guns Z to plus 60 standing barrage.

RATE OF FIRE.

Medium.

In the event of S.O.S. going up all guns will open fire immediately.

The S.O.S. Signal is

GREEN over GREEN over RED.

ACKNOWLEDGE.

(Sgd.) S.R. POCOCK
Captain & Adjutant,
for Lieut. Colonel,
Commandg. 18th Batt. M.G.C.

APPENDIX 105.

CASUALTIES INCURRED BY THE 18th Battn: M. G. Corps DURING THE MONTH OF OCTOBER 1918.

OFFICERS.

2/Lieut. W. H. G. Curtis.	Wounded in Action 30.9.1918.
Lieut. C. L. Davey.	Killed in Action 17.10.1918.
2/Lieut. E. C. Boughton.	Wounded in Action 17.10.1918.
Major H. S. Paterson.	Wounded in Action 24.10.1918.

-------------oOOoOOo-------------

OTHER RANKS.

Date.	Killed.	Died of Wds.	Wounded.	Wounded(Gas).	Missing.	TOTAL.
1st	-	-	2	-	-	2
2nd	-	-	1	-	-	1
18th	2	-	3	-	-	5
19th	-	-	2	2	-	4
20th	1	-	4	-	-	5
21st	-	-	1	-	-	1
22nd	3	-	5(1 at Duty)	-	-	8
23rd	1	-	6	-	-	7
24th	-	-	4	-	-	4
25th	-	-	4	-	-	4
26th	-	-	2	-	-	2
27th	-	-	2	-	-	2
28th	1	-	1	-	-	2
29th	-	-	-	2	-	2
30th	-	-	1	-	-	1
31st	1	-	1	-	-	2
TOTALS.	9	-	39	4	-	52

-------------oOOoOOo-------------

APPENDIX 106

CHANGES IN ESTABLISHMENTAND STRENGTH OF BATTALION DRAFTS RECEIVED, CHANGES IN OFFICERS ETC. DURING MONTH OF OCTOBER 1918.

Paper strength of Battalion (excluding attached):-

1st October 1918:- 49 Officers 868 Other Ranks.

DECREASES.

For Casualties in Officers during month see Appendix

Other Ranks.
Evacuated to C.C.S.............98
In Hosp. over 7 days........... 2

TOTAL DECREASES. 100
Casualties in action...... 54

TOTAL. 154

INCREASES.

Lieut. C.W. Thornton.) 2nd Lieut. A.J. Fenton.)	Joined Battalion from M.G.C. Base Depot and taken on strength 29.9.18		
2nd Lieut. N.S. Hearle.	Do.	Do.	8.10.18
Capt. T.C.T. Llewellyn.) Capt. C.G. Haselden.)	Do.	Do.	13.10.18
2nd Lieut. C. Pettitt	Do.	Do.	22.10.18

45 Other Ranks joined Batt. from M.G.C. Base Depot. 8.10.18
16 " " " " 9.10.18
1 " " " " 24.10.18
10 " " rejoined Batt. from C.C.S and taken on strength
TOTAL INCREASE (Other Ranks):- 62.

Strength 1st:-	49 Officers	868 Other Ranks.			
Decreases:-	10 "	154	"	"	
	39 "	714	"	"	
Increases:-	6 "	72	"	"	
Paper strength of Battn. 31st October 1918. (Less attached)	45 "	786	"	"	

C O N F I D E N T I A L.

W A R   D I A R Y   of   18TH BATTN. MACHINE GUN CORPS.

****

From 1st NOVEMBER, 1918.

To:- 30th NOVEMBER. 1918.

A P P E N D I C E S :-

107. NARRATIVE OF OPERATIONS from 25th October 1918, to 7th November 1918.

108. Battalion Operation Order No, 64.

109. Changes in Establishment and Strength of Battalion during the month of November 1918.

----------------oOo----------------

(V O L U M E   X)

****

Reference Map:- 57B N.E.
Scale 1/20,000

Instructions regarding War Diaries and Intelligence Summaries are contained in F. S. Regs., Part II. and the Staff Manual respectively. Title pages will be prepared in manuscript.

WAR DIARY
or
~~INTELLIGENCE SUMMARY.~~
(Erase heading not required.)

Army Form C. 2118.

Place	Date	Hour	Summary of Events and Information	Remarks and references to Appendices
BOUSIES.	Nov. 1.		Battalion in line. See narrative attached. appendix 107	[illegible] - app 1[illegible]
	2		appendix 108.	[illegible] app 10
	3		Order No 64 issued 1st. Attack on FOREST DE MORMAL launched. See appendix "A"	[illegible]
	4.		Attack continued as per narrative attached. appendix 107	[illegible]
PREUX au BOIS	5		Consolidation of line being completed.	[illegible]
	6.		Battalion relieved in the line and move to billets in PREUX au BOIS.	[illegible]
	7		Battalion moved to LE CATEAU	[illegible]
LE CATEAU	8.			
	9		Refitting and cleaning guns and equipment.	[illegible]
	10			
	11			
	12.		Battalion moved to PRÉMONT	[illegible]
	13		" Training.	[illegible]
	14.		-do-	[illegible]
	15.		Sunday. Church Services.	[illegible]
	16.		Battalion route march.	[illegible]
	17			

A5834 Wt. W4973/M687 750,000 8/16 D. D. & L. Ltd. Forms/C.2118/13.

Instructions regarding War Diaries and Intelligence Summaries are contained in F. S. Regs., Part II. and the Staff Manual respectively. Title pages will be prepared in manuscript.

WAR DIARY
or
INTELLIGENCE SUMMARY.
(Erase heading not required.)

Army Form C. 2118.

Place	Date	Hour	Summary of Events and Information	Remarks and references to Appendices
PREMONT.	Nov 18.		Battalion on Salvage operations.	R
	19		"	
	20		"	R
	21.		"	
	22		Battalion ceremonial drill.	R
	23			
	24		Sunday. Church Services.	R
	25.		Battalion drill.	
	26.		Battalion on Salvage operations.	
	27.			R
	28.		Practice review of Division by Brig. Genl. Sadleir Jackson.	
	29.		Battalion training	R
	30		Baths and cleaning guns and equipment	
	31.		Sunday. Church Services.	R
			For Changes in Establishment & strength of Bn during November see Appendix 109	app. 109

E. T. Megret Lieut-Colonel
Commanding 18th Bn Machine [illegible] Corps.

A5834 Wt. W4973/M687 750,000 8/16 D. D. & L. Ltd. Forms/C.2118/13.

SECRET. Appendix 108 Copy No. 15

Reference Map:- 57.A.N.W. 1/20,000. **1st November 1918.**

18th BATTN. M.G.C. ORDER NO. 64.

1.**GENERAL.** At Zero hour on "Z" Day the 18th Division will attack in conjunction with the 50th Div. on its right and the 38th Div. on left.

2.**PLAN OF ATTACK.**
Map "A" was issued to all Coys. giving boundaries, objectives and the proposed plan of attack of the 18th Division in Detail. Referring to this map, tasks were allotted as follows:-

RED. 54th Inf. Bde. to be withdrawn into Div. Reserve as early as possible after clearing up PREUX.

BLUE. 53rd Inf. Bde. to consolidate the RED LINE and to thin out as soon as the Green Brigade has passed through.

GREEN. 55th Brigade to capture the GREEN LINE and exploit success.

3.**SECRECY.** The strictest secrecy is to be observed, only such as are immediately concerned with preparations for the attack being told of its intention.

4.**ARTILLERY.** The creeping barrage will open on the initial line at Zero where it will remain for 4 minutes and will then lift at the rate of 100 yards in 6 minutes.
The barrage will halt on the grid between A.9., and 10., 15 and 16., 21 and 22., for one hour. It will halt on the protective barrage line clear of the Red Line for half an hour and then die down.

Through those parts of the forest where high trees are still standing the Barrage will be of H.E. Troops should be warned not to follow within 200 yards of it.

There will be a cessation of fire for 5 minutes prior to the hour fixed for the commencement of the barrage in front of the Red dotted line and four minutes intense fire before it moves on in order to indicate to the Infantry the hour for the next advance.

5.**COMMUNICATION.**
A Battalion line has been laid to F.29.b.2.9 and F.16.b.7.7. A line will be laid into PREUX as soon as possible and Adv. Bn. H.Q. will move to approx. A.15.c.4.3. Tank will lay cable along the ROUTE DE PREUX.

6.**SIGNALS.**(a) Red Flares will be carried as well as tin discs, to be shown when the contact aeroplane calls.
(b) S.O.S. Signal is GREEN over GREEN over RED.
(c) Aeroplanes will indicate signs of a counter attack to the Infantry by flying in the direction of the counter attack dropping white lights.

7. **TANKS.** 10 Tanks are allotted to the Division. These are reallotted:-

4 to 54th Infantry Brigade.
6 to 53rd Infantry Brigade.

two of the latter taking part in the clearing of the Eastern end of PREUX before advancing with 53rd Inf. Bde.

8. **MACHINE GUNS.**

(a) Barrage Guns.
8 Guns of "A" Company.
8 Guns of "B" Company.
8 Guns of "C" Company.
8 Guns of "D" Company.

(b) Consolidation Guns.
8 Guns of "B" Company) Operating with 53rd Inf.
8 Guns of "D" Company) Brigade.
8 Guns of "A" Company) Operating with 55th Inf.
8 Guns of "C" Company) Brigade.
O.C. "B" Company and O.C. "C" Coy. will be in Command in each case respectively.

(a) Barrage Guns.
Battery positions, targets, rates of fire are as shown on attached tracing, and fire Organisation Charts respectively.
Barrage guns will be grouped in Batteries of 8 under an Officer.
Battery positions will be dug and lines laid out ready for fire by dusk on 2nd inst.
S.A.A. dumps have already been formed at Battery positions.

(b) Forward Consolidation Guns.
Tracing showing approximate final defensive positions issued to Company Commanders herewith.
Guns will go forward with auxilliary mountings and 6 belt boxes to enable guns coming into action quickly.
Every effort must be made to help Infantry forward by bringing enfilade fire to bear on any point holding out.
Mules will take forward tripods and extra belt boxes.
Sections going forward will arrange for dumps under Company arrangements.
Gun Teams going forward should carry usual complement of picks, shovels, etc.,

9. **SYNCHRONISATION OF WATCHES.**
An Officer of each Company will report to Battn. H.Qrs at Zero minus 4 Hours for purpose of above.

10. ZERO HOUR. Will be notified later.

11. ACKNOWLEDGE.

[signature]

Lieut-Colonel,
Commanding 18th Battalion Machine Gun Corps.

Issued at ...... p.m.
Copies to:-

No.1.Copy C.O.
" 2 " Adjutant.
" 3 " "A" Company.
" 4 " "B" Company.
" 5 " "C" Company.
" 6 " "D" Company.
" 7 " Signals.
" 8 " 18th Division "G".
" 9 " 53rd Inf. Bde.
" 10 " 54th Inf. Bde.
" 11 " 55th Inf. Bde.
" 12 " C.M.G.O.
" 13 " 50th Division.
" 14 " 38th Division.
" 15/16" War Diary.
" 17 " File.

SECRET.

MEDICAL ARRANGEMENTS.
(To accompany 18th Bn.M.G.C.Order No.64)

1. O.C. 55th Field Ambulance is in charge of Advanced Evacuation. Hd.Qrs. BOUSIES. L.3.b.8.8.
He will have at his disposal the Bearer divisions, horsed ambulances, motor ambulances and wheeled stretcher carriers of 54th and 56th Field Ambulances.

2. O.C. 56th Field Ambulance will be in charge of Divisional Sick station, MAUROIS.

3. R.A.Ps. will be selected by Brigades concerned.
Ford Car Loading Post:- F.29.c.4.4.
Walking Wounded Collecting Post.) Near station BOUSIES
Advanced Dressing Station.) L.3.b.8.8.
Corps Main Dressing Station.)
Corps Walking Wounded Post.) LE CATEAU, K.34.a.8.8

4. METHOD OF EVACUATION.
Lying cases by hand carriage and wheeled stretchers to Ford Car post thence by cars to A.D.S.
Walking Wounded will be directed through ROBERSART to A.D.S. horsed ambulances will meet them as far forward as possible.
It is proposed to push Ford Cars as far forward as possible.

L.R. Porget Capt
for Lieut-Colonel,
Commanding 18th Battalion Machine Gun Corps.

2nd November 1918.
Copies to recipients of 18th Bn.M.G.C.Order No.64.

FIRE ORGANISATION CHART.

Group No.1. Commander:- Lieut. Campbell Davies. Battery "A"

Approximate positions.	Targets and Tasks.	No.of Guns.	Zero Time.	Rate of Fire.
F.12.a.3.3. to F.12.a.1.4.	Task.1. Barrage. from A.20.b.0.8. to A.20.b.4.3.	2	Z to plus 130.	130 R.P.M.
	Task.2. from A.20.b.45.65 to A.20.b.85.15	2	Z to plus 130.	130 r.p.m.
	Task 3. from A.15.c.15.45. to A.15.c.60.	4	Z to plus 50.	

Remarks:- No.3.Task will superimpose Nos. 1 and 2 Tasks at Z plus 50 to Z plus 130.

Group No.2. Commander:- Lieut.G.Young. Battery "B"

Approximate Positions.	Targets and tasks.	No.of. Guns.	Zero Time.	Rate of Fire.
F.17.c.9.4.	Task 1. from A.14.b.10.95. to A.8.d.60.00.	2	Z to plus 12.	130 r.p.m.
	Task 2. from A.9.c.0.2. to A.9.c.6.4.	2.	Z to plus 36.	130 r.p.m.
	Task 3. from Width (A.14.d.7.8. of (to Target(A.14.d.7.4. CREEP TO A.15.c.3.8. A.15.c.3.2.	4.	Z to plus 30.	130 r.p.m.
	Task 4. from Width(A.21.a.15.95 of (to Target(A.21.a.15.50. CREEP TO A.21.a.9.8.to A.21.a.9.4.	8.	Z plus 36 to Z plus 125.	130 r.p.m.

Remarks:- Task 1

These guns will cease fire at Z plus 12 and superimpose No.2.Task.

On completion of tasks Nos.1, 2, and 3 all guns lay on to and fire Task.4.

Group No.3. Commanded by Capt. LLewellyn. Battery "C".

Approximate Positions.	Targets and Tasks.	No.of Guns.	Zero Time.	Rate of Fire.
F.24.a.4.2. to F.24.c.4.9.	Task 1. From A.26.b.8.6. to A.27.a.4.2.	4	Z to plus 54	130 rpm
	Task.2. From A.21.d.2.8. to A.21.d.8.7.	4	Z to plus 155.	
	Task.3. From Width(A.21.d.70.65 of (to Target(A.21.d.80.20. <u>CREEP TO</u> A.22.c.50.60 to A.22.c.55.25.	4	Z plus 54 to Z plus 155.	

Remarks:- On completion of Task 1. these guns will lay on and fire Task 3. to Z plus 155.

Group No.4. Commanded by Lieut. LEITH. Battery "D"

Approximate Positions	Targets and tasks.	No.of Guns.	Zero time.	Rate of fire.
F.30.a.1.4	Task 1. From Width(A.20.d.1.4 of (to Target(A.26.b.1.7 CREEP TO A.20.d.8.3 to A.26.b.8.7	6	Z to plus 130.	130 r.p.m.
	Task 2. From A.20.d.15.45 to A.20.d.50.65	2	Z to plus 150.	130 r.p.m.
	Task 3. From Width(A.21.d.50.75 of (to Target(A.21.d.60.35 CREEP TO A.21.b.95.05 to A.22.c.20.80.	6	Z plus 130 to Z plus 150.	

Remarks:- Task 1. On completion of Task 1. these guns will lay on to, and fire Task 3. from Z plus 130 to Z plus 150.

Group No.5. Commanded by Coy.Comdr. 100th Bn. Battery "E"

Approximate Positions.	Targets and Tasks.	No.of Guns.	Zero time.	Rate of fire.
F.18.c.90.95	Task.1. from Width of(A.15.a.10.80.to Target (A.15.a.10.20. CREEP TO A.15.a.95.80 to A.15.a.95.20.	8	Z to plus 45.	130 rpm.
	Task 2. from Width of(A.10.c.50.35 to Target. (A.16.a.40.20. CREEP TO A.10.c.90.40 to A.16.a.90.20.	8	Z plus 45 to Z plus 180.	

Group No.6. Commanded by Coy. Comdr. 100th Bn. Battery "F"

Approximate Positions.	Targets and Tacks	No.of Guns.	Zero time.	Rate of fire.
F.18.c.75.40.	Task.1. from Width of(A.15.d.60.60.to Target. (A.15.d.60.00 CREEP TO A.16.d.10.60 to A.16.d.10.00.	8	Z to plus 90. (see remarks).	

Remarks:- From Z to plus 90 creep 100 yards every 5 minutes for 500 yards, then remain stationary on remainder of target to Z plus 174.

SECRET. 18th Dn.M.G.C.No.S.138.

To:- Recipients of Order No. 64.

Reference 18th Battn. M.G.C. Order No. 64, para 8, section a.

12 Guns of 100th Battn.M.G.Corps will form Group 5, Batteries "E" and "F" and will fire on targets as given in Organisation Chart.

A further 8 guns of "B" and "A" Coys of 18th Battn.M.G.C. will form an extra group (6) at approximately F.17.c.95.15 and barrage targets:-

Width of)	A.14.c.35.30 to	Rate
Target.)	A.20.a.35.80.	Time.
CREEP TO		
	A.15.c.0.3 to	Z to plus 113.
	A.21.a.0.8.	

Acknowledge.

for.
Lieut-Colonel,
Commanding 18th Battn. Machine Gun Corps.

2nd November 1918.

XXIV

6/24

2 Leinster Regt

Vol XX

War Diary
APPENDIX.107.

NARRATIVE OF OPERATIONS CARRIED OUT BY THE 18th Battalion Machine Gun Corps between the 25th October 1918 and 7th November 1918.

-0-0-0-0-0-0-0-0-0-0-0-0-0-0-0-0-0-0-0-0-0-0-

Reference Maps:- Sheets 57.B.N.E. & 57.A.,N.W. Scale 1/20,000

On the 25th October 1918, 24 Guns of this Battalion fired on selected areas to assist the 53rd Infantry Brigade's attack on MOUNT CARMOL. (Tracing of this barrage sent with War Diary for October.)

On the 26th October, the guns were disposed of to conform with the line of resistance and harassing fire programme arranged.

From the 26th to 31st October Battalion in Line. (See War Diary for October).

1.11.1918., Dispositions of guns of this Battalion are given on attached tracing "A".

Throughout the day and night harassing fire was brought to bear on selected areas.

A Conference of Company Commanders was held in the afternoon to discuss the attack ordered to take place on the 3rd November.

"A" Company relieved two guns of "B", "C", and "D" Companies. to enable these Coys. to rest their men prior to the attack.

On November 2nd, a barrage scheme was arranged to bring enfilade fire to bear on the enemy roads and approaches in the village of PREUX, machine gun nests and strongly held enemy positions.

The barrage was so arranged that the enemy was kept continually under fire during the advance of our Infantry. At dusk of this day Battery positions were dug, the location being as shown on tracing "A".

The attack ordered for the 3rd was postponed for the 4th.

On the 3rd the Commanding Officer interviewed all Section Officers going forward in the attack and gave them detailed instructions as to the method of advance, the positions to look for, and approximate positions of consolidation on reaching their objectives.

All Companies by midnight this day were in their Battle Positions. The guns of this Battalion plus 1 Company, 100th Bn.M.G.C. attached for barrage purposes were disposed of as given in Order No. 64.

The attack was launched on the morning of the 4th and was a complete success.

Nos. 1 & 2 Sections ("A" Coy) under the Command of Lieut. D. H. RIDDELL and Lieut. J. B. RUSSELL, M.C. moved forward with the 8th East Surreys and 7th Buffs, respectively, who reached their objectives without casualties, taking up positions for consolidation as per Tracing "B" attached. The Headquarters of this Company moved to A.21.c.75.90.

Nos. 5 & 6 Sections ("B" Coy) under Lieuts. BURR and BRINKMAN moved forward with the 8th Royal Berks.

No. 5 Section passed through HECQ to the second objective and reached its consolidation positions as per Tracing "B". During the advance these sections successfully engaged some enemy limbers. No. 6. Section moved to the second Objective and reached its consolidation positions as per Tracing "B".

During the advance these sections many times became engaged and secured good targets in the vicinity of PREUX, inflicting severe casualties on the enemy and greatly assisting in subduing the enemy's fire.

One section "C" Company under Lieut. J. LAURIE, M.C. moved forward with the 7th Queens, and one section "C" Company under Lieut. W. SANDIFORD moved forward with the 8th East Surreys. Both these sections reached their objectives with very slight casualties and took up positions for consolidation as per Tracing "B"

One Section "D" Company under 2nd Lieut. C. PETTITT moved forward with the 10th Essex Regiment. The attack was temporarily held up in A.15.d., A.21.b. and the guns of this section did excellent work by engaging and silencing enemy machine guns and snipers. They reached their objectives and took up consolidation positions as per Tracing "B".

By 12.00 all Coy. H.Qrs were established in PREUX AND Battn. H.Qrs moved to PREUX at 15.00.

The attack was contimued on the 5th by the 55th Infantry Brigade and 8 Guns "A" Company and 8 Guns "C" Company co-operated in the advance. The whole 16 guns being Commanded by Capt. E. J. BRETT. "C" Company, "A" Company taking up consolidation positions in B.18.a.9.2. - B.16.a.3.7.
2 Guns "C" Company went forward with the Vanguard formed by the 8th East Surrey Regt, and 6 guns of this Coy. went forward in support of the Main Body. They met with very little opposition and consolidated the line of resistance in B.18.a., B.19.d.

On the 6th inst. the 8 Guns of "A" Company were withdrawn to PREUX where "B" and "D" Coys of this Battalion were then concentrating. On the 7th inst. the Division was withdrawn and the Battalion concentrated in PREUX.

Lessons learnt during these operations is attached (Appendix "A").

[signature] Capt.
for
Lieut-Colonel,
Commanding 18th Battalion Machine Gun Corps.

APPENDIX. "A"

SUMMARY OF LESSONS LEARNT.

1. During the attack the guns were sent forward with the auxiliary mounting, the tripods following on Pack animals.
This method of advance proved to be a complete success.

2. The approximate positions were given for the guns going forward by the Commanding Officer prior to the attack; the route to be taken and the method of advance laid down. This also proved to be very successful.

3. Battalion Headquarters were at all times in closest touch with Company Commanders, and this appears to be absolutely essential in warfare of the above nature.

[signature] Capt. for
Lieut-Colonel,
Commanding 18th Battn. Machine Gun Corps.

APPENDIX 109

CHANGES IN ESTABLISHMENT AND STRENGTH OF BATTALION, DRAFTS RECEIVED, CHANGES IN OFFICERS, ETC. DURING MONTH OF NOVEMBER 1918.

Paper Strength of Battalion (excluding attached):-

1st November 1918:- 45 Officers 786 Other Ranks

DECREASES.

OFFICERS. (10)

Major W. Burns	Wounded 4.11.18.
Major P. Mathisen,	Transferred to 32nd Batt.M.G.C. 20.11.18
2nd Lieut, A.E.Ferguson.	To U.K. for Tour of duty. 16.11.18.
Lieut. J. Bryce.)	Evacuated out of Corps Area (Sick) and
2nd Lieut. A. Ferris)	struck off strength 9.11.18.
Lieut. E. Yeardley.)	
2nd Lieut. J.E. Pritchard.)	Do. Do. 22.11.18.
Lieut. H. Corran.	To M.G.T.C. GRANTHAM, for Instrnl. Staff Course. 28.11.18.
Lieut. J.R.Wood.)	Evacuated out of Corps Area (Sick)
Lieut. G.C.M.Jones)	and struck off strength 30.11.18.

OTHER RANKS.

Casualties in Action	55
Evacuated to C.C.S.	116
In Hosp. over 7 days	16
Other Causes	6
TOTAL DECREASES	193

INCREASES.

The undermentioned Officers joined Battalion from M.G.C. Base Depot on the dates stated:-

2nd Lieut. J.E. Pritchard	30.10.18.
Capt. A.M.Dick.	3.11.18
Lieut.C.B.Bridge)	
2nd Lieut. G.C.Beale.)	10.11.18
Capt.C.H.James.)	
Lieut. J.J.Melling.)	22.11.18
Lieut. A.R.Glaves.)	
Lieut. C.W. Proctor.)	
2nd Lieut. A.B. Neate.)	30.11.18

OTHER RANKS/

INCREASES (Continued).

OTHER RANKS.

The following reinforcements joined Battalion from M.G.C. Base Depot on the dates stated:-

25 O.R's	31.10.18
42 O.R's	1.11.18
52 O.R's	3.11.18
50 O.R's	12.11.18
35 O.R's	15.11.18
4 O.R's	18.11.18
32 O.R's	22.11.18
24 O.R's from H.T.Depot	22.11.18
5 O.R's	26.11.18
269	

16 O.R's rejoined Batt. from C.C.S. and taken on strength

285 O.R's. TOTAL INCREASE.

Strength 1st:-	45 Officers	786 Other Ranks
Decreases:-	-10 "	193 " "
	35 "	593 " "
Increases.	9 "	285 " "
Paper Strength of Battn. 30th Novr. 1918. (Less attached)	44 "	878 " "

C O N F I D E N T I A L

W A R D I A R Y of 18th BATTALION MACHINE GUN CORPS.

From:- 1st December 1918.

To:- 31st December 1918.

APPENDIX:-

110.. Changes in Establishment and strength of Battalion during Month of December 1918.

------------------o0o------------------

(V O L U M E XI)

Reference Map:- Sheet 57,b, 1/40,000.

Instructions regarding War Diaries and Intelligence Summaries are contained in F. S. Regs., Part II. and the Staff Manual respectively. Title pages will be prepared in manuscript.

WAR DIARY OF 18TH BATTALION MACHINE GUN CORPS.

Army Form C. 2118.

or

~~INTELLIGENCE SUMMARY.~~

(Erase heading not required.)

DECEMBER 1919-

Place	Date	Hour	Summary of Events and Information	Remarks and references to Appendices
PREMONT.	1st.		Church Parades.	CBH
"	2nd.		Divisional Review. Battn. marched past Major-General R. P. LEE. C.B.	CBH
"	3rd to 12th.		During this period Battn. were employed in salvaging. Companies working from 09.00 hours to 12.00 hours. Following squares being cleared:- Outskirts of PREMONT. B.5.b. and c. T.29.d. and 30.c. and USIGNY RAVINE. On the 4th His Majesty the KING visited the 18th Divisional Area passing through MARETZ - SERAIN and ELINCOURT.	CBH
"	13th & 14th.		Companies carried out training during the mornings in Squad, Arms, and Company Drill and Physical Training. The afternoons being devoted to Football, etc.,	CBH
"	15th.		Church Parades.	CBH
"	16th.		Training carried out by Companies.	CBH
"	17th.		Battalion Route March.	CBH
"	18th. to 22nd.		Education Classes commenced on the 19th for instruction of men in:- (i) Elementary Educational work. (ii) Commercial Training. (iii) Shorthand. (iv) Transport duties. (For men of Regular Army and men intending re-enlisting in Post Bellum Army). Classes were carried on throughout this period.	CBH CBH
"	23rd to 26th.		A holiday was observed during this period.	CBH
"	27th to 31st.		Educational Classes continued throughout this period. Afternoons devoted to Football etc., Statement showing changes in Establishment and Strength of Bn. during month attached.	CBH Appendix 110.

C.B. Hebbert [signature] Lieut.-Col.
Cmdg. 18th Bn. Machine Gun Corps.

(A7092). Wt. W12839/M1293. 750,000. 1/17. D. D. & L., Ltd. Forms/C.2118/14.

APPENDIX 110

CHANGES IN ESTABLISHMENT AND STRENGTH OF BATTALION, DRAFTS RECEIVED, CHANGES IN OFFICERS, ETC. DURING MONTH OF DECEMBER 1918.

****

Paper Strength of Battalion (excluding attached):-

1st December 1918:- 44 Officers 878 Other Ranks.

DECREASES.

OFFICERS. (2)

Lieut. D.H. Riddell.	Evacuated to C.C.S. 23.11.18. and struck off strength on transfer to U.K. 12.12.18.
2nd Lieut. W.F. Spree.	Struck off strength on evacuation out of Corps area 20.12.18.

****

OTHER RANKS.

Died	1
Evacuated to C.C.S.	33
Proceeded for duty at Transportation Depot, CALAIS	4
To M.G.T.C. GRANTHAM, for tour of duty	8
To U.K. as Miners	74
TOTAL DECREASES.	120

INCREASES.

The undermentioned Officers joined Battalion from M.G.C. Base Depot on the dates stated:-

2nd Lieut. J.E. Pritchard. 2nd Lieut. C. Cooke. 2nd Lieut. P. B. Brewer.	7.12.18.
2nd Lieut. T.C. Black.	12.12.18.
2nd Lieut. W.G. Slater. 2nd Lieut. C. Puttock. Lieut. R.H. Neale.	15.12.18.

INCREASES (Continued)

OTHER RANKS.

The following reinforcements joined Battalion from M.G.C. Base Depot on the dates stated:-

5 O.R's.....................29.11.18.
15 O.R's.....................5.12.18.
1 O.R'.................... 12.12.18.
2 O.R's................... 17.12.18.
12 O.R's.....................23.12.18.

35

6 O.R's rejoined from C.C.S.

41 O.R's. TOTAL INCREASES.

Strength 1st:-	44	Officers	878	Other	Ranks.
Decreases:-	2	"	120	"	"
	42	"	758	"	"
Increases:-	7	"	41	"	"
Paper Strength of Batt. 31st December 1918. (Less attached)	49	"	799	"	"

C O N F I D E N T I A L

Vol 12

W A R D I A R Y

-*- of -*-

18TH BATTALION MACHINE GUN CORPS.

From 1st January 1919.

To 31st January 1919.

APPENDIX:-

111. Changes in Establishment and strength of Battalion during January 1919.
ATTACHED.

(V O L U M E XII)

Map Reference:-
Sheet 57.B. 1/40,000.

Instructions regarding War Diaries and Intelligence Summaries are contained in F. S. Regs., Part II. and the Staff Manual respectively. Title pages will be prepared in manuscript.

Army Form C. 2118.

WAR DIARY OF 18TH BATTALION MACHINE GUN CORPS.

or

~~INTELLIGENCE SUMMARY~~.

(Erase heading not required.)

JANUARY 1919.

Place	Date	Hour	Summary of Events and Information	Remarks and references to Appendices
PREMONT.	1st.		New Years Day. Observed as a holiday.	
do.	2nd to 17th.		Battalion remained billeted in PREMONT. Throughout this period classes were held in all educational subjects, and training carried out. Areas in B.18 and B.24 were salved by the Battalion.	
do.,	18th,		Battalion moved to ELINCOURT at 09.30 hours and took over billets vacated by 55th Inf. Bde.	
do.,	19th to 31st.		Battalion remained billeted in ELINCOURT. A number of men proceeded to England for Demobilization daily. Training carried out during the mornings. Sports encouraged during afternoons, whilst evenings were devoted to Dances and Concerts.	
			Statement showing Changes in Establishment and strength of Battalion during month of January attached. (Appendix 111)	App.111.

S.R. Pocock Capt. for Major,
Commanding 18th Battalion Machine Gun Corps.

D. D. & L., London, E.C. (A8001) Wt. W1771/M2031 750,000 5/17 Sch. 52 Forms/C2118/14

APPENDIX 111

CHANGES IN ESTABLISHMENT AND STRENGTH OF
18TH BN. M.G.C. CHANGES IN OFFICERS
DURING THE MONTH OF JANUARY 1919.

-*=*-

INCREASES OFFICERS.

2nd Lieut. W. F. SPREE, Rejoined Bn. from M.G.C. Base Depot & taken on strength 23:1:19.

DECREASES OFFICERS.

2nd Lieut. H. J. BURR. To U.K. for final Demobilization & struck off:- 16:1:19.

2nd Lieut. H. P. G. DUPLOCK. To G.H.Q. Ordination Test School, & struck off:- 18:1:19.

Lieut. R. S. ROBERTSON, To U.K. for final Demobilization & struck off:- 28:1:19.

Lieut. H. CAMPBELL-DAVIES. To M.G.T.C, as Instructor, 27:1:19.

-*- -*- -*-

		Offs.	O.Rs.
PAPER STRENGTH OF BATTALION (1st JANUARY 1919)		49	799
INCREASES.		1	
4 O.Rs. joined Bn. from M.G.C.Base Depot,			4
5 O.Rs. joined Bn. from M.G.C.Base Depot,			5
6 O.Rs. joined Bn. from H.T.Depot, ABBEVILLE,			6
20 O.Rs. joined Bn. from M.G.C.Base Depot,			20
1 O.R. transferred from 8th East Surrey Regt.			1
		50	835
DECREASES.		4	
To:- C.C.S.	14		
U.K. as Miner,	1		
U.K. for demobilization,	136		
U.K. for Duty as Accountants,	2		
U.K. for Service in Regular Army,	10		
E.F.C. Hesiden & struck off strength,	1		
M.G.T.C. GRANTHAM as Instructor,	1		165.
PAPER STRENGTH OF BATTALION (31st JANUARY 1919)		46	670

Vol 13

CONFIDENTIAL.

W A R   D I A R Y

-*- of -*-

18TH BATTALION MACHINE GUN CORPS.

From:- 1st February 1919.

To:- 28th February 1919.

APPENDIX:-

112. Statement showing changes in Establishment and Strength of Battalion during February 1919

ATTACHED.

(V O L U M E XIII)

Reference Map:- Sheet 57.B.
Scale, 1/40,000.

Instructions regarding War Diaries and Intelligence Summaries are contained in F. S. Regs., Part II. and the Staff Manual respectively. Title pages will be prepared in manuscript.

WAR DIARY of 18TH BATTN. MACHINE GUN CORPS.

or

~~INTELLIGENCE SUMMARY~~.

(*Erase heading not required.*)

Army Form C. 2118.

F E B R U A R Y 1919.

Place	Date	Hour	Summary of Events and Information	Remarks and references to Appendices
ELINCOURT.	1st to 28th.		Battalion billeted during this period in the village of ELINCOURT. Training was carried out during mornings. Usual allotment of men proceeded to U.K. daily for final demobilization.	
			Statement showing changes in strength of Battalion during the month of February attached (Appendix 112)	App.112.

C B Hibbert Major,
Commanding 18th Battalion Machine Gun Corps.

D. D. & L., London, E.C.
(A8004) Wt. W1771/M2031 750,000 5/17 Sch. 52 Forms/C2118/14

APPENDIX 112.

CHANGES IN ESTABLISHMENT & STRENGTH
OF 18TH BATTN. MACHINE GUN CORPS,
CHANGES IN OFFICERS, DURING THE
MONTH OF FEBRUARY 1919.

-*=*=*=*=*=*=*=*=*=*=*=*=*=*=*-

DECREASES - OFFICERS.

Lieut. G. Young,	To U.K. for Demobilization 7:2:19.
Lieut. C. Pettitt,	do., do., 5:2:19.
Lieut. D. H. EBBUTT.	Retained in U.K. for Demob, and struck off strength from 27:1:19.
Lieut. W. G. Slater,	To U.K. for Demobilization 1:2:19.
Lieut. J. J. Melling,	do., do., 7:2:19.
2nd Lieut. J. E. Pritchard,	do., do., 9:2:19.
Lieut. H. J. Prout.	do., do., 8:2:19.
Major. C. G. Haselden, M.C.	do., do., 17:2:19.
Lieut. C. W. Proctor,)	To U.K. on duty under G.H.Q., A.G/7896/5
Lieut. W. Ramage.)	(O) dated 13:2:19 and granted 2
2nd Lieut. C. Cooke,)	months leave. Struck off strength
Capt. T. C. T. Llewellin,)	from 22:2:1919.

-*- -*- -*- -*- -*-

	Officers.	O.Rs.
PAPER STRENGTH OF BATTALION, 1st FEBRUARY 1919:-	46	670
INCREASES:-	-	
1 O.R. Joined Bn. from M.G.C. Base Depot 7:2:19.		1
1 O.R. Rejoined from C.C.S.		1
	46	672.
DECREASES:-	12	
Men to U.K. for Demobilization during the month:-		292
PAPER STRENGTH OF BATTALION, 28th FEBRUARY 1919:-	34 Offs.	380 O.Rs.

-*- -*- -*- -*- -*-

CONFIDENTIAL.

WAR DIARY

-*=*-

-*- of -*-

18TH BATTALION MACHINE GUN CORPS.

FROM:- 1st March 1919.

TO:- 31st March 1919.

APPENDIX :-

113. Changes in Establishment and strength of Battn. during month of March 1919.

- ATTACHED -

(VOLUME XIV)

Reference Map - France Sheet 57B 1/40.000.

Instructions regarding War Diaries and Intelligence Summaries are contained in F. S. Regs., Part II. and the Staff Manual respectively. Title pages will be prepared in manuscript.

WAR DIARY of 18th Bn. Machine Gun Corps

or

~~INTELLIGENCE SUMMARY.~~

(*Erase heading not required.*)

Army Form C. 2118.

MARCH 1919

Place	Date	Hour	Summary of Events and Information	Remarks and references to Appendices
ELINCOURT	1st to 26th		Physical Training and Squad Drill carried out during the morning together with checking of Mobilization Store Table and dumping stores at No 3 CCS CAUDRY. Athletics during the afternoons.	RD
	7th		Owing to Demobilization of animals authority was given on the 7th to reduce Bn to Cadre "A" Establishment. Bn was therefore organised on a 2-Coy Basis i.e. ① Cadre "A" Coy. ② Remainder of Bn Commanded by Major R.W. Butterell. MC	RD
	15th		The C-in-C paid a final visit to 18th Division - Bn represented by Lt-Col. E.C.T. Minet DSO. MC.	
	18th		18th Div ceased to exist - Bn now under GOC 55th Inf Bde - designated as 18th Div Cadre.	
	25th		Major J.W. Kwernham [?] assumed Command of "A" Coy	
	27th		Draft of 167 Other Ranks proceeded to join 42nd Bn M.G. Corps - (Army of Occupation) and Bn reduced to Cadre A	
	27th to 31st		Cadre "A" left Elincourt 1500 hrs on 27th and proceeded by March Route to CAUDRY and remained billeted there prior to proceeding to UK.	RD
			On 31st a further 13 ORs proceeded to join 42nd Bn M.G. Corps.	
			Statement showing Changes in Establishment & strength of Bn attached	App 113

D. D. & L., London, E.C. (A7883) Wt. W809/M1672 350,000 4/17 Sch. 52a Forms/C/2118/14

R. [signature] Lieut-Col.
Cmdg. 18th Bn. Machine Gun Corps.

APPENDIX 113.

CHANGES IN ESTABLISHMENT AND STRENGTH
OF 18th BATTALION MACHINE GUN CORPS;
CHANGES IN OFFICERS, DURING THE MONTH
OF MARCH 1919.

DECREASE - OFFICERS.

Lieut. R.H. Neale. — To U.K. on Duty under G3H.Q., A.G. 7896/5 (0) dated 13.2.19 and granted 2 months leave. Struck off strength from 1.2.19

2/LT. P.B. Brewer. — Proceeded for duty with No. 113 P. of W. Camp in the L. of C. Area on 6.3.19 and struck off strength accordingly. (Auth. A.G. 866/920 (M) dated 2.3.19)

Major C.B. Hibbert, D.S.O.	To U.K. for demobilisation		18.3.19
Lieut. C.B. Bridge.	Do.	Do.	18.3.19
Lieut. H.G. Harding.	Do.	Do.	19.3.19
Lieut. A.R. Glaves.	Do.	Do.	19.3.19
Lieut. (A/Major) N. Ryder. M.C.	Do.	Do.	19.3.19
Lieut. J.E. Braybrooke.	Do.	Do.	19.3.19
2/Lt. G.C. Beale.	Do.	Do.	19.3.19
2/Lt. J.B. Russell. M.C.	Do.	Do.	19.3.19
Capt. A.M. Dick.	Do.	Do.	19.3.19
Lieut. G.H. Leith. M.C.	Do.	Do.	19.3.19
Lt. (A/Major) R.D. Butterell. M.C.	Do.	Do.	19.3.19

Capt. C.H. James. — Transferred to Home Estab. while on leave to U.K. and struck off strength of B.E.F. 27.2.19. (Auth. C.R. No. 132939 B. dated 4.3.19.)

2/Lt. N.S. Hearle. — To U.K. for demobilisation 29.3.19.

T/Lt. (A/Capt.) J.O.R. Evans. M.C.
T/Lt. G.D. Loup. M.C.
T/2/Lt. T.C. Black.
T/2/Lt. G.E.T. Smith.
Lt. (A/Capt) E.J.Brett. M.C.
T/Lt. A.J. Fenton.
T/Lt. J. Laurie.
T/Lt. S.E. Puttock.
T/Lt. W. Sandiford.
T/2/Lt. W.F. Spree.
T/2/Lt. L. Jordan.

) Proceeded to join 42nd Battalion M.G.Corps on 25.3.19 and struck off strength. (Auth. G.H.Q. A.G. /9341 (0) dated 22.3.19.

2/Lt. A.B. Neate. — Posted from 18th Batt. M.G.C. to 6th Battalion Seaforth Highlanders and ceases to be employed with M.G.C. from 23.3.19. (Auth. G.H.Q. A.G. /2158/9522 (0)

	Officers.	O.R's.
PAPER STRENGTH OF BATTALION 1st MARCH 1919.	34	380
INCREASES.		
1 O.R. rejoined from Base Depot.		1
1 O.R. rejoined from C.C.S.		1
1 O.R. rejoined from Hospital in U.K.		1
	34	383
DECREASES.		
Men to U.K. for demobilisation during the Month:- 59		
Men evacuated to C.C.S.................... 6		
Other Causes........................... 8		
Men transferred to 42nd Battalion M.G.C.179		252
Officers struck off as on page 1.................	27	
PAPER STRENGTH OF BATTALION 31st March 1919:-	7 Offs.	131 O.R's

www.ingramcontent.com/pod-product-compliance
Lightning Source LLC
Chambersburg PA
CBHW080853010526
44117CB00014B/2242

* 9 7 8 1 4 7 4 5 1 0 8 0 6 *